A Question of Inheritance: Religion, Education, and Louisiana's Cultural Boundary, 1880-1940

A Question of Inheritance: Religion, Education, and Louisiana's Cultural Boundary, 1880-1940

by
James G. Dauphine

Published by The Center for Louisiana Studies
University of Southwestern Louisiana
Lafayette, Louisiana

ISBN Number: 0-940984-79-2
Library of Congress Catalog Number: 92-83847

Published by The Center for Louisiana Studies
P.O. Box 40831
University of Southwestern Louisiana
Lafayette, LA 70504-0831

CONTENTS

". . . for every one of the children of
Israel shall keep himself to the
inheritance of the tribe of his fathers."
Numbers 36:7.

PREFACE

This is a study of the relationship between cultural change and the persistence of cultural identities in two distinct sections of Louisiana in the late nineteenth and early twentieth centuries. From the early nineteenth century, Louisiana was culturally divided between northern and southern regions. North Louisiana, whose white population descended from Anglo Protestants, became culturally separate from the French Triangle parishes of South Louisiana—composed primarily of Catholics who are culturally indebted to the French, Spanish, and French Canadian heritages of the region.

The social dichotomy in Louisiana between Protestantism and Catholicism, already statistically apparent by religious census data in 1890, remained apparent into the twentieth century. By 1936, the date of the United States government's fifth and last religious census, North and South Louisiana had become more firmly differentiated by religious affiliation than in 1890, when the first government religious census was taken. From the beginning of Louisiana's settlement by different ethnic and national populations, religion was the primary social institution that reinforced ethnic, linguistic, economic, and other differences of custom, allowing cultural identities, once formed, to persist even once other cultural boundary-maintaining mechanisms weakened or disappeared. As anthropologists have theorized since the seminal work of Fredrik Barth in the 1960s, cultural or ethnic differences give rise to in-group identities that define the members of the culture, provide the basis for defining modes of behavior acceptable within the culture, and that define others across the boundary as culturally alien.

During the twentieth century, public education became the primary bearer of civil religious influence on Louisiana society, an influence oriented toward social standardization and modernization. As change associated with educational expansion and modern economic development occurred, such factors of cultural differentiation as language, rural isolation, and different economic pursuits became less germane to the existence of a cultural boundary between the two sections of the state.

Louisiana's cultural dichotomy perpetuated itself throughout the period of rapid social change between Reconstruction and World War II, largely through the survival of different cultural identities associated with Catholicism and with evangelical Protestantism. A close reading of religious statistical data suggests that religious patterns with origins in the state's early history persisted to 1940 in the face of growing socio-cultural secularism. This study looks at the way Catholics and Protestants co-opted the secular influence of public education to maintain and strengthen their own influence and to preserve the cultural boundary between North and South Louisiana.

Although I am not an anthropologist, I have incorporated anthropological theory into the basic framework of my historical study. What I have basically made of all the anthropological theory on cultural or ethnic boundaries is that a variety of factors cause boundary formation. Geography, economic practice, ethnicity, language, customs, etc. are all among such factors that group people together across boundaries from other groups. Once formed, however, a process of boundary maintenance helps to preserve cultural differences on each side of the boundary, perpetuating an "us and them" perception by the members of the opposing cultures—even though neither culture is static and both continue to evolve into forms completely unlike the cultures that existed when the boundary first formed. Religion is a factor that is central to this boundary maintenance process.

When members of one culture meet members of another across the boundary, they usually do not analyze each other as though they were anthropologists seeking to identify traits of difference. They have much simpler ways of determining whether individuals belong to "us" or to "them." Religious heritage or affiliation is one very common means of "pegging" people culturally. This is particularly true when people across a boundary are predominantly associated with two rival religious traditions, such as in Louisiana or, for that matter, in Ireland, Israel, Yugoslavia, or Canada.

Religion becomes a primary differentiator in these cases of absence of religious pluralism because it is the one social institution that adapts itself to cultural evolution in an integral way. Religion becomes part of the culture and is then a central component in the cultural process of adaptation to change as newer factors constantly contribute to the evolution of the society. Religion helps people to decide, in a collective way, what changes will be accepted into the culture and which will not. In this sense, religion fulfills a dynamic societal function that is very similar to the social function we know more commonly as "education."

Education, however, is not a simple process either. It takes place on different levels and in different ways for different reasons. The state, for example, promotes the education of its citizens in ways that are legally determined by government for specific reasons, usually of an economic and political nature. It is a broad, complicated process and no one presumes to be qualified to say definitively and completely what the educational system should and should not teach, or how it should do it, and to whom.

As a result, much of the education of society's members is of an informal nature. Religion, as a social institution, has great educational impact through the way that it both formally and informally teaches liturgy and morals as well as in the way that it indoctrinates people into the culture of which the religion has become an integral component. Through this educational function of churches, religion not only helps to define culture in the minds of the society's members, it also helps to introduce changes as part of the evolutionary process that all cultures continually undergo.

Religion's educational function within a society or culture affects not only people who are formally associated with the religious tradition as active communicants in churches. Religion also helps to educate culturally non-members of the dominant tradition by its impact on customs, rituals, and holiday observances in societies. For example, non church-goers in both North and South Louisiana were still influenced by either Catholic or Protestant heritages through such cultural preferences as support or non-support for alcohol, support or opposition to blue laws, or through their participation as members of the dominant culture in such cultural activities as Mardi Gras in South Louisiana or singing festivals and quilting bees in North Louisiana.

Because of the enormous impact on cultural formation and evolution by religion on both sides of Louisiana's North/South cultural boundary, it has been my purpose to examine the historical impact of religion on educational development during a formative period of Louisiana's history—the little more than sixty years from the end of Reconstruction to the outbreak of World War II. It is my hope that social scientists will not object to my simplifying of anthropology and sociology in order to fit findings of these disciplines into my framework. I hope, as well, that traditional historians will not object too strongly to the non-traditional manner in which I have constructed my historical framework. Inter-disciplinary cooperation is a concept in the academic pursuit of knowledge that one hears much about these days but yet, it remains a concept that few in any academic discipline attempt to employ.

I wish to point out, therefore, that my intention in writing this book has not been to "step on anyone's toes" by assuming mastery of the theoretical studies on cultural and ethnic boundaries, or by my abandonment of more traditional ways of writing history. I can only justify myself by claiming that my method was made necessary by the nature of my interest in this period of Louisiana history. With that disclaimer, I now invite students of Louisiana history to forge ahead with me and to cover some familiar historical ground in a slightly different way.

Tables

TABLE I
South Louisiana - Denominations as Percentage of
Religious Population: 1890/1936

	Catholic	Black Baptist	Southern Baptist	Black Methodist	Southern Methodist	Other
Acadia						
(1890)	86.7	0	1.4	5.4	5.5	1.0
(1936)	85.6	4.1	3.1	0.9	2.4	3.9
Ascension	58.5	30.3	0.9	7.9	1.2	1.3
	71.7	20.8	4.7	0.4	1.4	1.1
Assumption	80.6	13.5	0	5.0	0.3	0.7
	78.0	19.9	0	1.6	0	0.6
Avoyelles	82.6	8.0	1.8	2.0	5.3	0.4
	86.2	7.3	2.1	0.6	2.3	1.4
Calcasieu	53.0	4.5	17.8	8.4	10.4	6.0
	55.4	17.3	2.3	4.0	7.6	13.4
Cameron	0	24.8	0	0	75.2	0
	93.2	1.9	0	0	4.7	0.3
Evangeline	--	--	--	--	--	--
	92.6	2.1	3.8	0	0.2	1.3
Iberia	81.0	10.6	0	3.6	2.1	2.7
	83.5	10.1	0	1.1	2.3	3.0
Iberville	39.9	44.7	0	11.8	0.8	2.8
	56.0	39.1	0.9	2.3	0.3	1.4
Jefferson	66.0	23.0	0	5.5	0	5.5
	83.2	11.4	1.3	0	0.8	3.3
Jefferson Davis	--	--	--	--	--	--
	72.3	7.4	1.6	7.2	1.1	10.3
Lafayette	94.2	1.1	0	3.2	1.0	0.6
	93.3	0.9	1.5	1.1	1.8	1.5
Lafourche	86.6	8.9	0	3.4	0.2	0.9
	92.2	5.4	0	0.9	1.0	0.5
Orleans	69.6	2.8	0.6	6.6	2.4	18.0
	72.9	7.1	1.1	2.2	1.9	14.9
Plaquemines	95.8	1.8	0	1.9	0	0.5
	94.2	4.9	0	0	0	0.9

	Catholic	Black Baptist	Southern Baptist	Black Methodist	Southern Methodist	Other
Pointe Coupée	52.1 48.9	34.1 47.5	0.2 0.3	9.0 1.6	2.7 1.0	2.0 0.8
St. Bernard	95.6 91.0	4.4 7.3	0 0	0 0	0 0	0 1.8
St. Charles	35.9 86.7	62.6 11.7	0 0	1.5 0	0 0	0 1.6
St. James	86.1 86.5	12.5 13.1	0 0	1.4 0.3	0 0.1	0 0
St. John the Baptist	89.7 92.1	7.4 7.4	0 0	2.8 0.2	0 0.4	0 0
St. Landry	85.8 87.1	7.8 9.7	2.2 1.1	1.8 0.5	1.5 0.4	0.9 1.2
St. Martin	94.7 98.7	3.7 1.0	0 0	1.6 0	0 0.1	0.1 0.2
St. Mary	45.5 75.5	26.7 14.9	0 0.2	16.2 1.9	8.8 5.5	2.8 2.0
St. Tammany	53.4 55.4	5.3 5.0	1.7 13.8	23.7 5.3	13.5 9.2	2.4 11.4
Terrebonne	76.0 85.3	13.5 10.6	0 0	7.0 1.6	0.5 0	3.0 2.5
Vermillion	89.7 92.1	1.2 1.3	0 1.0	1.2 0.2	8.0 3.8	0 1.6
West Baton Rouge	43.3 43.1	16.6 51.8	0 0	29.0 5.1	3.9 0	7.2 0
TOTALS (1890)	73.7	9.5	1.0	5.7	2.7	7.5
(without Orleans)	76.1	13.3	1.2	5.2	2.8	1.5
TOTALS (1936)	78.6	9.7	1.3	1.6	1.8	7.1
(without Orleans)	81.8	11.2	1.4	1.2	1.8	2.6

TABLE II
North Louisiana - Denominations as Percentage of Religious Population: 1890/1936

	Catholic	Black Baptist	Southern Baptist	Black Methodist	Southern Methodist	Other
Allen (1890)	--	--	--	--	--	--
(1936)	46.1	11.2	13.4	8.4	9.5	11.3
Beauregard	--	--	--	--	--	--
	0	25.5	45.3	0.8	12.2	16.2
Bienville	0	41.2	21.3	12.0	22.9	2.6
	0	45.5	29.2	14.3	8.9	2.1
Bossier	4.2	41.3	5.5	41.3	6.3	1.4
	0	35.8	18.0	27.8	3.9	14.6
Caddo	10.3	42.7	9.2	17.0	10.1	10.7
	11.2	24.8	18.3	10.3	15.7	19.7
Caldwell	0	0	55.9	9.9	33.3	0.9
	0	24.1	47.4	2.4	11.8	14.2
Catahoula	6.4	63.6	24.8	0.4	3.2	1.5
	0	41.7	47.4	0	8.2	2.7
Claiborne	0.7	30.9	13.7	25.3	17.6	11.9
	0	26.0	10.6	43.5	8.3	11.6
Concordia	1.9	84.2	0	6.7	3.6	3.7
	3.4	69.0	6.6	0.7	5.1	15.3
DeSoto	44.2	12.0	17.4	10.4	7.8	8.2
	5.8	48.4	12.8	10.8	13.9	8.3
East Baton Rouge	28.7	0	19.4	18.4	20.9	12.6
	28.0	42.5	5.6	2.6	8.4	12.9
East Carroll	6.3	35.2	0	42.8	8.5	7.2
	7.2	74.1	11.9	2.9	0	3.9
East Feliciana	1.9	24.7	13.0	27.6	27.7	5.2
	1.0	66.9	6.9	9.1	11.9	4.3
Franklin	0	60.8	13.1	0.9	21.2	4.0
	1.9	55.2	25.2	0.7	11.9	5.0
Grant	8.0	6.6	34.6	13.9	30.7	6.3
	6.0	38.3	34.1	4.2	9.1	8.3
Jackson	0	48.9	16.5	0	11.8	22.9
	1.7	48.7	21.1	2.0	14.4	12.2
Lasalle	--	--	--	--	--	--
	0	12.2	61.1	2.9	16.2	7.6
Lincoln	0	58.7	18.6	4.8	13.4	4.5
	0	47.0	26.7	5.1	15.3	5.9

	Catholic	Black Baptist	Southern Baptist	Black Methodist	Southern Methodist	Other
Livingston	29.3	0	32.9	13.0	24.7	0
	34.9	5.5	41.8	0	15.6	2.2
Madison	3.5	45.6	0	46.8	0	4.1
	4.2	78.2	4.6	1.7	7.3	4.1
Morehouse	2.2	35.1	2.9	39.2	15.4	5.2
	0.5	52.3	8.6	28.0	6.3	4.4
Natchitoches	67.5	13.3	6.4	9.8	1.1	1.9
	47.8	17.8	19.6	6.3	4.2	4.3
Ouachita	11.2	30.7	6.8	24.0	19.1	8.2
	6.4	52.1	15.6	5.0	10.1	10.8
Rapides	23.9	36.5	12.9	13.9	7.1	5.8
	35.7	17.5	21.4	5.9	4.9	14.6
Red River	0	51.8	6.2	21.4	17.6	3.0
	0	33.9	41.9	4.4	13.5	6.3
Richland	1.3	40.3	8.8	20.3	6.2	23.1
	1.9	41.3	8.7	29.2	11.2	7.6
Sabine	18.6	6.2	43.2	4.6	27.5	0
	29.6	6.4	46.1	1.1	8.9	7.8
St. Helena	0	0	35.2	25.3	38.8	0.7
	0	0.7	19.3	45.6	32.6	1.8
Tangipahoa	20.5	0	29.2	29.3	8.6	12.4
	40.2	7.7	17.3	19.0	6.6	9.3
Tensas	3.9	60.9	0	26.1	2.6	6.5
	1.6	84.6	1.3	1.2	0	11.4
Union	0	19.9	60.0	4.1	11.4	4.6
	0	53.6	32.6	1.9	4.7	7.3
Vernon	0	0	56.1	4.8	33.8	5.3
	1.1	16.1	53.7	3.4	8.1	17.7
Washington	0	0	80.3	19.7	0	0
	7.5	13.7	26.6	6.9	10.8	34.5
Webster	1.6	60.0	13.1	11.8	6.6	6.9
	2.1	39.9	20.4	20.0	9.8	7.8
West Carroll	0	0	18.3	33.7	27.3	20.7
	2.2	29.9	38.8	2.1	16.4	10.6
West Feliciana	6.2	20.7	1.5	37.4	19.1	15.0
	2.7	78.0	0	2.3	8.6	8.4
Winn	0	2.6	66.2	3.6	13.4	14.3
	0	35.2	43.5	6.1	8.7	6.4

	Catholic	Black Baptist	Southern Baptist	Black Methodist	Southern Methodist	Other
TOTALS						
(1890)	14.4	31.0	18.1	17.1	12.9	6.5
(1936)	13.5	35.4	19.6	10.2	9.9	11.5

A Question of Inheritance: Religion, Education, and Louisiana's Cultural Boundary, 1880-1940

I

Introduction: Some Overall Perspectives on Cultural Boundary Formation and Maintenance in Louisiana, 1880-1940

Since statehood in 1812, Louisiana has contained two distinct sections—each with cultures influenced and perpetuated by different religious traditions. Far-reaching, increasingly rapid social change became characteristic of Louisiana, as with other states in the region and nation, following the Civil War and Reconstruction. North and South Louisiana were not divided by loyalties to either the region or nation. Rather, as both sections of the state incorporated similar economic, political, and educational changes as a result of the advent of increased industrialization and urbanization between 1880 and 1940, regional ties and American nationalism grew stronger.

While processes of national unification developed over the latter part of the nineteenth and first part of the twentieth centuries, the regional and national economies integrated and grew. As southerners returned to national politics in the twentieth century, greater political unification took place. Similarly, educational expansion and improved communications served to standardize social institutions and to tie people across the region and nation closer together. However, within the broad social processes of standardization and unification encouraged by the centralization or integration of social institutions such as government, public education, and the economy, one other of the four major social institutions, religion, retained the denominational diversity and autonomy that had historically characterized American religion.

Religions in Louisiana, as elsewhere, faced the enormous task of accommodating the cultural traditions of their religious adherents to social change. Just as public education became the purveyor of civil religion and the state's agent in educating people to participate in desired economic change, religious education expanded in order to co-opt the economic and political influences of progressive education in an attempt to expand the influence of religion on the changes taking place.

Although social change occurred after 1880 and became more rapid after World War I, a number of well-developed social customs in North and South

Louisiana survived up to and beyond World War II. A few broad examples suffice to demonstrate that different folkways in North and South Louisiana—which developed and were perpetuated largely through the influence of competing religious traditions—persisted amidst increasing social change, producing separate cultural identities. Continuing religious dominance by evangelical Protestantism in North Louisiana and by Catholicism in South Louisiana was central to the survival of these differing cultural identities. By World War II, the nineteenth-century pattern of dominance by different religious traditions in each section of the state had become more easily demonstrable statistically than in 1890. This fact is of central importance, historically, in understanding how Louisiana's cultural dichotomy between north and south persevered during an age of externally imposed mass standardization and centralization.

Anthropological research concerning the formation and maintenance of cultural boundaries has shown that factors of climate, economic resources, racial composition, language, and religion are all involved in the social processes causing cultural groups to view themselves in terms of a subjective "in-group" identity. Up to World War II, factors of language, race, economics, and the environment—previously important to the formation of separate cultural identities in North and South Louisiana—began to have less impact on the maintenance of the cultural boundary dividing North and South Louisiana.

Economic differences historically associated with the cultivation of different cash crops—cotton in North Louisiana, sugar and rice in South Louisiana—became less a dividing factor during the twentieth century as Louisiana industrialized and urbanized. As the educational system expanded in the twentieth century, laws requiring compulsory school attendance and the use of English began to reduce linguistic differences between French Louisianians and Anglos. Separate nationalism in French South Louisiana, already largely subsumed by the processes of statehood and participation in the Civil War, declined further with the growth of American nationalism before and after World War I. As a consequence of the decline or disappearance of such factors relating to economic, national, and political differences, Louisiana became increasingly unified during the period from Reconstruction to World War II.

Cultural differences continued to persist, however. Different musical traditions, reflecting cultural difference between North and South Louisiana, were well established by 1940. Distinctive to South Louisiana were three different traditions associated with the French-speaking population: that of mostly urban French colonial descendents, of mostly rural French Acadians (or Cajuns), and of "French" Negroes, who preferred the term "Creoles" as a distinction from both white groups of French inheritance and from non-French-speaking, mostly Protestant blacks. Common to all three French traditions was the usage of French, of accordions and stringed instruments, and non-religious inspiration for songs lending themselves to dance, gaiety, and extended occasions for fun and frolic.[1]

In contrast, North Louisiana's musical traditions were more church-inspired. Unlike the zydeco music of black Creoles, black music in North Louisiana derived more inspiration from the tradition of slave spirituals and became oriented more to what we know as "the blues" and to gospel singing. North Louisiana whites also developed a musical tradition inspired by Protestant religions. Common throughout North Louisiana were "singing conventions," often sponsored by evangelical churches, which were representative of a wider Anglo-Saxon Protestant tradition in uplands areas of the South. The largest of Louisiana's "singing conventions" was an annual event attracting upwards to 70,000 people, sponsored by the Shreveport Chamber of Commerce.[2]

Culinary practices also helped to distinguish North from South Louisiana. Known today as Creole or Cajun cooking, South Louisiana methods of cooking developed dishes that often featured ingredients such as seafood and rice and which were prepared with pungently-seasoned sauces derived from sauteed flour, known as a "roux." The origins of Creole and Cajun cooking were described in 1941, by a writer employed by the Work Projects Administration, as the result of "French love for delicacies and the Spanish taste for pungent seasoning, . . .the culinary skill of the Negro," and "roots and herbs contributed by the Indians, particularly the Choctaw." Choctaws contributed powder prepared from sassafras leaves—called filé by the Creoles—which is an ingredient of gumbo.[3] Cooking in North Louisiana featured none of the distinctive characteristics of South Louisiana and was not unlike culinary preferences common to most southern states. According to one commentator on culinary difference between southern and northern Louisianians, an important difference "is that the latter do not eat crawfish," whereas the former group harbors "passion for the creature" that "verges on the absurd."[4]

In the matter of social customs, generally, South Louisiana deviated from patterns found in North Louisiana and in other southern states. North Louisiana folkways, featuring logrollings, corn huskings, and quilting bees, were not much different from customs across the border in Arkansas or

Mississippi. In South Louisiana, however, Catholic Church pageants, ceremonies, and holidays contributed to folkways that were not only distinctive to Catholics, but which exerted social influence over non-Catholics as well, causing South Louisiana, as a sub-region, to be socially and culturally cohesive and distinct from areas of the state where Catholic influences were absent or minimal.[5]

Catholic influences had a large impact, not only on the white population, but also on the black population, despite the postbellum strength of Protestantism among South Louisiana blacks. As an unidentified writer for a WPA-sponsored guide to the state observed in 1941, many South Louisiana blacks were as culturally different from blacks in other places "as is the Cajun from the Ozark hillbilly or the New England farmer," a cultural difference he attributed to South Louisiana Catholicism and "Latin influence."[6]

Such cultural differences between the sections of Louisiana began to abate during the present century in the face of standardization resulting from modern industrial and urban development. Cultural differences, however, tend to create cultural identities that persist within changing cultures. In-group identities, once formed, become a cultural inheritance and continue to contribute to cultural distinctions that are readily apparent to outsiders or to new settlers wishing to fit in. In commenting on cultural identities as he perceived them only fourteen years ago, Christopher Hallowell wrote that "in Louisiana, identities are assigned with jarring offhandedness." To the South Louisiana Cajun, a northern Louisianian "is a redneck Protestant, sure to be unfriendly," while to North Louisianians, "the southern third of the state is coon-ass country. The whole thing is as plain and simple as that."[7]

During the present century, much has happened to alter nineteenth-century patterns. A prominent development has been the growth of secular, or non-religious, influences on society. Secular social values came to have a greater and greater impact in Louisiana from 1880 to 1940, representing change. A prominent agent for secular change was public education, as this social institution expanded during the twentieth century and began to challenge formal denominational religion's role in American, and Louisiana, society. After 1900, public educational development was rapid and widespread, forcing religions to respond to its impact on cultural evolution by introducing new strategies of religious aggrandizement through religious education.[8]

Scholars like Robert N. Bellah and Martin E. Marty contend that secularism, defined as a world outlook pertaining to non-spiritual or non-sacred personal and social values, became transformed into something of a religion in itself. Bellah introduced the idea of a secular American religion, calling it "civil religion."[9] As the concept has been further defined and articulated by a number of scholars, civil religion has come to be identified as a secular religious system, complete with symbolism, mythology, and ritual. Having grown out of intense nationalistic sentiment corresponding to the growth of American influence in the world, the American civil religion has become the means by which Americans can express their devotion to America's democratic and free institutions, ideals, and form of government—as well as belief in the superiority of American forms of culture and economic practice. The symbolism behind civil religion has been supplied by the glorification of the deeds of great Americans of the past, the mythology has been supplied by distortion and simplification of American history, and the ritual is evident in everyday life—in the form of observance of holidays, displays of the flag, and oaths of allegiance or other such pledges of national loyalty, whether in formal or informal application. Its influence is pervasive and undeniable regardless of whether or not it can properly be termed a religion.[10]

An important aspect of "civil religion," besides its secular, or temporal nature, is its unitary character. Its appeal is to all, and there is nothing to prevent communicants of any religious denomination from adhering as well to this secular, American creed, so long as he or she is willing to view the nation as indivisible "under God," supplying the guiding divinity of their own choosing. In this way, the civil religion is not necessarily incompatible with traditional, formal religious practice.[11]

Of central importance to the process in which secularism achieved respectability in society and began to increase its influence on culture was the erection of a universal system of public education. Beginning about the turn of the century, southern states began to alter their constitutions to allow counties or school and tax districts to collect public funds for the purpose of building and maintaining schools. State Departments and Boards of Education were given administrative control of the burgeoning systems, and educational growth became pronounced as public education assumed its place at the head of the reform programs of southern progressivism.[12]

Among southern reforms contemporary to educational expansion, besides programs for improved public health and road construction, was Negro disfranchisement. Far-reaching in its implications for future southern development, the system of segregation formally implemented and legally justified in southern states by the turn of the century retarded the educational efforts of these states in that a significant proportion of their populations—embodied by southern Negroes—was practically and effectively denied adequate access to educational attainment.[13]

Separate and unequal access to educational opportunities was the practical effect of segregation. As late as 1910, there was not a single public high school for blacks in any southern state. In the continuing absence of state-sponsored educational facilities, following demise of Reconstruction programs for black education, Louisiana's blacks turned to religious denominations for educational financing and organization. Protestant denominations became particularly involved in the late nineteenth century with black schools, a development that expanded Protestant influence among blacks on both sides of the cultural boundary—endangering the boundary's integrity by reducing Catholic influence in South Louisiana.[14]

Although racial segregation did not achieve legal status and justification until the 1890s and later, segregation had been the accepted pattern of southern church organizations—except for Catholics—since the Civil War.[15] Only in southern Louisiana did any significant population of Negro Catholics exist, and here the segregation of Catholic parishes into black and white congregations had its beginnings in a program inaugurated by the Archdiocese of New Orleans in 1895. Moving in step with the spirit of the times, the idea of building separate churches for Negroes quickly gained the social acceptance of white Catholics. By the 1920s, most black Catholics worshipped in segregated churches and chapels. Catholic schools, hospitals, and orphanages, however, had always been segregated.[16]

Among southern Protestants, segregation had long been the rule. Over the first half of the nineteenth century, antebellum planters began to consider conversion of slaves to Christianity part of their social duty within the paternalistic system of slavery. Separate worship services for slaves developed into slave religion—the one black social institution allowing slaves free participation without interference by whites.[17] During the twentieth century, leaders of southern white society continued to encourage religious worship by Negroes because they regarded religion as a useful deterrent to criminal, unruly, or otherwise socially troublesome behavior.[18] Accordingly, racially segregated religious worship became acceptable and desirable to both the black and white populations of the South.

One reason for the change in practice by Louisiana Catholics toward the end of the nineteenth century was alarm on the part of the Catholic hierarchy that Negro Catholics were converting to Protestantism. Another was that most white Catholics favored conformity with the regional trend toward separation of the races in all social institutions. By the end of the century, the Catholic Church had recognized the necessity of flexibility toward local conditions and conformed to norms established by the southern Protestant majority. Nowhere else in the United States did segregated Catholic parishes become the accepted pattern.[19]

Acceptance of segregation went beyond acknowledgment of the southern racial setting in Louisiana. It also reflected the desire of the Catholic hierarchy to achieve Catholic aggrandizement within the black population. Cognizant of the success Protestants achieved in the conversion of blacks in both North and South Louisiana following the Civil War, Catholics recognized that provision of educational facilities for blacks had to become a priority for the Catholic Church to expand its influence in the black community.[20] Lack of funds on the part of the Catholic Church in Louisiana, which barely escaped financial bankruptcy during the 1880s, precluded any extensive program of school construction for black Catholics. Under these conditions, Catholic racial segregation became a precondition for obtaining the educational funds and services provided by Catholic philanthropies and religious orders—founded for the exclusive benefit of black Catholics. Further motivation for the Catholic Church's sanctioning of segregation was that in 1890, black Protestants outnumbered black Catholics in Catholic South Louisiana by about two to one.[21]

Itself a costly procedure, the establishment of separate church buildings for black congregations postponed further the implementation of a program of black Catholic school construction, until after 1910.[22] By this time black Protestant congregations were well established, though financially unable to build schools of good quality in sufficient numbers to adequately feed the Negro universities built by northern Protestants in New Orleans during Reconstruction.[23] Following the founding of Xavier University for black Catholics in 1915, a proliferation of black Catholic parochial schools in the 1920s initiated the beginnings of an ultimately successful effort to enlarge the number of black Catholics in South Louisiana.[24] By 1960, Catholicism had become the religious affiliation of the majority of blacks in about half of the southern section of Louisiana, though not in the parishes closest to New Orleans or in the rest of the state. Also by 1960, segregation of churches was no longer enforced, and Catholic schools in

New Orleans were about to become the first schools in Louisiana, both public and private, to desegregate during the early 1960s.[25]

Catholic success in enlarging the church's influence over South Louisiana's black population during the twentieth century is a testament to the power of religion in maintaining the cultural boundary. The initial Catholic failure to enlist blacks to the church following the Civil War constituted a serious threat to the integrity of the cultural boundary. Though blacks had been segregated by slavery before the war and by white prejudice and legal devices after the war, blacks and whites in both North and South Louisiana were still members of the cultures that prevailed in each section. By the unusual circumstances introduced by black emancipation and the rapid spread of Protestantism among Louisiana's blacks, a sizeable portion of the South Louisiana population came under the spiritual and cultural guidance of an alien cultural force—Protestantism.

The Catholic Church, which had once attempted, through the colonial Code Noir, to ensure Negro Catholicism in Louisiana by mandating that blacks receive education under Catholic auspices, watched helplessly as blacks deserted the Church en masse for its postbellum failure to provide access to education for blacks.[26] The Catholic hierarchy in Louisiana had reason for further alarm in that blacks deserted the Catholic Church after the Civil War to become Protestants, and most often, Baptists.

By its postbellum actions, the Catholic Church demonstrated awareness that its continued dominance in South Louisiana depended on its ability to preserve the section's cultural distinctiveness. Among blacks as well as among whites, the Church recognized the importance of co-opting educational influences leading to cultural divergence. In South Louisiana, that meant expanding the influence of Catholic education in order to combat the cultural influence of black Protestant schools and of black public schools pervaded by Protestant influences dominant elsewhere in the southern region. It abandoned the practice of integrated congregations employed elsewhere in the country in order to accommodate the peculiar social imperatives of the bi-racial South and ultimately succeeded in closing the breaches in Louisiana's cultural boundary created by the rapid postbellum spread of black Protestantism. In applying segregation as a policy, the Catholic Church in Louisiana completed the transition it had been undergoing since 1803 and became fully a southern church.

Despite the challenges of secular civil religion and black Protestantism to the maintenance of Louisiana's North-South cultural division, such cultural boundaries as Louisiana's reflect the tendency of cultural groups to retain distinctive subjective identities. Rapid social changes within cultures can produce the disintegration of the culture if the changes are introduced by a competing culture across the boundary. Social institutions within a culture tend, therefore, to resist external cultural influences and to protect the culture. Religion is one social institution that has been particularly associated with the process of cultural conservatism.[27] Politics and economics also contribute to cultural formation and maintenance, though these factors are more subject to rapid change and are less responsible than religion for the persistence of cultural traditions.

All cultures are produced, in part, by factors of climate and topography, which contribute to the economic strategies that people in any one area employ for the purpose of utilizing available resources.[28] The same climatic, topographical, and racial conditions that led to the rise of plantation agriculture elsewhere in the South, apply as well to Louisiana, which developed reliance on plantation agriculture and black slavery to no lesser extent than most other southern states during the nineteenth century. What made Louisiana different from other states was the existence of a population of French Catholics in South Louisiana. Predominantly Anglo-Saxon Protestant people from other southern states moved into Louisiana and took up residence in North Louisiana and the Florida parishes during the nineteenth century.[29] A cultural boundary took shape all along the outer fringe of existing French Catholic settlement, which had begun during the eighteenth century.

As part of the southern region characterized by black and white racial composition, whites in both sections of Louisiana came to share a common outlook towards their bi-racial society. By 1850, whatever Francophone nationalism once existed in South Louisiana had been subsumed under both an American and a southern regional identity. Invasion of South Louisiana by people of Anglo-Saxon origins during the nineteenth century produced an end to the political dominance of French Louisianians by about 1850. By the end of the Civil War, the white population of Louisiana was seventy per cent Anglo-Saxon.[30]

Whites in South Louisiana, because of soil conditions and rainfall amounts, developed an agricultural economy that featured the production of staple crops other than cotton during the nineteenth century. Whereas cotton production characterized North Louisiana, first sugar and later rice as well became staple crops in the southern parishes. Both sections developed a reliance on slave labor, however.[31] Following the Civil War, economic differences that arose between the two sections had a bearing on politics in the state. Because of competition from sugar producers in the West Indies, South Louisiana sugar planters favored a protective tariff, while North Louisiana cotton planters retained a political stance in opposition to tariffs put in place by the northern oriented Republican party during and after the Civil War.[32]

During Reconstruction, different agricultural methods employed in the production of cotton and sugar resulted in different systems of farm labor. Sharecropping and tenantry became predominant in North Louisiana, and South Louisiana developed greater reliance on a wage labor system. Despite such differences, white planters in both sections tended to be members of the Democratic party after the Civil War, shared a common desire to regain control of the black labor supply, and shared common outlooks toward the politics and economics of other regions in the country.[33] That is, the problems and aspirations they shared in common outweighed the specific economic and political differences that sometimes affected state elections.

In any case, an urban political machine in New Orleans, which held the balance of power between the elites of North and South Louisiana, appeared by the end of Reconstruction and allied its interests most often with planter elites in North Louisiana. The result of that alliance was political behavior on the state level that largely accorded with political behavior in other southern states.[34] If anything, the political hegemony of the state's economic elites was more complete in Louisiana than in other southern states. In this regard, Louisiana was more "southern" than other southern states, despite the atypical presence of a powerful urban machine.[35]

The most significant difference between North and South Louisiana was a difference in culture, reinforced and perpetuated through the dominance of evangelical Protestantism on one side of the cultural boundary and of Catholicism on the other side. One by one, during the nineteenth and twentieth centuries, all other differences of language, politics, economics, and outlook toward race either disappeared or reached accommodation across the cultural boundary. What has survived are subjective identities of distinctiveness. These ascriptive social identities, founded on cultural traits exhibited in customs, music, crafts, observance of holidays, and attitudes toward work, are all rooted in different cultures that have evolved into forms vastly different from the original cultures of the early nineteenth century. Despite social change, brought on by political and economic changes introduced from the national and regional socio-political arena, as well as by emigration, immigration, and cultural contact and exchange across the cultural boundary, the boundary has persisted in giving evidence of separate cultural identities on either side of it. Religion, acting as the social institution that it is, has been the cultural force most responsible for maintaining the cultural boundary and the subjective identities of cultural difference that persist, despite the rapidity of social change, shared American and regional identities, and shared accommodation to secular, or non-religious, social influences.[36]

Public education, society's prime disseminator of secular information, developed into a social institution separated from religion only in the twentieth century. Before the erection of public school systems featuring both primary and secondary education, religious organizations shouldered the bulk of society's perceived responsibilities toward the education of children. This was particularly true of places in the South, such as Louisiana. Louisiana's public educational system was initiated in 1845 and grew slowly from that point until the twentieth century.[37] Public schools rarely offered courses past the elementary school level until the 1890s, when semi-public high schools began to appear in significant numbers only in the cities and larger towns of the state, and only for the white population. Rapid proliferation of high schools ensued after 1900, prompting the State Department of Education, in 1908, to appoint a State High School Inspector and to begin assuming the same responsibilities toward high schools it had exercised toward primary schools since 1845.[38]

Public primary schools were also too few to meet educational demand in the state before 1900. Denominational schools and private non-denominational schools continued to operate in numerous localities across the state. Centralized direction of the state system remained weak because of the importance of local funding to public school operation, and in this situation, religion retained influence over what children were taught in the schools.[39]

Because Catholics continued to attempt expansion of their own underdeveloped school system, public schools in both sections of the state were usually under the direction and control of Protestants. Much like non-denominational private schools, run by Protestant ministers, public schools offered religious instruction that did not attempt to favor one Protestant denomination over another, but that did conflict with Catholic dogma.[40] The fact that the majority of Louisiana's denominational schools were Catholic, by 1900, did not imply that Protestant religious influence on education was absent in the state.

To the contrary, non-denominational private, and many public, schools tended to function as Protestant parochial schools, a fact that helps to explain the relative absence of Protestant denominational schools.[41] Once public school expansion became more rapid in the last decade of the nineteenth century, Catholic complaints about the Protestant version of the Bible being taught in public schools grew louder. The issue forced attention to the reasoning of some Catholics that fairness demanded partial public tax support for Catholic parochial school expansion. As it happened, the issue of public aid for private and denominational schools was also part of the national political debate in the 1890s.[42] In Louisiana, as in other states across the country, legislators reacted adversely to the question of public aid for private schools by passing laws explicitly denying the validity of the concept. The other part of the issue, Bible-reading in schools, remained unaddressed in many states, including Louisiana, for a number of years. Ironically, a Jewish lawyer named Sidney Herold, from Shreveport in Protestant North Louisiana, became the central figure taking the issue to the state courts in 1913. His victory in a case disputing the legality of Bible-reading in the public schools of Caddo Parish brought Louisiana into conformity with the national pattern of religious exclusion in public schools.[43]

A further irony is that secularization of public schools followed the court decision, which was justified as a means of preserving constitutional provisions for church-state separation. The irony derives from the fact that church-state separation had been the justification for outlawing public aid to Catholic parochial schools during the 1890s. Despite the removal of religion from public school curricula, religion continued to exert influence on education in Louisiana. Denominational colleges and parochial schools continued to exist and religion's influence on people's outlooks preserved a conservative social posture on the part of rural Louisianians, especially, serving to retard the process of public educational expansion, although largely unconsciously. The fact that public school improvement and expansion depended on the educational interest of localities—which provided the bulk of funds for schools through local taxes until 1935—meant that the largely rural parishes, with low property valuations, had to tax themselves more heavily in order to achieve educational outlays proportional to those in more prosperous areas, such as in the cities and larger towns.[44] Not surprisingly, the socially conservative and largely poor Baptists and Methodists of rural North Louisiana, as well as many socially defensive rural Catholics in South Lousisiana, chose not to equate progress with the expansion of educational opportunity. The cost in property taxes would have been too imposing, even had the religiously conservative rural people of Louisiana been inclined to regard education in higher esteem than they did.

The majority of both evangelical Protestants and Catholics in Louisiana were rural before World War II. They were mostly poor, mostly from backgrounds of low educational attainment, and usually did not place a high priority on formal schooling.[45] The Catholic Church and the denominations of Southern Baptists and Southern Methodists in Louisiana all began to sponsor expanded programs for denominational education after the turn of the century.[46] These programs required support in contributions from their church members, however, and failed to meet the expectations and desires of church leaders in the years before World War II. The problem was that, before people can be induced to support educational expansion, they must have both the ability to pay for it and social recognition of education's benefits to their culture. Being mostly poor and mostly agricultural, Louisiana's rural people possessed neither attribute.

Something that rural Louisianians did possess was their culture. The economic, political, and racial problems of rural people were similar in both sections of Louisiana, but because the dominant religious traditions in each section were different, religious antipathy caused the cultural boundary to persist, preventing rural people in the opposing cultures from cooperating politically in the solution of their problems. "Differences between the Protestant north and the Catholic south," according to V.O. Key, "furnished a convenient advantage to those who, with their eye on the main chance and unencumbered by ecclesiastical prejudice, would divide and rule."[47]

For its role in championing competing cultures, religion in Louisiana was necessarily conservative; it was cautious and halting in its function of socializing religious adherents to changes introduced from outside the culture. Rapid educational expansion was one reform that sought to effect social change introduced to Louisiana and the rest of the South by the example of educational progress and industrial expansion in the North. As the seminal reform of the Progressive Era, education that was secular and standardized in curricular content reflected a strengthening of American nationalism, as well as the growing cultural influence of the American "civil religion."

Faced with powerful new cultural influences, seeking to break down cultural barriers in the way of increased national unity and social integration, southern religions struggled to accommodate acceptance of education's social beneficence with their value systems, based on conservative theologies rooted in social traditions of racial segregation and loyalty to the subjective idea of regional distinctiveness. While white Catholics in South Louisiana fought to retain the distinctiveness of their own sub-culture and to resist the encroachment of Protestantism, they shared with white Protestants a belief in the myth of the Lost Cause.[48] That Catholics and Protestants in separate sections of Louisiana faced the problem of social accommodation to externally introduced change separately, in different ways, does not diminish the fact that Louisiana's religions faced the common problem of guiding the social transformation of their adherents from agriculture to industrialism. In their attempts to do so, Louisiana's religious leaders had to accept new ideas and to attempt to convince church communicants of the correctness of those ideas. The method was, of course, education.

Louisiana's religions did not succeed in guiding a completely smooth transformation. In the years of industrial expansion and rapid rural dislocation following World War II, the accommodation of religious leaders to changed political, social, and economic conditions resulted in increasing numbers of defections from the major religious denominations, as the phenomenon of ultra-conservative sectarianism became noticeably widespread for the first time during the 1950s. Denominational support, on the part of both Catholic and Protestant leaders, for the "radical" idea of increased racial integration in society was a prominent cause of sectarian defections but not the exclusive one.[49]

Religions in Louisiana did succeed, however, in advancing programs of education that helped to prepare people born after the turn of the century for social adjustments they would be forced to undergo during their lifetimes. Such programs as the Baptist Sunday School movement after 1910 and the parochial school expansion of the Catholic Church, also after about 1910, were limited in scope, but significant for two reasons. Firstly, they represented acceptance by church leaders that the progressive concepts of organization, communication, and education could help better prepare church members meet the problems of daily life while helping to forge a broader consensus among church members in regard to both church doctrine and social morality.

Secondly, the educational programs of Louisiana's religions reflected accommodation to the right of the state to impose curricular standards in schools for the purpose of imparting patriotism and secular knowledge deemed appropriate for the economic advancement of the state. Protestant Sunday Schools reflected Protestant dissatisfaction with the secular curricula in place in public schools after 1915, but because they served as religious supplements to public education, they also sanctioned Protestant reliance on public schools for the education of children. Catholic parochial schools reflected mistrust of both the secular orientation of public schools and the influence of Protestant administrators, principals, and teachers in those schools. They also reflected acceptance of the educational aims of the public schools in that Catholic schools cooperated with the state by maintaining public school standards and adopting the texts and secular curricula of the public schools.[50]

Through partial co-option of the the state educational system, religious educational programs in Louisiana helped to sanction acceptance of secular changes in society by church members. Religious education also had the significant effect of producing accommodation to external change and to new ideas without disturbing the integrity of the cultural boundary. Through the different means by which Catholics in South Louisiana and Protestants in North Louisiana accomplished the same ends, they were able to protect their religious dominance and to maintain cultural influence on the changing societies in each section of the state.

Not to recognize the influence of religion on cultural evolution in Louisiana is to miss the central importance of religion in maintaining the subjective identities of cultural distinctiveness that exist on either side of Louisiana's cultural boundary. From antebellum times to the present day, the cultures of North and South Louisiana shared similar problems of politics, economics, race, rural isolation, backwardness, and the persistence of external cultural influences from the North and other regions. Both cultures have changed dramatically since their antebellum origins and largely as the result of incorporating identical external influences into their cultural systems. From antebellum to present times, the outstanding difference between the two cultures is religious affiliation. Considering that, by the twentieth century, many South Louisiana "French Catholics" were at least partly of Anglo-Saxon origin, religion—and not language, ethnicity, or national origin—is the one outstanding difference between antebellum North and South Louisiana that still survives.

The ascriptive group identities that label members of the culture across the boundary as "different," or "other," no doubt originated because the mostly French people who lived in Louisiana when the nineteenth century immigrations of mostly Anglo-Saxon people occurred, *were* different. Between 1880 and 1940, however, differences of national origin, language, economic practice, racial views, and politics became less easily discernible as South Louisiana and its Catholic Church became an integral part of the southern region instead of the foreign country within a country that it once constituted.

Americanized, at last, South Louisiana yet remained different after World War II because of its Catholicism and its peculiar heritages of music, cooking, and "joie de vivre" that survived the Americanization process through adoption or toleration by Anglos. In large measure, these peculiarities, which help give the southern section its distinctiveness, have survived because of the social influence that Catholicism exerted on its side of the cultural boundary. Conversely, South Louisiana cultural traits were prevented from spreading into the northern section of the state by the Protestant influences dominant there.[51]

Social development in Louisiana between 1880 and 1940 demonstrated a process, not of social continuity, but of social and cultural persistence in both sections of the state. By the beginning of World War II, both sections had undergone extensive social change, a process best measured by the growth of educational systems, both public and religious. Largely developed beyond the crude, first stages of their evolution by 1940, public and religious systems of education in Louisiana needed only more money in order to enter into their final stages of development following the war. The patterns of development had become settled.

Both black and white Protestants had become reliant on public education, supplemented by religious education in Sunday Schools. Catholics continued to expand their parochial school system and to duplicate, as far as possible, the administrative procedures, curricula, class materials, and educational philosophies of the public schools, except for the religious education provided. The state had finally wrested control of educational outlays away from local governments and had begun to equalize the public system both in terms of urban-rural and black-white disparities. Accomplishment of educational parity for blacks was, unfortunately, never accomplished, despite the de-segregation of public schools in more recent times. However, the equalization of qualifications and teacher salaries of blacks and whites, as well as the increased outlays of funds for black schools in the years after 1935 (up to the end of the dual system in the 1970s), attest to an effort by the state to give the phrase "separate but equal" a sounder basis in fact than it had before 1935.

By 1940, the dominant religious groups in Louisiana, Baptists and Catholics, had settled on the educational methods by which they continued to guide cultural accommodation to change by their church members on each side of the cultural boundary. Having accomplished successful religious aggrandizement in their respective sections, Baptists and Catholics would prove able to increase their proportional percentages among church populations in the postwar period of even greater and more rapid social change than characterized the period between Reconstruction and World War II. Although sometimes disparaged by the non-religious, or by those impatient for rapid social reforms that religious groups often opposed, religious denominations necessarily respected and encouraged the social conservatism of their adherents in order to retain their confidence and loyalty. Religious educational programs have consequently been slow in accommodating church members to new ideas that foster social and cultural changes. However, the fact that they did so—while serving as a force for cultural stability amidst the bewildering pace of change in society—was historically significant to the social and cultural development of the state.

II

Definition and Delineation of Louisiana's Cultural Boundary

Louisiana's cultural boundary is the geographical line separating North Louisiana, as a cultural region, from the French Triangle. All the various factors involved in the maintenance of separate cultures in the state during the nineteenth century were components of cultural systems prominently associated with the competing religious traditions of Protestantism and Catholicism. As social institutions, Louisiana's religious traditions supported and perpetuated the cultural systems associated with them. After 1880, broad social changes resulted in cultural transformation as the competing cultural systems in the state absorbed external cultural influences and altered or discarded existing factors of cultural differentiation. One constant in both cultural systems was the continuing dominance of their religious traditions.

Over time, the numerical strength of Catholicism in South Louisiana and of evangelical Protestantism in North Louisiana increased as other factors of cultural difference diminished. Consequently, of all the factors involved in the maintenance of Louisiana's separate cultures, religious affiliation is the one most appropriate for use in defining the cultural boundary's geographic location at any point in time. All five religious censuses conducted by the United States government—which enumerate memberships of various denominations on the county, as well as the state, level—were conducted between 1890 and 1936, affording statistical comparisons over a time period roughly coincident with the time frame of this study.

Analysis of the religious data for individual parishes clearly demonstrates the existence of a boundary along lines of religious affiliation. Rather than showing the gradual appearance of Protestant and Catholic majorities along either side of a mixed population zone between sections of the state, Louisiana's pattern of religious affiliation reflected sharp religious differences from one parish to the next along a clearly recognizable line between Protestant North and Catholic South Louisiana. Sustained or even strengthened over time, such sharp religious differences were not anomalies suggested by flawed data at individual points in time. Rather, religious differences in Louisiana were strikingly revealed by the censuses of 1890, 1906, 1916, 1926, and 1936. Despite flaws that cast doubt as to whether Catholics outnumbered Protestants in the state as a whole, as the censuses indicated, margins of error in the censuses were not so large as to suggest any doubt over the validity of figures showing solid Protestant or Catholic majorities in individual parishes.

As already suggested, religious difference was the most prominent of social divisions tending to perpetuate Louisiana's cultural boundary amidst profound social changes resulting from and following the Civil War and Reconstruction. Political, ethnic, and racial divisions also existed, which had a bearing on the formation and maintenance of the cultural boundary. North-south political division was a partial consequence of cultural differences, but also of economic factors deriving from the production of different staple crops in the two sections of the state. Ethnic divisions were minor in impact because Louisiana attracted few immigrants between 1880 and 1940. However, what immigration did take place affected the cultural boundary in that the majority of Louisiana's immigrants were Catholic and tended to settle in the Triangle parishes—strengthening already-existing religious and cultural divisions in the state. A more prominent factor affecting cultural and religious differences was racial division, as Louisiana contained, proportionally, a larger black population during the late nineteenth century than any state other than Mississippi and South Carolina.

A majority of the state's black population resided in North Louisiana between 1880 and 1940. Following the Civil War, small enclaves of black Catholics continued to reside in Natchitoches, Rapides, and Sabine parishes in North Louisiana, but the overwhelming majority of North Louisiana's blacks became and remained Protestants over the years before World War II. In South Louisiana, the majority of blacks also became Protestants, at least by 1890. About one of every three black religious adherents remained Catholic up to 1890 and the ratio of Catholics among the black religious never declined from that point—even into the post-World War II period, when the bulk of Louisiana's black population had shifted to the southern parishes. Because enough of the black population of South Louisiana remained Catholic after the Civil War, augmenting an overwhelming Catholic influence on whites, South Louisiana remained predominantly Catholic, despite a large number of black Protestants.

Up to World War II, Louisiana had a tri-partite political division between urban New Orleans, the rest of rural South Louisiana, and North Louisiana. The state's only true metropolitan center before World War II, New Orleans, with about one-fifth of the state's population, came to be dominated by urban machine politics by the end of Reconstruction. After Reconstruction, a political alliance between Orleans Parish and the parishes of the state dominated by planter elites assumed control of state politics. While both the northern and southern sections of the state were largely rural in character, both containing black-belt parishes, North Louisiana cotton planters generally prevailed over the sugar planters of South Louisiana, when the interests of these two groups differed.[1]

Because of different economic interests, politically evident most often in dispute over the tariff, the more common political alliance prior to the 1930s was that between the city machine and North Louisiana planters and cotton farmers. Louisiana differed from the classic southern political dualism between black-belt planters and hill-county poor whites. Rather, in Louisiana, bi-factionalism was more apparent in terms of North-South economic and political differences, although such differences began to have less impact as the state industrialized and urbanized.[2]

Economic and cultural differences, separating the North Louisiana cotton-belt from the South Louisiana sugar and rice parishes, were reflected by the pattern of settlement in the state. The South Louisiana prairies, wooded swamps, and farm lands along rivers and bayous, lined by live oak trees, generally represented the limits of settlement of French and Acadian Catholics in the eighteenth century. The cotton-belt areas of the Florida parishes and North Louisiana became settled in the nineteenth century by Anglo-Saxon Protestants immigrating from southern states to the east, where cotton cultivation dominated the agricultural economy.[3] By the late nineteenth century, when the last remaining areas of the state were populated, Louisiana's cultural boundary became stabilized. Roughly as it existed in 1890, the boundary remains evident to travelers through Louisiana today.[4]

Anthropologists and folklorists, who have studied Cajun and Creole culture, still refer to the French Triangle which, when imposed on a map of Louisiana, indicates broadly the geographical boundary lines that separate French Catholic Louisiana from the Protestant, Anglo-Saxon population of North Louisiana and the Florida parishes. Beginning in Cameron Parish in the southwestern part of the state, a line runs northeast to the tip of Avoyelles Parish. From here, at the apex of the triangle, another line runs southeast to St. Bernard Parish, completing the triangle, the base of which is the coastline of the Gulf of Mexico. Everything within the triangle is a cultural area characterized by Catholicism and the influences of French colonial heritage. Outside the triangle are areas characterized by Protestantism and the cultural influences of the Anglo-Saxon people who moved to Louisiana from other southern states during the nineteenth century.[5]

Of course, there has always been communication and intercultural exchange across the boundary, which has never been completely rigid. During the nineteenth century, enclaves of French-speaking white and black Catholics lived in DeSoto, Natchitoches, Rapides, and Sabine parishes west of the Red River in the northern section of the state. Over time, these

Catholics either emigrated or were absorbed by the surrounding dominant population of Protestants, as population growth occurred in the twentieth century. Few people in these parishes speak French any longer and the percentage of Catholics has dwindled in relation to a growing percentage of Protestants, mainly Baptists and Methodists.

Similarly, descendants of Anglo immigrants in the southern part of the state tend now to be Catholic and to be willing participants in perpetuating the surviving remnants of nineteent-century Cajun and Creole culture. Students of French culture in southern Louisiana often comment on the assimilative power of that culture, especially in its ability in the past to have absorbed immigrants of Spanish, German, Italian, and even English or Irish backgrounds. To the present day, there remain isolated rural communities within the French Triangle where the inhabitants speak French, or speak English with a Cajun accent, despite the prevalence of surnames of German, Italian, Spanish, or English origin. Especially in the area of southwestern Louisiana, where Cajun influence was strongest, did rural isolation survive into the twentieth century and French cultural influence remain strongest. Catholic influence and French-speaking among black Creoles was also strongest and most persistent in southwestern Louisiana.[6]

Since World War II especially, the isolation and continuing dominance of Cajun and Creole culture within the southern part of the state has broken down. Public school systems that demanded English language instruction, a burgeoning oil industry that rewarded increased levels of educational attainment, and increased immigration of people, attracted from across the cultural boundary by oil-induced economic prosperity, have brought increased social change. Weakening of traditional religious influence brought on by the increased strength, in the present century, of secularism had the effect of eliminating the cultural isolation of Louisiana's cultural groups from the national mainstream.[7]

Southern Louisianians are no longer as easily distinguishable from their fellow Louisianians in Alexandria, Bogalusa, Shreveport, or Monroe. In the cities of Lafayette, Houma, or Donaldsonville, newly arrived residents from Texas or Michigan have little difficulty in adapting to the cultural mix that characterizes South Louisiana today. As long as there are Protestant churches to attend, NFL football games to watch, Parent-Teacher organizations to join, and a modern infrastructure around which an industrial economy survives, newcomers to South Louisiana find no reason not to support programs for bilingualism in the schools, or to attend functions that feature Cajun music and spicy seafood. In fact, where once anything "Cajun" had a pejorative connotation to outsiders, Cajun music, food, and cultural "joie-de-vivre" are now considered fashionable, even in such far-off locations as San Francisco or New York City.

The two sections of the state have become less different from each other than before, but only because they have independently incorporated some of the same external influences from outside the state and from outside the southern region. Much change in Louisiana society and culture was induced by post-World War II economic prosperity. Particularly important to economic change was development of the oil, petrochemical, and oil well service industries originating in Texas and controlled by northern-based corporations. For this reason, Shreveport and environs have more cultural contact with Dallas, Texas than with South Louisiana. Conversely, southern Louisiana has more cultural contact with Houston, Texas than with northern Louisiana cities such as Alexandria, Monroe, or Shreveport. To the present day, there are only two four-lane highways connecting South Louisiana with any part of North Louisiana—Interstate 55, which runs northward from near New Orleans through the Florida parish of Tangipahoa, and then on to such cities as Jackson, Mississippi and Memphis, Tennessee, and Interstate 49, stretching from Lafayette to Shreveport.[8] In Louisiana, both in the nineteenth century and in more recent times, the generalization holds true that Protestants have predominated in North Louisiana—which, as a cultural area, includes the Florida parishes—and Catholics form the majority within the French Triangle.

In thirty-eight of fifty-nine parishes where the religious population was overwhelmingly Protestant in 1890, all were outside of the French Triangle except for Cameron, Iberville, St. Charles, St. Mary, and West Baton Rouge Parishes. In 1890, Cameron Parish, composed largely of coastal marshland, was sparsely populated, difficult to travel through, and devoid of Catholic churches. Consequently, the census in Cameron was incomplete and erroneously reflected an absence of Catholic influence. In later years, as Catholic churches were constructed to serve the Catholic population and as transportation through the parish improved, subsequent religious censuses more accurately reflected the religious composition of the parish. The 1936 religious census reported Cameron Parish to be over ninety-three per cent Catholic.[9]

Aberrant religious composition of the other four Triangle parishes reported as Protestant in 1890 is explained by the predominance of Protestantism among majority black populations. These parishes ranged from sixty-four per cent black in St. Mary to seventy-four per cent black in St. Charles Parish. In all four parishes, black Baptists and Methodists overshadowed white Protestants and Catholics. Blacks in Iberville Parish, converted to Protestantism during the Reconstruction period, accounted for fifty-seven per cent of the religious communicants of the parish. White

Protestants, on the other hand, accounted for only two per cent of the religious. Other South Louisiana parishes that did not contain black majorities, were statistically Catholic because few whites in South Louisiana were Protestant. By 1936, when the black population had declined relative to the white, four of the five parishes showing Protestant majorities in 1890 had become majority Catholic. The other, West Baton Rouge Parish, remained majority Protestant because it retained a majority black Protestant population. In addition, Pointe Coupee Parish, heavily black but Catholic in 1890, developed a slight Protestant majority by 1936, due to the influx of large numbers of blacks from heavily Protestant West Feliciana Parish during the twentieth century.[10]

There were other exceptions to the cultural boundary's rigid separation of Protestants and Catholics. Of the twenty parishes in 1890 with Catholic religious majorities, two—Natchitoches and St. Tammany—were located outside of the Triangle. A third parish, DeSoto, contained a large number of Catholics even though its majority was Protestant. Natchitoches, which was nearly sixty-eight per cent Catholic in 1890, and DeSoto, which was over forty-four per cent Catholic, are located in the northwestern part of the state. These parishes have a history of French and Spanish Catholic settlement that pre-dates the arrival of Anglo-Saxon Protestants in the nineteenth century. The first permanent French settlement in Louisiana, in fact, was at Natchitoches in 1714.[11]

The same is true of the other exception, St. Tammany Parish, which is located north of Lake Pontchartrain, directly across the lake from Jefferson and Orleans parishes. Throughout the history of the parish, the largest number of people in St. Tammany lived along the northern shore of the lake, and happened to be largely French Catholic. Population growth in the central and northern parts of the parish, which are predominantly Protestant, has since managed only to keep up with the growth of largely Catholic towns as Covington, Mandeville, and Slidell, which are within easy reach of Catholic New Orleans. Regular steamship service connected New Orleans to the southernmost parts of St. Tammany as early as the 1860s. In more recent times, United States and interstate highways, as well as the causeway bridge spanning the lake, have strengthened the ties between St. Tammany and Orleans and Jefferson parishes. Consequently, the close ties between New Orleans and the southernmost portions of St. Tammany have caused the parish to display statistical characteristics that are different from the other Florida parishes. Although the greatest part of the land area of the parish is inhabited by a predominantly Protestant majority, the denser population along the shores of Lake Pontchartrain is predominantly Catholic, making St. Tammany statistically one of the Triangle parishes.[12]

After 1890, the Catholicity of Natchitoches and DeSoto parishes succumbed to Protestant conversion, Catholic out-migration, and cultural absorption by a surrounding majority of Protestants. By 1936, DeSoto Parish had become 94.2 per cent Protestant, while Natchitoches, from where North Louisiana's bishopric headquarters was moved to Alexandria in 1910, had become almost fifty-three per cent Protestant. After Bishop Cornelius Van de Ven moved his diocesan headquarters from the city of Natchitoches to the city of Alexandria in Rapides Parish, the Protestant majority of Rapides declined slightly, but the parish remained over sixty per cent Protestant by 1936. By 1936, the Diocese of Alexandria, comprising all of North Louisiana exclusive of the Florida parishes, contained only one parish with a Catholic majority: Avoyelles Parish, which is inside the French Triangle.[13]

In conformity with the national pattern of Catholic concentration in cities, Catholics have made proportional gains since the nineteenth century in such North Louisiana cities as Alexandria, Monroe, and Shreveport. Although these urban gains have been both noticeable and significant, Protestants retained sizeable majorities in cities outside the Triangle. Whether because rural Catholics in North Louisiana moved to North Louisiana cities or migrated out of the section, Catholicism had become an urban phenomenon in the northern section of the state by 1936.[14]

Within the dominant cultural areas of Louisiana, separated by religious affiliation, were ethnic enclaves that were neither Anglo-Saxon Protestant nor French Catholic. In the case of European immigrants, most tended to settle in the southern part of the state, where they were usually absorbed by the dominant French Catholic culture. In conformity with the pattern that prevailed in all areas of the South where Anglo-Saxon Protestants dominated, foreign immigration to North Louisiana never amounted to more than a trickle, even during the periods of heaviest immigration to the United States between the 1880s and 1920s.[15]

The largest single group of foreign immigrants to Louisiana by 1930 were Italians, who made up one-third of all foreign-born whites in the state. Another third originated from Germany, France, Ireland, and Great Britain, of whom only Great Britain did not have a substantial Catholic population. The remaining third were from scattered origins, Russians being the largest group in this category at 2.4 per cent of the total foreign-born. No other national group was represented by more than two per cent of the total foreign-born. At a glance, one observes that the majority of foreign-born Louisianians were from Catholic countries, a probable reason that most settled in the southern part of the state. The majority of these immigrants either lived in New Orleans, or in surrounding parishes where they engaged predominantly in truck farming to supply the food demand of the city of

New Orleans. The only distinctive enclaves of foreign culture to be found in the state were either in New Orleans and vicinity, or in fishing communities along the southern coast. Everywhere else in the rest of the state, the foreign-born were scattered individuals who quickly assimilated into the surrounding population and culture.[16]

Another group of newcomers to Louisiana was the sizeable immigration of Americans, mostly from Iowa and parts of the Midwest, in the 1880s. These people came in response to a promotional campaign backed by the Louisiana Grange, the state government, and private companies involved in land speculation to attract immigrants interested in agricultural opportunities. Begun in the early 1870s, efforts to attract immigrants to Louisiana were, for the most part, a failure in that widely distributed literature extolling the state's agricultural blessings failed to attract many foreign immigrants. However, with the aid of the venerable Seaman A. Knapp, the prospect of growing rice in southwestern Louisiana did attract the interest of a number of midwesterners. During the 1880s, towns in Acadia Parish, such as Crowley, and Lake Charles in Calcasieu Parish, along the route of the new railroad being built between New Orleans and Houston, sprang up nearly overnight. Within a short time, rice fields dominated the landscape around Crowley, Lake Charles, and such other new towns as Iowa and Vinton, whose names reflected the state of origin of the towns' founders.[17]

Religiously, these midwesterners came from an area of the country strongly represented in 1890 by Lutherans, but also by Catholics, who made up twenty-five to fifty per cent of the total population (not just of the religious population) in both of the Dakotas, Illinois, Iowa, Minnesota, Nebraska, and Wisconsin. The 1890 census reported only one Lutheran church outside of the New Orleans area—in Calcasieu Parish. By 1936, the majority of Lutherans in Louisiana were still to be found in New Orleans. Small Lutheran congregations of 100 to 200 members could also be found in the Florida parishes, in Baton Rouge, and in Acadia and Calcasieu parishes. In both 1890 and 1936, Acadia Parish was overwhelmingly Catholic (over eighty-five per cent). Calcasieu Parish was mostly Catholic in 1890 despite the fact that the parish contained the predominantly Protestant area that would be split off in 1911 to form Allen and Beauregard parishes. The overwhelmingly Catholic area that became Jefferson Davis Parish was also split off from Calcasieu Parish in 1911, explaining why Calcasieu's religious population of 1936 was only fifty-five per cent Catholic as compared to fifty-three per cent in 1890. Most of Calcasieu's Catholics lived in the eastern portion of the parish, around Lake Charles, while most Protestants occupied the western part of the parish, in proximity to the Texas border. Clearly, the rice-growing areas of eastern Calcasieu,

Jefferson Davis, and Acadia parishes were religiously dominated by Catholics in both 1890 and 1936. Consequently, the majority of midwestern immigrants to this area in the 1880s and 1890s were either Catholic when they arrived or else they adapted to the predominantly Catholic religious influences of southern Louisiana. In either case, the effect was a greater concentration of Catholics in an area sparsely populated before the 1880s—and a strengthening of the cultural boundary defined by religious affiliations.[18]

The majority of Louisiana's Protestants were Baptists in 1890. Methodists were prominently represented in the Florida parishes, in Grant Parish, and in the northwestern and northeastern parts of the state. Elsewhere in North Louisiana, Baptists were the overwhelming majority. Because most of the state's antebellum black-belt areas were located along the Red, Mississippi, and Ouachita rivers in the northern part of the state, blacks made up the majority of the population in much of northern Louisiana as well as the majority of Louisiana's Protestants.[19]

In 1890, blacks made up fifty-one per cent of the state population but declined relatively to thirty-seven per cent in 1930, a reflection of black out-migration and growth of the white population, particularly in southern Louisiana. Out of thirty-three parishes with black majorities in 1890, only eleven were within the French Triangle. By 1936, only three of sixteen parishes with black majorities were inside the Triangle.[20]

Protestant religious bodies, other than Baptists or Methodists, comprised only five per cent of Louisiana's religious population in 1890.[21] The highest percentage among religious communicants of any religious group other than Catholics, Baptists, or Methodists in any parish, was a 7.7 per cent representation by Episcopalians in West Feliciana Parish. Episcopalians represented twenty-two per cent of the white religious in the parish, an unusually high percentage for any group other than the three major denominations. West Feliciana's atypicality was explainable in terms of unique historical and geographical conditions. It is the only parish along the Mississippi border that has frontage along the Mississippi River, but yet is not separated from Mississippi by the river. West Feliciana's strong connections with Mississippi during the nineteenth century gave the parish stronger economic and social bonds to Mississippi counties than with surrounding Louisiana parishes and contributed to the strength of its Episcopalian population, which originated in Mississippi. Also, for some years, the Catholics of this parish were unique in being served by the Diocese of Natchez in Mississipi, rather than by the Archdiocese of New Orleans or the Diocese of Natchitoches, as with every other Louisiana parish in 1890. By 1936, Episcopalians made up over forty per cent of the white religious population. West Feliciana, however, contained a majority black population in which nearly eighty per cent of the parish's total religious population were black Baptists.[22]

Jews have never been numerous in Louisiana, as is true for the South in general. In 1890, Jews made up less than one per cent of the religious population of the state, and the percentage becomes miniscule if represented in relation to the total state population. A total of 2750 of the approximately 3500 Jewish people in the state resided in New Orleans, while Baton Rouge and Shreveport contained small communities of 375 and 150. By 1936, the Jewish population had grown to about 13,500, representing 1.2 per cent of the religious population of the state. Substantial growth since 1890 had made Jews about as representative throughout the state as Presbyterians or Episcopalians. Over half still resided in New Orleans, but Baton Rouge and Shreveport also contained Jewish communities of significant size. Indicative of the national pattern of Jewish settlement, Louisiana's Jews lived in cities or large towns. By 1936, nearly every Louisiana city of any size and economic importance contained a small population of Jewish people. Excluding New Orleans, there was no sectional pattern to the growth of the Jewish population. For its small size, Louisiana's Jewish population exerted an unusual degree of influence over such matters as economic and educational development in the state and must be considered a significant factor in the relationship that evolved between religion and education as social institutions.[23]

The same characterization holds true for Presbyterians and Episcopalians, who tended to be well represented in the state's planter and merchant classes. As with the Jewish minority, Presbyterians and Episcopalians exhibited no sectional pattern of concentration, except that they tended to be more urban than the state's three dominant religious groups, though not exclusively so. Also, like the Jewish population, the majority of Louisiana's Presbyterians and Episcopalians resided in New Orleans. The only other significant religious group in Louisiana was the slightly fewer than four per cent of the religious population who belonged to one or another of the various sectarian offshoots of Baptist and Methodist groups. As was true for the parent bodies from which these groups originated, they were most proportionally represented outside of the French Triangle in both 1890 and 1936.[24]

The cultural boundary's definition by religious affiliation was already stable and well-established by 1890—except for the four southern parishes where black Baptists predominated and except for the Catholic majority of Natchitoches Parish. By 1936, only two southern parishes, Pointe Coupee and West Baton Rouge, contained black Protestant majorities. The twenty-five parishes (including St. Tammany, but not Natchitoches) that made up the southern, French Catholic section of the state in 1890 were 73.3 per cent Catholic. By 1936, with the break-up of Calcasieu Parish, the southern section had grown to twenty-seven parishes (including Pointe Coupee and West Baton Rouge) and had increased its percentage of Catholics, among the religious, to 78.5 per cent. The next largest religious group in South Louisiana was the Negro Baptists, who grew from 9.6 per cent of the religious in 1890, to 9.7 per cent in 1936. White Southern Baptists grew from one per cent to 1.3 per cent. Altogether, all of the white and black Baptist and Methodist groups declined, in southern Louisiana, from 19.1 per cent in 1890 to 14.4 per cent in 1936.[25]

In the northern section of the state, Protestantism was dominant by 1890 and remained so in 1936. While the numbers of Catholics outside the Triangle grew from just over twenty thousand in 1890 to over fifty-four thousand in 1936, the Catholic percentage among the North Louisiana religious population declined from 14.7 to 13.6 per cent. While Catholics predominated in Natchitoches Parish in 1890, Baptists and Methodists predominated in all North Louisiana parishes by 1936.[26]

In both Orleans Parish, containing the city of New Orleans, and in the rest of the southern parishes, only Negro Baptists ever mounted any challenge to the religious dominance of the Catholic Church, a challenge offset in the twentieth century by a declining percentage of South Louisiana blacks relative to whites, who were overwhelmingly Catholic. In the northern section of the state, including the Florida parishes, a great deal more competition between Protestant denominations took place from 1890 to 1936. In this contest, largely between Baptists and Methodists, among both the white and black populations, Baptists were the clear winners by 1936.[27] By 1970, every parish in the state was either majority Baptist or majority Catholic except for East Baton Rouge, which was mostly Protestant although Catholics slightly outnumbered Baptists.[28]

A part of the cultural boundary's definition could not be furnished by religious census data. Although the religious censuses enumerated black Protestants in both North and South Louisiana, they did not distinguish between black and white Catholics until 1936. Moreover, the 1936 enumeration of black Catholics was incomplete, including only black Catholics attending exclusively black churches at a time when Catholic Church racial segregation was not a completed process.

The Catholic Church began to segregate black Catholics after establishment of the first exclusively black church in New Orleans in 1895. By the 1920s, the majority of black Catholics were in attendance at segregated churches and chapels. At all times before World War II, however, an unknown number of black Catholics continued to attend predominantly white churches, where separate black churches had not yet been established.[29]

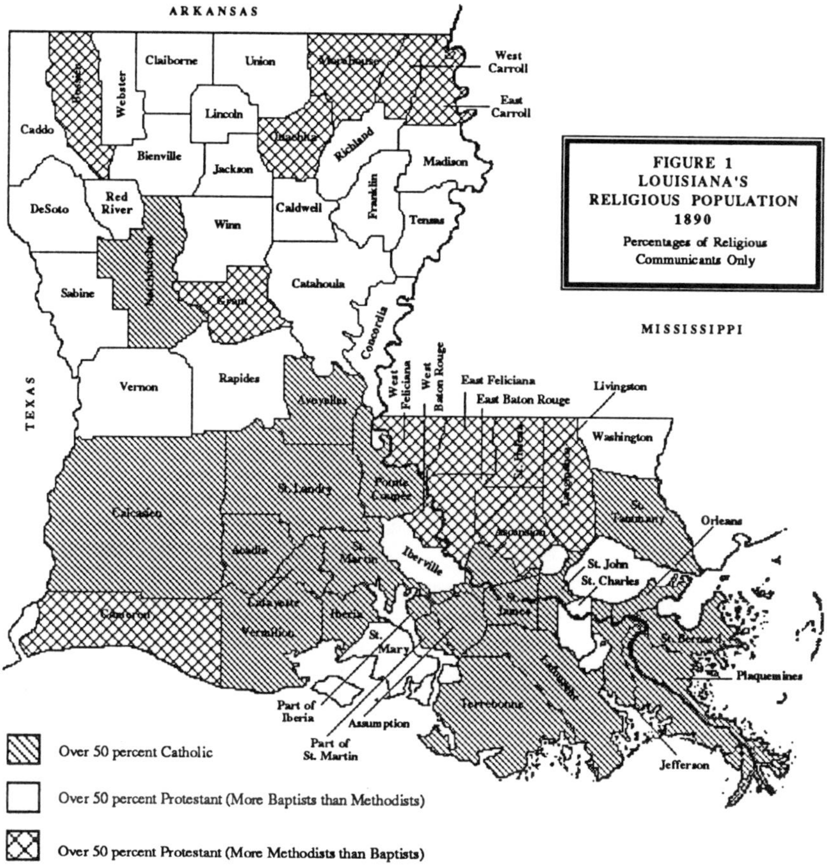

FIGURE 1
LOUISIANA'S
RELIGIOUS POPULATION
1890
Percentages of Religious
Communicants Only

Map outline from William Ivy Hair, ***Bourbonism and Agrarian Protest: Louisiana Politics, 1877-1900*** (Baton Rouge, 1969), p. 117; Statistics from U. S. Bureau of the Census, ***Report on Statistics of Churches at the Eleventh Census: 1890*** (Washington, 1894).

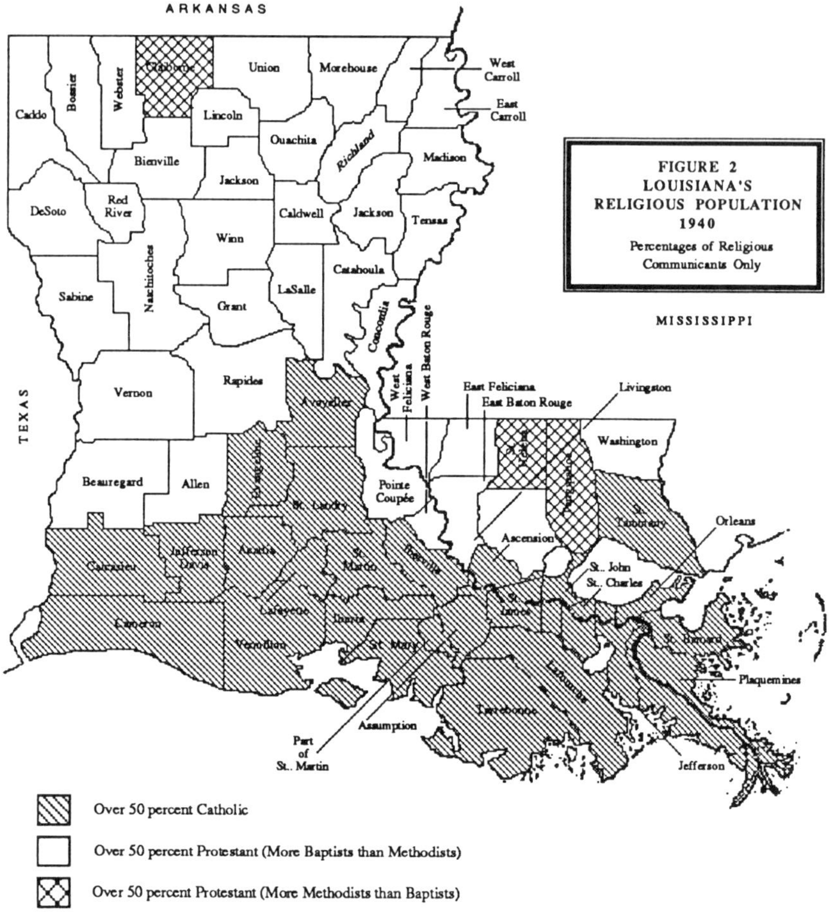

FIGURE 2
LOUISIANA'S
RELIGIOUS POPULATION
1940
Percentages of Religious
Communicants Only

Map outline from William Ivy Hair, *Bourbonism and Agrarian Protest: Louisiana Politics, 1877-1900* (Baton Rouge, 1969), p. 117; Statistics from U. S. Bureau of the Census, *Religious Bodies: 1936* (Washington, D. C., 1941).

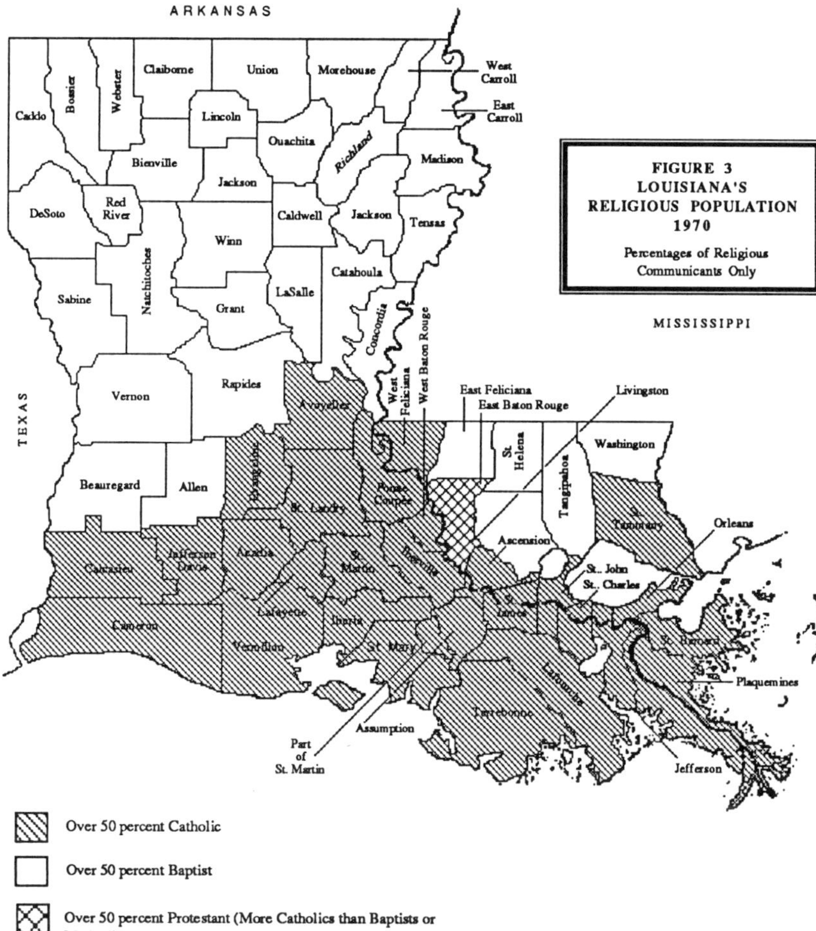

Map outline from William Ivy Hair, *Bourbonism and Agrarian Protest: Louisiana Politics, 1877-1900* (Baton Rouge, 1969), p. 117; Statistics from Edwin S. Gaustad, *Historical Atlas of Religion in America* (New York, 1976).

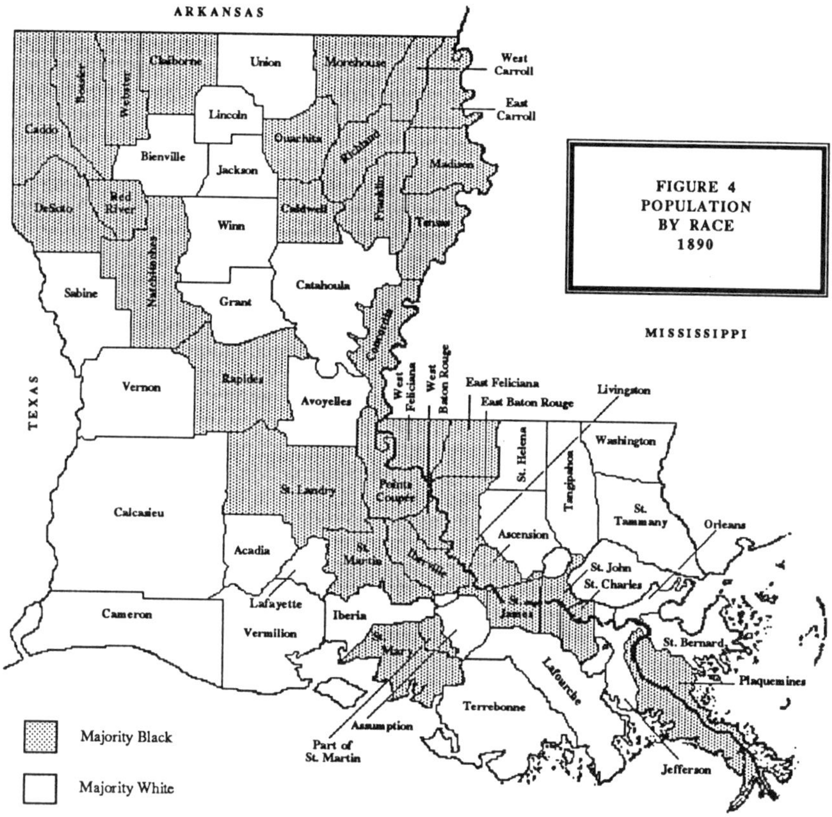

FIGURE 4
POPULATION
BY RACE
1890

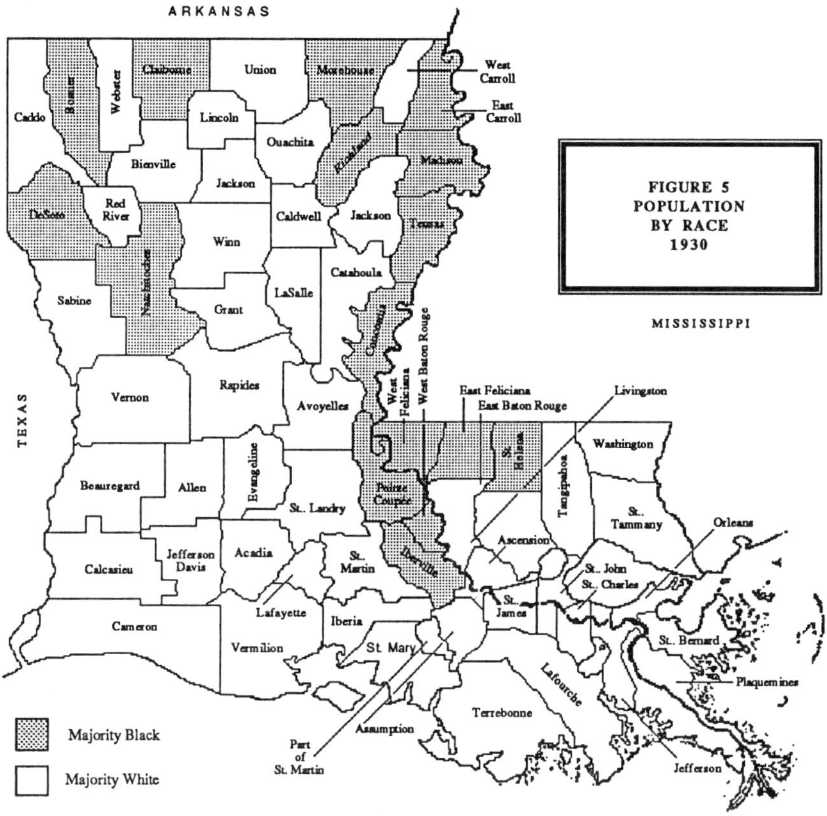
ARKANSAS
TEXAS
MISSISSIPPI
FIGURE 5
POPULATION
BY RACE
1930
Caddo
Webster
Claiborne
Union
Morehouse
West Carroll
East Carroll
Lincoln
Ouachita
Bienville
Jackson
Madison
Red River
DeSoto
Caldwell
Jackson
Tensas
Winn
Catahoula
Sabine
Grant
LaSalle
West Baton Rouge
Vernon
Rapides
Avoyelles
West Feliciana
East Feliciana
East Baton Rouge
Livingston
Washington
St. Helena
Beauregard
Allen
Evangeline
St. Landry
Pointe Coupee
Tangipahoa
St. Tammany
Orleans
Calcasieu
Jefferson Davis
Acadia
St. Martin
Ascension
St. John
St. Charles
St. James
Lafayette
Iberia
Cameron
Vermilion
St. Mary
St. Bernard
Plaquemines
Lafourche
Terrebonne
Assumption
Part of St. Martin
Jefferson
Majority Black
Majority White

Consequently, the 1890 census had no enumeration of black Catholics and the 1936 enumeration was incomplete.

Catholic Church records are no help in determining how many Catholics were black because reports on church membership by church pastors did not indicate the racial composition of church memberships. For all of North Louisiana and for some civil parishes (counties) in South Louisiana, the 1890 census enumeration of blacks and of black Protestants established that black Protestants were the majority of the black religious population. For most of South Louisiana's parishes, there was no reliable way to determine whether the majority of the black religious were Protestant or Catholic, though estimates for South Louisiana and the state, as a whole, are possible.

Archbishop Francis Janssens ordered a census of black Catholics in the Archdiocese of New Orleans in 1889. At the time, the archdiocese contained all South Louisiana parishes, except Avoyelles, which was part of the Diocese of Natchitoches. Unfortunately, only eight of approximately one hundred churches responded to Janssens' directive. Subsequently, the archbishop publicly estimated that there were 75,000 black Catholics in his archdiocese, a figure that probably represented the number Janssens thought should have existed in relation to total black population. It is not known how Janssens arrived at his estimate, though it is beyond question that the estimate was too high.[30]

For North Louisiana, which contained few Catholics of either race, the 1890 census revealed that approximately twenty-three per cent of the black population belonged to religious denominations, in contrast to nearly thirty-six per cent for the South as a whole. Acceptance of Janssens' estimate for black Catholics would raise the 1890 percentage of black religious to black population in the state from twenty-three to thirty-three, more in line with the southern average. However, if just South Louisiana parishes are considered, which contained nearly all of the black Catholics in Janssens' estimate, then the percentage of black religious in South Louisiana rises to forty-four—eight points higher than the southern average and nearly twice the percentage in North Louisiana.

A better estimate for South Louisiana's black Catholics is one assuming that South Louisiana's percentage of black religious was comparable to the percentage in North Louisiana, where a majority of the state's blacks resided. Accordingly, if twenty-three per cent of South Louisiana blacks belonged to religious denominations, then the number of black Protestants reported by the 1890 religious census should have been augmented by approximately 20,000 black Catholics—a figure representing approximately ten per cent of South Louisiana's total Catholic population in 1890.

Unspecified Catholic authorities estimated in 1865 that there were approximately 63,000 black Catholics in Louisiana, at a time preceding the missionary efforts of white northern Protestants through the Freedman's Bureau and through northern church missionary agencies.[31] After 1865, the establishment of black Protestant churches in South Louisiana became a source of concern to Catholic authorities, who recognized that the church's influence on the black community was dwindling as black Protestant churches multiplied during the late nineteenth century. The 1890 religious census reported approximately 40,000 black Protestants in the southern parishes, a Protestant increase since 1865 likely gained at the expense of the Catholic Church's reported membership in 1865. Subtracting the census enumeration of black Protestants from the estimate for black Catholics in 1865 leaves 23,000 black Catholics, out of which 3,000 is a reasonable estimate for North Louisiana.

Although only an estimation, the figure of 20,000 black Catholics in 1890 South Louisiana is the identical product of two different estimation procedures. In the absence of verifiable, accurate counts, the figure of ten per cent of the total Catholic membership represents a reasonable estimate for the number of black Catholics in Louisiana in the late nineteenth century.

On the basis of that estimate, an apparently valid assertion is that black Protestants outnumbered black Catholics in 1890 by approximately two to one in Catholic South Louisiana—a serious breach in the integrity of the religiously defined cultural boundary. Had such Protestant hegemony over South Louisiana's black population continued into the twentieth century, the Catholic Church would have lost its cultural influence over a sizeable segment of the South Louisiana population, endangering both the cultural cohesion of South Louisiana and the continued maintenance of the cultural boundary by force of religious tradition and the cultural activities perpetuated by religious traditions.

Twentieth-century statistical evidence, however, does not show that Catholic membership losses in the late nineteenth century became a continuing trend. Continued dominance of Catholic religious traditions within South Louisiana's white population served to arrest further numerical losses relative to Protestant traditions since the black population—once the majority of Louisiana's total population as late as 1890—became a constantly decreasing minority in the first decades of the twentieth century.[32] That trend of population growth served to reduce the total impact of black Protestant strength on the integrity of the cultural boundary, since white Catholic majorities assured that Catholic majorities among the total population would continue to characterize the southern parishes.

In addition, statistical information on black religious adherents suggests that nineteenth century Catholic losses among blacks in South Louisiana ceased by the turn of the century, as Catholic segregation of churches after 1895 began to promote significant growth in the numbers of South Louisiana black Catholics. The 1936 religious census, which reported only the black Catholics in segregated churches, indicated that on the eve of World War II, South Louisiana black Protestants outnumbered black Catholics by about 80,000 to 60,000—figures representing equal increases of about 40,000 since 1890 by both religious traditions. Since the 1936 census figure for black Catholics is a low figure, not including blacks in predominantly white Catholic churches, the evident conclusion is that Catholic influence among South Louisiana blacks increased relative to Protestant influence between 1890 and 1940.

Black Protestantism, however, became the dominant religious tradition in some South Louisiana parishes during the late nineteenth century. Protestantism also became and remained the dominant religious tradition among blacks in North Louisiana. At a time during the late nineteenth century when the state largely ignored educational needs of blacks and before either the Catholic Church or industrial philanthropists became extensively involved with black education, black educational aspirations became one reason for the tendency of blacks to affiliate with Protestant, and particularly of Baptist, churches. As institutions largely controlled and directed by blacks, churches became social agencies to which blacks turned for the organization of self-help efforts, such as school construction, in order to enhance black economic opportunities in the post-Reconstruction South.

Because of the influential role played by black Protestant churches in the development of black education in the late nineteenth century, Protestantism became influential among blacks in both sections of Louisiana, contributing to the potential weakening or altering of Louisiana's religiously defined cultural boundary. Black Baptists were particularly involved in the expansion of denominational education programs in Louisiana and are the subject of the next chapter on black religion and its co-option of public educational influence on Louisiana's black population.

III

Religion and the "Great Detour" in Louisiana: Black Baptists and Education

After 1880, Louisiana's black population constituted a sub-culture within the two sections of the state, dominated by whites. Segregated in both sections, Louisiana's black population experienced not only the effects of the cultural boundary, but also of the invisible, omnipresent, and geographically undefined racial boundary that became known in the South as the color line. While white culture had influence on the black sub-cultures in both North and South Louisiana, the cultural boundary itself had less impact on the black population than it had on the white.

Louisiana's black population constituted an important exception to the general rule that Catholics and Protestants resided on different sides of the cultural boundary. During antebellum times, slaves usually followed the religion of their masters. Once freed of direct supervision by white masters in the postbellum period, blacks in both North and South Louisiana began to develop their own social institutions. Because blacks were denied equal access to political and economic opportunites in post-Reconstruction Louisiana, religion became the one social institution that allowed blacks the freedom of self-determination.[1]

An unidentified white representative of the American Baptist Home Mission Society (Northern Baptists) explained the reasons for blacks' affinity for religious organization in 1908:

> When the Negroes found themselves free men, they found that they were shut up to the church as the only organization that they were reasonably free to form and maintain. . . . No other organization is so generally encouraged now by the white neighbors of the Negroes. In this way the church came to have a very large place in the life of the Negro people.[2]

The Baptist faith attracted more black communicants after the Civil War than other faiths because it was the only one that did not feature the existence of a white-dominated hierarchy. By fitting the need of blacks for institutions beyond regulation or interference by whites, Negro Baptist denominations became a prime example of black non-conformity to social patterns determined by the cultural boundary. While the majority of whites in North Louisiana were Baptists and North Louisiana blacks conformed to that social pattern, the majority of blacks in South Louisiana eschewed the dominant white pattern of Catholicism in favor of attachment to Protestant congregations.

One important desire of blacks was to obtain better educational opportunities than white-dominated southern state governments provided. More so than with whites, black educational aspirations depended upon the commitment of religious organizations toward providing educational facilities. As a result, the missionary efforts of various religious denominations tended to produce competing efforts aimed at improving Negro education, beginning in the 1860s. Competition for the religious loyalty of Louisiana's blacks partly explains the motivation behind the educational philanthropy of mostly white, mostly northern, missionary agencies during Reconstruction and beyond.

Northern whites, interested in aiding the transition of the black population from slavery to freedom, quickly realized both that education was a necessary component in the transition process and that southern blacks sincerely desired educational opportunities. Partly because of southern white animosity and resistance to the efforts of "Radical Reconstruction" governments to provide public assistance to blacks, public educational systems were unable to meet demands for education in the black community. This would be hardly surprising, without white animosity, since the educational aspirations of white citizens could not be met by southern state governments—even after the installation of "white men's governments," following the Compromise of 1877. Consequently, the story of southern black, as well as of white, education in the last quarter of the nineteenth century was, in large measure, a story of campaigns for religious conversion as well as for religious education.

Of the four major northern missionary organizations which became involved in building and operating schools for southern blacks after the Civil War, only the Board of Missions for Freedmen of the Presbyterian Church was not active in Louisiana. Eleven of the twenty-one schools maintained by this organization in 1908 were located in North and South Carolina, while there were two in Arkansas, and one in every other southern state except Louisiana. Presbyterian influence was smaller in Louisiana than anywhere else in the South in the late nineteenth and early twentieth centuries. Not only were Northern Presbyterians not involved in educating Louisiana blacks, but neither were Southern Presbyterians involved in educating Louisiana's whites to any significant measure.[3]

The American Missionary Association (AMA), the American Baptist Home Mission Society, and the Freedmen's Aid Society of the Methodist Episcopal Church did maintain schools for blacks in Louisiana. For the most part, the educational efforts of these groups were stronger in other southern states, although the Negro universities established in New Orleans by these northern religious agencies in the 1860s and 1870s played a significant role in the overall development of education for blacks in Louisiana. All of the missionary agencies placed special emphasis on the establishment of higher educational institutions, where students of theology could be trained to improve the quality of the black ministry. More important than this function of northern missionary colleges was the training of teachers who could be sent back into rural areas to improve primary and secondary education for southern blacks.[4]

The colleges established in New Orleans by religious groups were of inestimable importance toward the improvement of black education in Louisiana and in the rest of the South. Northern Methodists established New Orleans University, which included the Flint Medical College, in 1873. Northern Baptists opened Leland University in New Orleans in 1870, and the AMA opened Straight University in New Orleans in 1869. These colleges were the only institutions of higher education for Negroes in Louisiana until the founding of Southern University in New Orleans by the state in 1880 and Xavier University by the Catholic Church in 1915.[5]

By 1940, the only surviving black colleges in Louisiana were the state-operated Southern University in Scotlandville, near Baton Rouge, the state-operated Grambling College in the small town of the same name, near Ruston, the Catholic Xavier University in New Orleans, and Dillard University, which resulted from the merger of Straight and New Orleans universities in 1935.[6] While these schools could hardly match the number, quality, and geographic accessibility of white colleges and universities, their growth, improvement in quality, and attainment of adequate endowments by 1945 were a far cry from the disparity in evidence between these schools and white colleges in the late nineteenth century.

In reporting to the Corresponding Secretary of the AMA in New York, concerning the quality of Straight University in 1876, Reverend Walter S. Alexander of the AMA commented that Straight "is not a school of high grade, merely a grammar school with a large *primary* department . . . ." Furthermore, it was Alexander's "firm conviction that the school will never advance beyond its present state, but rather steadily and surely decline under its present management." Alexander did maintain that improvement was possible, but only by "self-denying and persistent labor, by the highest enthusiasm and devotion, and by the wisest administration."[7]

Alexander's implicit conclusion was that financing of the school was inadequate. More explicit evidence of the tight budget under which such schools were run can be gleaned from the constant appeals to the AMA Secretary by Straight's teachers for advances and raises on their small salaries. More telling still was the difficulty that James A. Adams, the school's president, had in convincing the AMA of the necessity of fire insurance for the school's buildings. Fortunately, a policy for $15,000 had been taken out before the main building at Straight was destroyed by a fire in February, 1877. Otherwise, the school might not have survived this calamity.[8]

Despite financial problems and its poor quality, Straight University represented the best educational opportunity for blacks that could be found in the state of Louisiana during the 1870s. Adams reported to the AMA in 1876 that students of the other two missionary schools in New Orleans were leaving those schools to attend Straight, even though Leland, the main competitor, had "finer accommodations, better buildings, . . . [and] a state full of Baptist ministers to help them." Further, when the state government reorganized the public educational system after 1877, it appointed a school board to administer the public schools of New Orleans. Because of the lack of any public high school for blacks, the New Orleans Board proposed financing a normal department for Straight and assuming the salaries of the school's teachers in exchange for AMA agreement in making Straight "the High School for colored people in New Orleans." Although Straight University was evidently the finest secondary school for blacks in Louisiana, it had a long way to go toward living up to its designation as a "university."[9]

Straight University had shortcomings that were due, not only to inadequate financial support, but also to social and political conditions prevalent in the South following the Civil War. In commenting on the detrimental effects of southern politics on education in the South, Straight's president succinctly put his finger on the true nature of the problem. "Nothing can flourish on grinding poverty, corruption, fraud, turmoil, and strife," he said.[10]

Little improved by 1915 as Louisiana's black denominational colleges remained inadequate substitutes for well-funded, state-supported colleges. Unfortunately, Louisiana's black state college, Southern University, did not begin to receive adequate funding from the state until the 1930s. In 1939, Southern University's president, Felton G. Clark, described the condition of state-supported Negro land-grant colleges, like Southern, in 1915. There were seventeen such colleges in the South, which represented the future for southern black higher education because state funding offered the potential of better financial support than missionary agencies and black religious denominations could give black denominational colleges. Yet, Clark maintained that the quality of black land-grant colleges fared badly in comparison to the Negro colleges run by religious denominations and agencies. The Louisiana legislature's appropriation to Southern University in 1915 amounted to $10,000.[11]

After 1915, Louisiana began to do better by Southern University. In 1939, Southern University's legislative appropriation was $790,000. Southwide, by 1939, more than half of all southern Negro college students were enrolled in Negro land-grant colleges like Southern. Another indication that public higher education had begun to displace denominational colleges was that the seventeen black land-grant colleges in the South in 1939 accounted, for the first time, for over half the total value of southern Negro college physical plants.[12]

Before the beginnings of decline after 1915, denominational colleges in New Orleans represented the best opportunities for higher education available to blacks in Louisiana. They also performed the important function of supplying teachers to black primary and secondary schools throughout the state. Being religious schools, the denominational colleges' influence on black education in Louisiana tended to support the growth of denominational primary and secondary school programs in the state. For its influence among Louisiana's Negro Baptists, Leland University became particularly important, after 1892, to the supply of teachers for a rapidly expanding system of schools sponsored by Louisiana's Negro Baptists.[13]

As the single largest Protestant religious denomination in Louisiana from 1890 and probably for some years before then, Negro Baptists constitute the best example of Negro religious influence on educational development in Louisiana.[14] However, when referring specifically to southern Louisiana, one must recognize the significant influence of the Catholic Church, and of Negro Catholics, as well, particularly in years after 1915 and the founding of Xavier University.[15]

Despite the philanthropic generosity of private foundations, of northern missionary agencies, and of southern religious groups as well (although to a much smaller extent), development of the rudimentary structure that constituted Louisiana's system of education for Negroes before 1915, depended in large measure on the self-help contributions of Louisiana's black population. Black Baptists were particularly well-organized and involved with educational programs in localities across the state, as they constituted an overwhelming majority of Louisiana's religiously affiliated blacks.[16] This extensive organization was part of a Southwide expansion of Negro Baptist educational activity.

In 1892, the National Baptist Convention (the largest national body of Negro Baptists) established a separate National Baptist Educational Convention which was to meet annually and to work toward the success of a four-part educational program. The four objects of the educational convention were: 1) to collect statistics on Negro schools, 2) to assist graduates of Negro schools in finding jobs, 3) to provide a fund for the financial assistance of promising Negro students, and 4) to make the convention serve as a national forum for Negro and white educational leaders.[17]

By 1898, the educational convention made little headway toward the success of its program and became reunited with the parent National Baptist Convention (NBC), as its Educational Board. A good deal of self-criticism was expressed by this Educational Board in its report to the convention in 1898. Among self-criticisms of the Board was that it had spent too much time and money since 1893 publishing the quarterly *National Baptist Magazine*. Although the board claimed this magazine was "among the finest literary periodicals published among the Negroes of this country," it had also made it "necessary to partially abandon the legitimate effort of fostering educational work." However, the board also reported:

> That we have not accomplished more since our existence [since 1892] is no evidence of signal failure. We have been in a constructive stage gathering material, getting into position for the launching of plans which we trust will be productive of great results in the near future.[18]

By 1900, the outline of these plans had become clear. The board's purpose would be to discover and provide aid to Negro schools that were owned and operated by Negroes, usually Negro Baptists. That is, the board would seek to find and aid Negro schools that were unconnected with missionary agencies or with philanthropic organizations. In addition, the board intended to work out better relations between white missionary agencies—especially the American Baptist Home Mission Society—and Negro Baptists, so that blacks might have better input into the formation of black educational policies and programs. A final concern was the proposed establishment of a national theological seminary for Negro Baptists, which never came to fruition.[19]

The central idea of the NBC Educational Board became to organize a confederation of independent Negro schools in the South, and to have the national convention "take under our nurture and control such institutions. . . ." Because independent Negro schools were often supported by contributions to local Negro Baptist Associations, it became difficult to organize a system in which local contributions changed channels and were redirected to the Educational Board of the national convention—rather than to local boards of individual Associations or state conventions. As a result, the Educational Board of the national body became a gatherer of statistics, seeking to have local boards report the amounts of contributions received from their sources so that the national board could serve to channel its funds where they were most needed.[20]

"We have found," the board reported, "a number of institutions, such as high schools, academies, seminaries, colleges, and universities, scattered throughout the country, maintaining themselves by their own individual efforts, . . . and supported by contributions from Negro Baptists alone." The NBC Board saw its function as a central agency through which funds solicited from philanthropies could be channeled into schools to supplement their meager resources. Additionally, the board would serve as a central advisory body which could help to standardize and upgrade teaching practices and curricula. In effect, the NBC Educational Board wished to bring the schools associated with it into wider public view so that these schools might benefit by the resources of the national body and its contacts.[21]

Also, the NBC Board wished to expand its own involvement in Negro education so as to increase its influence upon the educational policies, programs, and financial resources of such missionary agencies as the American Baptist Home Mission Society. Members of the NBC Educational Board became disillusioned with northern white missionary agencies for their unilateral control of the progress and direction of religious educational efforts in the South. The board complained in 1899 of collusion between northern and southern white Baptists, charging them with refusal to allow Negroes any influence over the shaping of Negro educational policies in the South:

> They counselled and planned together as to what they should do for and with the Negro, but refused to consult his wishes, thereby declaring that they knew better what the Negro needed than he knew himself.[22]

The following year, the board felt compelled to answer charges by the Home Mission Society (of the northern white Baptists) that the NBC sought to disrupt educational efforts for Negro Baptists, by its competition for Negro Baptist educational loyalties. "None among us," the NBC's board appealed, "are so ignorant as to think for a moment that the colored Baptists are able to support all the educational work necessary for [Negro Baptists]." However, the board continued to insist that the Home Mission Society should agree to cooperate with the NBC and to allow it a voice in the determination of educational policies for Negro Baptists.[23]

By 1901, seventy-two independent Negro Baptist schools, mostly secondary academies, had become affiliated with the NBC. Fifteen academies in Louisiana were among these—the largest number of such academies in any single state. Southwide, the seventy-two schools in the NBC confederation were valued at just over $520,000. These were, in the main, very poorly equipped educational institutions. By comparison, the twenty-two schools for Negroes maintained by northern Methodists were valued in 1908 at over $1,450,000. The twenty-six schools of the American Baptist Home Mission Society were valued at over $1,800,000, and the thirty-seven schools of the American Missionary Association were valued at over $1,600,000.[24]

Despite the poor quality of the physical plants of these Negro Baptist academies, their impact on black education was significant. Unlike the northern missionary schools, Negro Baptist academies attempted to supply the educational demands of localized, rural areas, although many of these schools did offer boarding facilities. Many of the black academies in Louisiana were located in small towns in areas of dense black population, such as in Bunkie, Cheneyville, Cherryville, Gibsland, and Lake Providence. Others, however, were in larger towns and cities such as Shreveport, Baton Rouge, Houma, Monroe, and New Iberia.[25]

An indication of the importance placed on these schools was the amount of money raised among Negro Baptists for their maintenance. The fifteen NBC schools in Louisiana were valued, in 1901, at $40,000. However, the state convention of Negro Baptists raised $45,000 in 1901 for their maintenance. In addition, $2500 more in contributions, originating from Louisiana, found its way to the national convention's Educational Board, which channeled these funds back to Louisiana's Negro Baptist academies. Altogether in 1901, the national Educational Board of Negro Baptists distributed nearly $130,000 among seventy-two Negro academies.[26]

For the time, and considering the meager financial resources of the largely poor, rural Negro Baptist contributors, these were impressive sums. Consider, for example, that in 1923, the best year of a five-year campaign by Louisiana's white Methodists to raise one million dollars for educational purposes, only a little over $33,000 in contributions were received. Louisiana's relatively more prosperous white Methodists, during a decade of greater general prosperity, could not match the educational contributions of Louisiana's Negro Baptists in 1901.[27]

Similarly, white Southern Baptists initiated a five-year drive to raise seventy-five million dollars for Baptist education in 1919. Just over one million of this total was earmarked for Louisiana College, the college of the Louisiana Baptist Convention. By 1927, only $450,000 had been collected, due to reneging on pledges made by Southern Baptists. As a result, Louisiana College spent money it did not have during the 1920s, and entered the depression years in a state of heavy indebtedness. Again, the educational commitment of Louisiana's Negro Baptists compared favorably to the best educational efforts of their white Protestant counterparts.[28]

By 1903, Louisiana's fifteen associated Negro Baptist academies had increased the value of their physical plant to over $75,000. In addition, nine of the academies had become affiliated with Leland University in New Orleans. As part of a centralized educational program by Louisiana's black Baptists, graduates of black Baptist academies were sent to Leland for further training. Upon completion of their courses in New Orleans, new teachers returned to the academies to improve their quality of instruction.[29]

Leland began its formal affiliation with Negro secondary schools in 1892, shortly after dropping affiliation with its founding body, the American Baptist Home Mission Society. Because of slow improvement in the quality of denominational colleges like Leland, educational progress among Negro Baptist academies and primary schools was correspondingly slow. In the absence of an adequate public system for blacks, expansion of the black Baptist educational system after 1892 provided educational opportunities for a growing black elite that would otherwise have had little educational recourse. A consequence was enhancement of black Baptist influence on the cultural evolution of Louisiana's segregated black population.

Leland's break with northern white Baptists reflected dissatisfaction with northern white control of Louisiana's only Negro Baptist institution of higher education—at a time of growing confidence among Negro Baptists in their ability to direct educational efforts in line with their own societal aspirations. The NBC Education Board's campaign to increase its influence on educational policymaking began in 1892 with the first meeting of the National Baptist Educational Convention. State and national conventions of Negro Baptists had small influence over Negro Baptist educational policies up to that time. After 1892, financial contributions steadily grew as organization improved and as a Negro Baptist educational program became better defined.

In its first year of existence, in 1880, the National Baptist Convention received a total of $317.06 in contributions. By 1899, it was operating with over $37,000 in contributions, largely for educational purposes. However, it still controlled only a small portion of the total educational contributions by Negro Baptists. With the introduction of the Educational Board's plan for coordinated direction and control of a confederation of Negro Baptist secondary schools in 1900, contributions to the NBC suddenly jumped to over $142,000. Obviously, the NBC's decision to enlarge the range of its educational activities had struck a responsive chord among Negro Baptists.[30]

The initiative of Leland University's directors after 1892, to expand the educational role of the college in Louisiana, appeared to have struck the same responsive chord among the Negro Baptists of the state. By 1908, Leland was formally affiliated with ten Negro Baptist academies and, informally, with the other five. Affiliation with Leland gave Leland's president the presidency of all the affiliated schools as well. This empowered Leland's directors to appoint teachers at these schools and to determine the courses of study.[31] Between 1902 and 1908, Leland's Normal

Department graduated fifty-eight students. Of these, fifteen became principals of Negro academies, thirty more found teaching positions in Negro academies, and some of these became involved, additionally, with state-operated summer normal courses for prospective Negro teachers.[32]

As part of a centrally coordinated effort to improve the teaching in Louisiana's Negro schools, Leland's contribution to Negro education in Louisiana was highly significant. Despite the leading role that Leland apparently assumed in Louisiana Negro education by the turn of the century, the college's efforts to upgrade Negro education only scratched the surface of black educational needs in the state. Although Leland, the other denominational colleges, and the Negro academies produced a majority of Louisiana's best-educated blacks, these individuals represented a miniscule portion of the black population. All efforts by philanthropies, by missionary agencies, and by Louisiana Negroes themselves to provide educational opportunities remained unable to affect the vast majority of the 650,000 Negroes in Louisiana at the turn of the century.[33]

Following the Civil War, associations of Negro Baptists, largely without any aid from outside sources, began to construct their own churches, meeting-houses, and schools. Meagerness of financial resources most often meant that buildings had to serve multiple purposes. Although Negro Baptists built twenty-five schools in Louisiana between 1865 and 1908, the bulk of educational activity took place in small, usually one-room, structures which served as both churches and schools. By 1908, about eight hundred such buildings had been constructed by Louisiana's Negro Baptists. About one hundred of these were in use in 1908 as "public" schools of the state of Louisiana. Three hundred more served as private schools for Negroes.[34]

In such schools as these the great majority of Louisiana's Negroes received what little and inadequate educational opportunities existed—forty-five years and two generations removed from the Emancipation Proclamation of 1863. Writing during the depression of the 1930s, Edwin R. Embree, president of the Julius Rosenwald Fund, described southern Negro education "not [as] a system but [as] a series of incidents: bizarre, heroic, pathetic, romantic." Rural Negro schools were most often taught "in a church or a dilapidated shack. . . . If the school [was] in a well-constructed building, the chances [were] that it [had] been erected by the combined donations of the Negro community, white friends, and the Rosenwald Fund in addition to public funds. . . . In the typical school from sixty to ninety per cent of the pupils [were to] be found in the first three grades."[35]

In writing his memoirs after retirement in 1940, Louisiana's long-time state superintendent of public education, Thomas H. Harris, commented:

"The Negro schools have always been neglected, and still are." However, Harris could point to some progress, particularly in the years after 1916 when the "Negro School Division" became a part of the state's administrative apparatus in public education. The state did not pay the salary of the director of the Negro School Division, nor did it do much to direct or to finance its activities. This became the function of the General Education Board, without whose aid, Southern University could not have erected needed buildings or have met the salaries of its teachers. In a sense, the state of Louisiana relinquished control and development of its "public" system of education for Negroes to the General Education Board after 1915. The GEB, in supplementing meager state financing, in acting as the central channel for the contributions of other philanthropic agencies, and in largely determining how and where funds would be spent, became the true administrative body involved in directing Louisiana's system of public schools for blacks.[36]

In his memoirs, Harris credited the few improvements in black education after 1916 to several philanthropic organizations and to individuals who directed their activities in Louisiana. Specifically, Harris credited Leo M. Favrot, the first director of Louisiana's Negro School Division, both for his efforts in this capacity and for later activities as general agent for the GEB. Others whom Harris cited were Arthur C. Lewis, Favrot's successor as director of the Negro School Division, James H. Dillard, for his role as director in Louisiana of both the Anna T. Jeanes Foundation Fund and the John F. Slater Fund, as well as Samuel L. Smith, who directed the Rosenwald Fund in Louisiana and in the rest of the South.[37]

To Harris' mind—as one who should have been qualified to know—the important, lasting contribution of these men was not the improvement they oversaw in physical plants, length of school terms, and teacher quality of Negro schools. Rather, their largest single contribution came in the efforts these men made in breaking down public opposition to Negro education in Louisiana and in the South—making growth of appropriations by local and state governments possible. Harris realized that, despite the growth of the public educational system he administered in Louisiana between 1908 and 1940, little could be done by the state to improve Negro education until state and federal governments assumed more responsibility for educational funding and policymaking. Writing about 1915, Harris lamented that, despite growth of the state's appropriations to education, eighty-five per cent of the state's educational outlay still came from parish and community governments. Due to legislative passage of a bill to provide for a state "equalizing fund" in 1934, state funding for education exceeded that of local governments for the first time in 1935-36. Dramatic increases in state funding during the war years continued until, in 1950, total expenditures on education were more than five times what they had been fifteen years earlier. By 1952, the state was providing over sixty-eight per cent of funds for education and education for blacks had come out of the Dark Ages.[38]

Continued control of the pursestrings by local governments before World War II meant that Negro education would continue to depend on the generosity of the educational foundations and on the limited resources of the Negro community as essential, but incomplete supplements to inadequate local and state funding. Further, because the activities of the foundations depended, to a large extent, on aquiring and maintaining the good will of the white population, the main thrust of their guidance of Negro education was the furtherance of vocational and agricultural education. As Harris described the education of Negroes in Louisiana during his tenure as superintendent:

> . . . in the main the policy has been followed of establishing small schools in the country upon the theory that the negroes [sic] should be kept on the farms, and the way to realize that ideal is to train the negro [sic] children where they live to take care of themselves properly on the farms. In these small country schools the negro [sic] children are taught the fundamental principles of agriculture and homemaking, the importance of home ownership and of industrious effort.[39]

Under the educational expansion fostered by northern industrial philanthropy after 1916, blacks' own educational aspirations were ignored, leaving only the black denominational schools as institutions seeking to meet educational aspirations defined by blacks themselves. After 1916, expansion of the public system for blacks presented educational competition that denominational schools could not match in terms of financial ability to expand and to reach the uneducated masses of blacks in the state. After 1916, the educational influence of black Baptist associations and schools declined as public school influence correspondingly increased. By 1940, most of the black Baptist academies had ceased to exist.

With the demise of black Baptist academies, public and GEB-supported County Training Schools redirected black secondary education away from college prep toward agricultural and vocational training. County Training Schools resulted from a concept for Negro secondary education advanced by the John F. Slater Fund after 1911. Because of the prevalence of rural, one-room schools in the South and because of the difficulty of finding teachers to staff these schools, the idea evolved of a central secondary school in each county where teachers for the one-room rural schools could be trained. Beginning with four schools in 1911, the Slater Fund's program expanded to 389 County Training Schools in thirteen states in 1930. The vocational and agricultural nature of these schools made them the formal channels of an educative process which attempted to provide education that was "realistic" and proper for a black population that was mostly rural and agricultural. Blacks, however, who attended denominational academies considered themselves socially superior to the students of the County Training Schools, marrying from among their own group.[40]

The "Great Detour" as Henry Allen Bullock termed it, involved a reorientation in Negro education away from the postbellum ideal of assimilation—which had been the goal of the northern denominational schools for Negroes. With continuing neglect of black education by southern states and the drying up of the funds of northern missionary agencies after 1910, educational philanthropies assumed the leading role in Negro education. Moreover, as the educational foundations expanded their role and influence, the ideal in Negro education changed to accommodate prevailing notions in southern white society as to what purposes Negro education should seek to realize. As Bullock phrased the change:

> Unlike the benevolent and religious societies that sponsored the freedmen's school movement, the various funds established by the industrial philanthropists were not used to launch a crusade of racial equality. Remaining personally aloof from the racial conflict that was still active in the South, the industrialists accepted the great detour as the best policy for the region and so prescribed as the conditions of their gifts that the region's peace not be disturbed.[41]

Post-Reconstruction realization that black educational needs were not a primary concern of the state government had led Louisiana blacks to seek other means to accomplish the end of improved educational opportunity. The northern missionary agency schools in New Orleans provided higher education that improved the black ministry, provided the black community with a small cadre of professionals, and supplied teachers and administrators to black primary and secondary schools throughout the state. However, the denominational colleges were handicapped by a lack of black secondary schools to supply them with qualified students. The system of black Baptist academies in Louisiana attempted to rectify that problem. The Baptist academies also represented an attempt by black religious leaders to assume a greater measure of control over educational policymaking from first, the northern white denominations and second, the northern educational philanthropies.

By World War II, the poverty of Louisiana's blacks and increased state funding led to the decline of Baptist-sponsored schools and the growth of a more comprehensive system of public schools that included black high schools and teacher training programs. As public education expanded, black religious denominations began to assume an educational philosophy more in line with that of white denominations—with greater emphasis on Sunday

Schools and ministerial training, rather than on secular education featuring classical curricula. During the 1930s, Louisiana's white Baptists became involved in sponsoring a program for black ministerial education, at approximately the same time that the northern missionary agencies were leaving the field of black education in Louisiana.

In South Louisiana, the Catholic Church also began to enlarge its involvement in black education. Expanded black educational programs in South Louisiana by the Catholic Church, after 1915, sought to effect the conversion of blacks to the Catholic faith. Limited success was evident in that Catholic aggrandizement among South Louisiana blacks had outpaced the growth of Protestantism among blacks between 1890 and 1940. In North Louisiana, demise of the black Baptist educational program had little effect on religious affiliation. Blacks remained Baptists in majorities that increased during the twentieth century. In southern Louisiana, however, religious competition by the Catholic Church resulted in the inauguration of a strong program of black education by Catholics after 1915—just as Protestant academies were beginning to decline.

By 1940, white Protestant denominations had begun to demonstrate greater interest in the development of black ministerial education, while the state had begun to assume larger responsibility for the secular education of blacks. The unusual circumstances surrounding the sudden rise of black Protestantism following emancipation and the Civil War created a serious breach in the integrity of Louisiana's cultural boundary. Black Protestantism in Louisiana threatened the hegemony of the Catholic Church in South Louisiana and the influence of northern white Protestants on the development of black Protestantism threatened racial beliefs that Louisiana's white churches helped to perpetuate among the white community. Black educational aspirations and black Baptist efforts to provide educational opportunities had served to reinforce the predominance of black Protestantism in both sections of the state. By World War II, however, black Baptist-sponsored schools had become unable to compete with public schools in North Louisiana and with public and Catholic schools in South Louisiana.

Initially of small impact on the development of black religion, during the formative period following the Civil War, the cultural boundary had begun to assert noticeable influence on black religious affiliations by World War II. Already dominant in the northern part of the state by 1890, Protestantism retained its hold on the black population, as it did on whites as well, despite the failure of black Protestant denominational schools to survive first, Louisiana progressivism in the 1920s and secondly, the depression of the 1930s. In South Louisiana, the demise of Protestant schools had a different effect. Existing competition by a rival religious tradition resulted in Catholic co-option of black Baptist educational efforts after 1915. As the Catholic parochial school program for blacks in South Louisiana expanded, so did the numbers of black Catholics. In the end, the cultural boundary came to have an important and growing influence on the distribution of black religious affiliations in the state.

No longer the obvious exception to the general rule of North Louisiana Protestantism and South Louisiana Catholicism that it had been in 1890, the black population increasingly began to conform, after 1915, to religious patterns that had always held true for the white population. The cultural boundary had survived a most serious threat to its integrity—a threat caused by unusual social circumstances in the wake of the Civil War and Reconstruction—and re-assumed its traditional function of defining the limits of separate, persisting cultures identifiable by Protestant or by Catholic religious dominance.

IV

Waiting for Men and Society: Catholics and Black Education

While Baptists were assuming a large share of the effort to provide educational opportunities for Louisiana's freedmen in the last quarter of the nineteenth century, other religious groups became either unwilling or unable to expand much into this field.[1] Besides the Negro Baptists, Methodists and Catholics were, by far, the religious groups with most influence in Louisiana's black community. Unlike Baptists, these two groups had an episcopal hierarchy that was white-dominated and which created barriers to effective involvement in Negro education.[2] Methodists never overcame their educational difficulties in Louisiana and Negro Methodist memberships declined relative to the numerical strength of both black Baptists and black Catholics during the twentieth century.[3]

Religious educational programs played a vital role in the process of religious aggrandizement by competing religious traditions on either side of the cultural boundary. A particularly significant development that helped strengthen the religious definition of Louisiana's cultural boundary was the Catholic Church's expanded effort to provide education for black Catholics in the years after 1906. Post-Civil War developments caused near financial insolvency in the Catholic Archdiocese of New Orleans and the Catholic educational system had virtually no impact on Louisiana's black community in the late nineteenth century.[4] During the next century, the significant events leading to success in attracting blacks into Catholic schools were the segregation of blacks into separate church parishes after 1895 and retirement of the heavy archdiocesan debt by 1904. However, these developments would have little impact on blacks outside of South Louisiana, as Catholic educational programs in North Louisiana never succeeded in converting black Protestants to Catholicism, but rather succeeded only in retaining the small communities of North Louisiana blacks who had historically been Catholic.

A successful program of education for black Catholics became important to the church leadership at the turn of the century because of the significant inroads made by Protestant denominations in enlarging memberships within Catholic South Louisiana. Growth by black Baptist associations, in particular, threatened the Catholic Archdiocese of New Orleans with loss of influence among an entire segment of South Louisiana's religious population. The United States government's religious census of 1890 revealed that membership in black Protestant denominations had reached 40,000 in the twenty-five parishes that constituted South Louisiana as a distinct section—a development indicating significant penetration by Protestantism across the cultural boundary into Catholic South Louisiana.[5] Rapid Protestant growth following the Civil War portended further penetration across the boundary unless Protestant growth could be arrested by greater Catholic influence within the South Louisiana black community.

The Catholic clergy recognized, by the 1890s, that black children who attended schools sponsored by Protestant denominations joined Protestant churches and that public school attendance also often led to Protestant affiliation because of Protestant religious instruction in public schools—which were dominated by Protestant teachers and administrators.[6] The obvious counter to Protestantism's growing influence through black education in South Louisiana was an expanded educational effort by Catholics. Barriers to effective black Catholic education, however, first had to be overcome.

Catholic churches, unlike Protestant denominations, remained racially integrated following the Civil War. Catholic schools, however, had been racially segregated since the 1830s and continued to be until the 1960s. A consequence was that whites, who dominated within parish churches, often opposed the use of church parish funds to build black schools.[7] Whites' opposition to black education was exacerbated by the highly unpopular experiment with public school integration by Louisiana's state government during Reconstruction. That experiment largely affected only New Orleans and led to white flight from public schools and the construction of over ninety denominational schools for whites between 1868 and 1875. Forty-one of these, all in New Orleans, were Catholic schools built during a time of severe financial strain following the Civil War. A predictable result of this burdensome school construction of the early 1870s was that the Archdiocese of New Orleans incurred a heavy burden of debt that it could not escape until the first decade of the following century.[8] Financial paralysis, combined with growing racial prejudice on the part of dominant whites within church parishes, prevented the Catholic Church from implementing an effective educational program for black Catholics.

These events occurred during a time of great demand for education by blacks. State and local governments demonstrated neither the capability nor the will to adequately supply that demand following Reconstruction.[9] Consequently, Catholic absence from the field presented Protestant denominations with great opportunities for success in their missionary efforts among South Louisiana's blacks. Schools built by black Baptist associations and by missionary agencies of northern Protestant denominations flourished in the late nineteenth century as thousands of South Louisiana blacks converted from the Catholic to Protestant faiths.

In the antebellum period, Louisiana was known for having the largest population of free Negroes in the South. Known in French Louisiana as the "gens de couleur libre," Louisiana's free black population was strongly influenced by the Catholic Church. About two thousand had emigrated to Louisiana from the French Catholic colony of Saint-Domingue during the 1790s, and others had gained freedom under a French slave regime characterized by greater frequency of manumission than in English colonies. One important reason French colonies treated slaves and free blacks more liberally than other colonies was the influence of the Catholic Church.[10] The Code Noir of both the French and Spanish colonies in Louisiana mandated that planters provide Catholic education and make Catholic church services available for their black slaves. Jesuit missionaries and Ursuline nuns were primarily involved in supplying the educational and ministerial needs of both slaves and the gens de couleur libre. When Louisiana became an American state in 1812, Catholic practices and traditions continued to predominate for a number of years. Until the 1830s, the gens de couleur libre of Louisiana could avail themselves of any available educational opportunities that existed without the stigma of segregation. Beyond the 1830s, some communities of free Negro Catholics continued to enjoy a respectable standing in antebellum society, as Gary B. Mills related in his history of the colony of gens de couleur libre on Cane River, in Natchitoches Parish. However, growing fear among whites that free blacks represented a threat to the docility of slave populations resulted in laws that severely restricted the freedom of the gens de couleur libre after 1830.[11]

A law of 1830 effectively repealed the Code Noir by making it illegal to teach slaves to read. Free blacks could no longer attend schools in a desegregated setting, and were excluded altogether from participation in the public school system created in 1845. Ostensibly, the fear of slave rebellion caused Louisiana slave-owners to deny literacy to slaves and to restrict the freedom of free Negroes in order to reduce the likelihood that free Negroes might incite rebelliousness among the slaves. The revolutionary origins of both Haiti and the Dominican Republic exacerbated such fears and mistrust of Louisiana's free Negroes and led to the state law of 1842, banning the immigration of free Negroes into Louisiana. As did the rest of the South, in response to northern abolitionism, Louisiana clamped down on the freedom of Negroes in an attempt to subjugate their aspirations as citizens to the survival of slavery—as the indispensable element of the agricultural economic system.[12]

Following Reconstruction, when white public sentiment against white involvement in Negro education became more pronounced, the Sisters of the

Holy Family became increasingly involved in the education of Negro Catholics. Founded by two free Negro women in New Orleans in 1842, this numerically small order of nuns had operated a home for elderly free Negro Catholics in New Orleans prior to the Civil War. After 1848, they also became involved with several primary schools for free Negroes and then began expanding their educational work after the war and Reconstruction. They founded St. Mary's Academy in 1882, which was the first secondary school in New Orleans for colored girls. They also opened the Holy Ghost School for Negro Catholics in Opelousas in 1874, marking their involvement outside of New Orleans for the first time. In 1895, the Holy Family Academy opened in Baton Rouge, followed by a primary school in Mandeville the following year. In 1903, another school was built in Lafayette, and the educational activities of this colored sisterhood continued to expand in subsequent years. By 1944, thirty-eight Holy Family Sisters were involved in staffing six primary schools and three high schools in the Diocese of Lafayette alone. These black sisters, however, were too few to provide the numbers of teachers necessary for the Catholic educational expansion taking place after 1915.[13]

White religious orders encountered resistance in many of their efforts to establish private and parochial schools for blacks in southern Louisiana. The white Sisters of the Sacred Heart, who had maintained a private school for white girls since 1821 in Grand Coteau, opened a school for black children nearby in 1875, in addition to another school in New Orleans, opened in 1867. Such schools were rare, however, and other attempts by white religious orders met with failure. An effort by Redemptorist priests in New Orleans to operate a parochial school for blacks, in conjunction with a nearby white school under their management, was abandoned in the 1870s after the school had three times been burned to the ground. In the small town of Arnaudville, in the Teche Country, the parish priest, Charles Denoyel, opened a small school for Negroes in 1893. Within one week of the school's opening, whites from the area had set it on fire, though the school was saved and remained open. In 1894, Denoyel was approached by a group of whites who asked him to leave the parish because of the Negro school that was being staffed by one white Marianite Sister. Denoyel and the brave sister persisted, however, and the school remained open until 1919.[14]

The school in Arnaudville was an early example of the influence of Katharine Drexel on Catholic education for Negroes, and for American Indians. A devout Catholic as well as a wealthy heiress from Philadelphia, Drexel dedicated her entire fortune to the education of Negro and Indian Catholics. She also founded a religious order, the Sisters of the Blessed Sacrament for Indians and Colored People, in February 1891, whose sole mission was the furtherance of educational work among these Catholic minorities. After 1894, schools staffed by Sisters of the Blessed Sacrament opened in New Mexico, Arizona, Nebraska, South Dakota, Oklahoma, and Pennsylvania for the benefit of American Indians. Schools for Negroes were started in Virginia, Texas, Tennessee, Georgia, Alabama, Mississippi, Pennsylvania, and Louisiana. Until 1915, Drexel's influence on Negro education in Louisiana was limited to helping fund several small Negro Catholic schools such as the one in Arnaudville in 1893.[15]

Earlier, the Catholic Church had shown concern over the problem of Negroes and their adjustment to freedom following emancipation. The meeting of the Second Plenary Council of American Bishops, in Baltimore in 1866, entertained discussion over the matter but organized no formal program to aid freedmen until 1884. The meeting of the Third Plenary Council in 1884 had been called primarily because of Catholic opposition to an educational bill pending in Congress since 1881. However, organization of the Commission for Catholic Missions Among the Colored People and Indians resulted from this conference of the American hierarchy, as well as a decree commanding that every Catholic parish see to the construction of a parochial school. The Commission for Catholic Missions was to receive funds for its aid of Negro and Indian missions and schools from a yearly collection for that purpose. Such aid to Negro education came rather belatedly in time and failed to have much significant impact. The yearly collection for Negro missions was more than southern religious denominations contributed for Negro education, but placed the Catholic Church far behind the educational efforts of northern Protestant missionary agencies.[16]

Only in southern Louisiana was any significant population of Negro Catholics to be found, and here the financial condition of the church was extremely poor in the late nineteenth century. In 1883, the last year of Archbishop Perché's administration, there were mortgages on ninety per cent of properties held by the archdiocese. The new archbishop, Francis X. Leray, discontinued all church expansion upon taking over the archdiocese, closed the archdiocesan seminary, and attempted to do what he could to prevent the complete financial collapse of the archdiocese. Despite some success at making arrangements with creditors, a Catholic parish in Baton Rouge went bankrupt in 1885, and the church building was sold at public auction. Understandably, beset with these kinds of pressing financial problems, Leray did little to comply with the decrees of the Third Plenary Council, or to do much for black education in the archdiocese. In fact, Leray did not even announce to his people until 1886 what the decrees of the Third Plenary Council had been two years earlier. Where finances were available, Leray attempted compliance, but few parochial schools were built in Louisiana in the late nineteenth century.[17]

In South Louisiana, especially, where Catholic ceremonies and holiday rituals contributed to the customs of society and encouraged survival of the French language, free blacks both influenced and borrowed from the culture of white Creoles.[18] Following emancipation, former free blacks continued to constitute an elite within a rapidly growing black Creole culture. Black Creole culture, and black Catholicism, was also heavily influenced by former slaves and their descendants, many of whom were only nominally Catholic. Catholic rituals were widely adapted to surviving forms of African and Caribbean worship as Catholic saints often became substitutes for Voo Doo or other gods from African religions.[19] Consequently, Catholic schools for blacks became desirable not only to accommodate blacks' desire for expanded educational opportunities, but also to eliminate deviant forms of worship in South Louisiana that masqueraded as Catholicism.[20]

The Catholic Church in South Louisiana found itself in a situation in which rapid population growth made the construction of new churches a higher priority than the founding of schools—despite the 1884 directive by the Third Plenary Council, calling for parochial schools in every Catholic parish. In Louisiana, financial indebtedness and the necessity of first *forming* parishes around new churches in numerous Catholic communities, precluded parochial school construction.[21] In the case of black parishioners, parochial schools were, in any event, closed to them unless the parish was both prosperous enough and willing to construct both a white and a black school. In the face of strong white hostility to black education in any form in the years after Reconstruction, few Catholic parishes provided black parochial schools.

During the late nineteenth century, then, black Catholics found themselves at educational disadvantage and had cause, additionally, to resent the second-class status assigned to them by whites in their parish churches. As a result of blacks' dissatisfaction with white-controlled Catholic churches and organizations, defections to black Protestant churches, employing black ministers and often sponsoring black schools, became widespread.

The black Creole elite had less cause for dissatisfaction than the majority of black Catholics because they occupied a higher level within Louisiana's caste system. However, even this elite core of black Catholicism in South Louisiana became dissatisfied with the lack of educational opportunities offered by the Catholic Church. Particularly in New Orleans, black Catholics who could afford private school tuition resented the Church's failure to provide good secondary schools and a college, such as northern Methodists, Baptists, and Congregationalists built in New Orleans following the Civil War. The black Creole elite resented having to attend these Protestant institutions and began to pressure the Archdiocese of New Orleans to build a black Catholic college comparable to Straight University, to New Orleans University, and to Leland University.[22]

Upon appointment as archbishop of New Orleans in 1888, Francis Janssens became heir to the growing problem of black conversion to Protestantism and recognized the need in Louisiana both for parochial and private schools for black Catholics. Basic problems were the archdiocesan debt and white hostility to black education, problems too large during the 1890s for Janssens to eliminate. To his credit, however, the archbishop undertook to establish a working relationship with religious orders that had been founded for the purpose of promoting black Catholic education. In particular, Janssens aroused the interest of the Sisters of the Blessed Sacrament and of the Society of St. Joseph, both of which became important to eventual expansion of Catholic educational opportunities for blacks in Louisiana.[23]

The Sisters of the Blessed Sacrament were particularly crucial to black Catholic education because of their role in founding Xavier University. Xavier resulted from the purchase of school property in New Orleans, vacated when Southern University moved to Scotlandville, near Baton Rouge, in 1915. Katharine Drexel and her Sisters of the Blessed Sacrament purchased the property and opened Xavier Academy—the Catholic Negro secondary school that Negro Catholics of New Orleans had been asking the archdiocese to sponsor since the 1880s. Although the secondary school would continue to operate at Xavier (Becoming Xavier University Prep School), Drexel's nuns had plans for expansion that would result in a teacher's college and the school's evolution, by 1925, into Xavier University—the first Catholic Negro University in the United States.[24]

In addition, the Sisters of the Blessed Sacrament built two new Negro high schools for segregated Negro parishes in Lake Charles and in New Iberia in 1923 and 1925. Along with the normal school at Xavier, these Negro high schools became a source of lay Catholic teachers for an entire system of rural primary schools being planned as free, mission schools in isolated, rural areas of the southern parishes. By request of the State Board of Education, the last year of the high school course at the Sacred Heart High School in Lake Charles became an abbreviated normal course to bolster the inadequate supply of teachers in rural Negro public schools in the Lake Charles area. In 1930, the one-year normal course became additional to the completion of the high school course, and the entire program was eventually eliminated in 1938 when the state upgraded its requirements for Negro teachers by mandating the completion of a four-year normal course.[25]

By 1939, Drexel's Sisters of the Blessed Sacrament had opened fourteen small rural schools for Negroes, some in places—mostly in the Diocese of Lafayette—where not even public schools had been available. All of these schools were being staffed by teachers from Xavier University. Besides these rural schools, Drexel's nuns also opened eight new elementary schools in such larger towns as Lake Charles, New Iberia, St. Martinville, and New Orleans. The construction of these schools, at a time when private, Negro Protestant schools were being forced to close as a result of the depression, and at a time when the public system for Negroes remained inadequate, served to strengthen the influence of the Catholic Church on, literally, many more thousands of Negroes in southern Louisiana than the church had previously been able to reach.[26]

Once started, the expansion of black Catholic schools became rapid, having great effect in preventing defections to Protestantism as well as in reaching thousands of nominally Catholic black Creoles in rural areas across South Lousisiana. This expansion brought more orthodox religious practice to black Catholicism and strengthened it by facilitating the formation of new black Catholic parishes. However, before this educational expansion could take place, changes in the way that the Catholic Church handled race relations in Louisiana were introduced. Such change was among the legacies of Archbishop Janssens, who first introduced the concept of a separate church for blacks in New Orleans in 1895.

Janssen's purpose was not to formally implement racial segregation as church policy, but to offer blacks (and other Catholic minorities) churches for their use in the event either of dissatisfaction with predominantly white churches or of lack of space in them. By the turn of the century, however, racial segregation had become the dominant pattern in southern and Louisiana society. Most whites favored the idea of separate churches for blacks and many blacks also approved of the greater autonomy and freedom of action that exclusively black churches could offer. Once the archdiocesan debt was removed by Archbishop Louis Chapelle in 1904, more money became available within church parishes for the construction of separate church buildings and church segregation became a rapidly advancing movement. By 1918, segregation of blacks into separate churches had become the rule rather than the exception in South Louisiana.[27]

Black Catholic elites in New Orleans initially resisted the concept of separate churches, preferring that attention be given to construction of a black college. Rural black Catholics received the idea more positively, having greater interest in freedom from white prejudice and the possibility of parochial schools that separate black parishes might offer. Segregation into separate church parishes had the educational advantage of creating greater availability of funds from philanthropies created for the exclusive benefit of black Catholics. Under the traditional system of racially mixed parishes, funds from the Katherine Drexel Foundation or from the Commission for Catholic Missions Among the Colored People and Indians were often withheld because of the difficulty of spending the money only on black Catholics within church parishes. The same held true for services intended for blacks' benefit, such as the teaching services of the Society of St. Joseph, an order of priests dedicated to the work of black education.[28]

Upon becoming the new archbishop of New Orleans in 1906, James Hubert Blenk described Louisiana's Catholic parochial system as "defective in every way," and made improvement of that system a priority of his administration.[29] Segregation of blacks into separate church parishes, a process already begun in many of South Louisiana's rural parishes, became central to Blenk's effort to expand Catholic education for blacks. Over the course of Blenk's administration, up to 1918, the segregation process accelerated, affecting Orleans as well as the rural parishes, and black Catholic parochial schools began to proliferate.[30] The timing of this process was significant in that black Catholic educational expansion began to take place just as northern Protestant missionary agencies began to terminate their involvement with black education in the South during the 1910s and 1920s.

Northern white Protestant organizations, such as the American Missionary Association or the American Baptist Home Mission Society, had long experienced difficulty in adequately funding their educational activities in the South. These organizations began to relinquish control of black schools and to turn over funding responsibilities to northern industrial philanthropies, such as the Rockefeller Foundation. This great philanthropy, and others, had become involved in a campaign to improve southern education under the auspices of the General Education Board after the turn of the century. The G.E.B., funded and controlled by the Rockefeller Foundation, was created in order to coordinate the activities of the Rockefeller, the Julius Rosenwald, Anna T. Jeanes, John F. Slater, and other foundations and to orient these educational funds toward supplementing the secular educational efforts of southern state governments.[31]

After 1915, the black public school system, supported and overseen by administrators appointed by the state and by the educational foundations, began to expand and to overshadow previous school systems operated by northern religious agencies. Public school expansion after 1915 was significant, but slow, leaving ample room for competition from religious denominations. After 1915, the Catholic Church in South Louisiana became more aggressive in the field of black education than Protestant groups, except perhaps for black Baptist associations, which continued to operate secondary academies affiliated with Leland University—which supplied teachers and administrators to black Baptist schools across the state. Leland, however, was moved to Baton Rouge in 1923 and never successfully reorganized there. The black Baptist system of numerous primary and seventeen secondary schools declined, especially once the depression of the 1930s began to force many black Baptist schools to close.[32] By the 1930s, Protestant denominational schools were becoming rare while Catholic schools for blacks grew in numbers apace with the continuing establishment of separate black parishes.

Racial segregation in the Catholic Church severely restricted the interracial cultural exchange that had once largely characterized South Louisiana. It also caused decline in the social status of the black Creole elite, which became confined exclusively within the segregated black community. The ethnic gulf between whites and blacks widened as a result of segregation's removal of religion as an important area of racial interaction. Catholic segregation did, however, enable the Church to extend Catholic education to blacks by removing white interference through the creation of exclusively black church parishes. Within the segregated secular social environment that existed after the turn of the century, religious segregation became necessary for the Catholic Church to improve its freedom and ability to meet the religious needs of blacks.[33]

One important need in the black community continued to be education and adoption of segregation in church life preceded increased educational growth. By the 1920s, Catholic education in South Louisiana became better able to meet that need than could Protestant education. Also, the outlawing of Bible-reading in public schools after 1913 initiated a prohibition on partisan religious instruction in public schools, preventing public schools from being virtual Protestant parochial schools, as had often been the case in the late nineteenth century.[34] By 1920, Protestant denominations had lost the recruitment advantages they enjoyed during the late nineteenth century and South Louisiana blacks began to embrace Catholicism in growing numbers.

Between 1890 and 1940, black Catholics—so long a minority—grew into the majority of South Louisiana's black religious population. As a result of this significant growth in black Catholicism, South Louisiana's cultural identity became more firmly linked with Catholicism and the religiously defined boundary between North and South Louisiana retained its important historical impact on Louisiana's social and cultural development. Unfortunately, it is not possible to determine the precise extent of black Catholic growth after 1890, because religious censuses did not distinguish between white and black Catholics as they did between white and black Protestant denominations. Even after Catholic segregation became widespread, an indeterminate number of black Catholics continued to attend predominantly white churches. The number of blacks in mixed congregations is uncertain because church pastors did not keep records indicating the racial composition of church memberships.[35] Consequently, government religious censuses counted only black Catholics in separate black parishes and the true number of blacks who were Catholics between 1890 and 1940 can only be estimated.

The numbers of black Catholics in Louisiana at the starting date of 1890 must also be estimated, since there is no absolutely reliable data that exists to provide this information. However, as explained in Chapter Two of this volume, if the percentage of black religious communicants in South Louisiana was approximately equal to that of North Louisiana, then South Louisiana contained about 20,000 black Catholics in 1890 in addition to the 40,000 black Protestants counted by the 1890 census.[36] Consequently, it is fair to assert that black Protestants outnumbered black Catholics in South Louisiana by about two to one in 1890.

For 1940, partial census counts of black Catholics makes estimation of the total number easier than for 1890. In addition to counts of blacks in Protestant denominations, the 1936 census of religion in the United States counted blacks in segregated black Catholic parishes, leaving only those black Catholics still attending predominantly white Catholic churches uncounted. A 1939 estimation by the Archbishop of New Orleans for his archdiocese and an actual census of black Catholics in the Diocese of Lafayette in 1943, produced the fair estimation of 28,000 South Louisiana black Catholics in addition to the 60,000 accounted for by the census count of black Catholics in separate black parishes. The 1936 religious census reported about 80,000 black Protestants in South Louisiana, suggesting that black Catholicism had overcome the minority position it occupied in 1890 in the southern part of the state.

By how much Catholic influence increased over that of Protestantism after 1890 was unclear because neither the government nor the Catholic Church undertook to count accurately the number of black Catholics in Louisiana at any time prior to the 1960s, except in the Diocese of Lafayette in 1943. The Catholic Church did undertake national surveys in 1928 and 1940 to determine how many Catholics were black, but the procedures employed in these Catholic surveys produced estimations that were too high.[37] The procedure was to count the number of Catholics in exclusively black churches and then to rely on estimations by bishops and archbishops to determine the additional number of blacks in white churches.[38] In Catholic dioceses, such as the Diocese of Alexandria in North Louisiana, where Catholics were the religious minority and where relatively few Catholic churches existed, estimates of black Catholics can be assumed to have been reasonably accurate. That was not the case for the South Louisiana Archdiocese of New Orleans or for the Diocese of Lafayette, which easily contained the largest percentage of both white and black Catholics to total population of any diocese or archdiocese in the United States up to 1960.[39]

The 1940 Catholic survey reported 60,201 black Catholics in thirty-nine segregated churches and chapels. Estimations for black Catholics in attendance at predominantly white churches brought the total to 115,040. Subtracting the total for the Diocese of Alexandria in North Louisiana, which reported slightly over 6000 black Catholics in both 1928 and 1940, leaves an estimate for the South Louisiana dioceses of approximately 109,000 in 1940.[40] This estimate relied on figures supplied by the Archdiocese of New Orleans and the Diocese of Lafayette, which claimed 35,000 black Catholics in the Archdiocese of New Orleans and 74,000 in the Diocese of Lafayette. The latter figure was suspect at the time, being the result of calculations based on population figures and Catholic Church records of baptisms—which were the only Catholic records that reflected racial distinctions among South Louisiana's Catholics.[41] These calculations produced an estimation greatly at variance with Bishop Jules Jeanmard's guess in 1933 that there were about 43,000 black Catholics in his diocese. In 1943, Jeanmard sponsored a complete census that showed 35,376 Catholics in sixteen exclusively black parishes (one black parish not reporting) and 17,834 black Catholics in twenty-three other racially mixed parishes—producing a total of 53,210 black Catholics.[42] Accepting that figure in substitution for the one reported in the 1940 survey revises the estimate of black Catholics in South Louisiana downward to about 88,000. Accordingly, Catholic gains among the South Louisiana black population between 1890 and 1940 amounted to well over 60,000 religious adherents, as opposed to an increase by black Protestants of about 40,000. This finding securely supports the assertion that Catholic aggrandizement among South Louisiana blacks outpaced that of Protestantism during the twentieth century—a development that not only indicated survival of Louisiana's North/South religious boundary, but a strengthening of its impact on the state's cultural dichotomy.

An implicit conclusion grounded in the facts of black Catholic educational expansion and growth of black Catholic numbers after 1906 is that Catholic Church segregation improved the Church's effectiveness in reaching the South Louisiana black population. In later years, during the 1940s and 1950s, the Church came under criticism for its acquiescence in racial segregation. However, as Loyola University Chaplain, Reverend Harold L. Cooper, pointed out in answer to such criticism in 1956:

> . . . the Church has not been so slow to see the injustice involved in segregation. As with all problems (especially where the State is involved) the Church does not speak out precipitously. She often waits for men and society to see their own mistakes.[43]

Indeed, segregation had not been official Catholic policy, but instead represented the necessity of adapting Church activities to social and political realities in southern racial relations following Reconstruction. In 1949, the archbishop of New Orleans explicitly stated the Church's official policy in directing that "Negroes must be allowed to worship in whatever church they please and must not be asked to sit in specially designated pews."[44] A year later, the Commission on Human Rights of the Catholic Committee of the South declared its objective to be "ultimate removal of the color-bar from our Catholic universities, colleges, seminaries, academies, high schools, and elementary schools." In 1962, voluntary desegregation of Catholic schools in New Orleans preceded the forced desegregation of public schools in Louisiana by nine years.[45]

In a perceptive study of southern Catholicism in the nineteenth century, Randall M. Miller pointed out that the Catholic Church, like southern Protestant denominations, "won social and political acceptance in the South by sanctifying the secular order of slavery and states' rights." In doing so, southern Catholicism became captive "to southern culture and society."[46]

Although South Louisiana has traditionally contained a majority Catholic population, it has never been isolated from the larger economic and political unit constituting the majority Protestant southern region. The social imperatives dictated by perceived economic and political necessities in the southern region could not be and were not ignored by the Catholic population of South Louisiana. In that sense, what was true of Catholic complicity in southern political and economic practices in the nineteenth century, described by Miller, proved no less true for Catholic participation in southern Jim Crowism during the twentieth century. Just as Catholicism in the United States differs from Catholicism in other areas of the world, Catholic priorities in the South have differed, in the past, from Catholic priorities in the North or West.

During the 1950s, anti-segregationists in the Catholic Committee of the South—whose activities were concentrated in South Louisiana—attempted a civil rights education campaign, which "showed that Catholics were interested and bent on doing something on problems of the South, instead of just conducting services and running Catholic schools."[47] Such activities were similar to those of a minority of Southern Baptists involved in activities of the Southern Baptist Convention's Social Service Commission, founded in 1948. However, neither the Catholic Church nor the Southern Baptist Convention proved able to accomplish much in the way of change through the activities of these committees and commissions. Both religious bodies had to wait for "men and society to see their own mistakes." What was most important, between 1880 and 1940, to both Catholic leaders in South Louisiana and Protestant leaders in North Louisiana was that when men came to see their errors, they would do so as members of their denomination and not as members of the rival religious body dominant on the other side of the religious boundary.

V

Cultural Captivity: Evangelism and Education Among Louisiana Baptists

While Catholics were resisting the cultural challenge of black Protestantism within the French Triangle during the late nineteenth and early twentieth centuries, Protestant growth outside of the triangle served to overcome the challenge of Catholicism in North Louisiana and in the Florida parishes. Among North Louisiana's white religious population, Southern Baptists became predominant by 1890, but then faced newer challenges in the twentieth century, such as accommodation to secular public education, rapid social change, and the desire to spread the Baptist faith across the cultural boundary into South Louisiana. The ways in which these challenges were met may best be described by examining the ideals of religious education formulated and adopted by Louisiana's Southern Baptists in the years after 1880.

The Southern Baptist Convention (SBC) is and has been the largest, most influential southern white denomination since its inception in 1845. Having split from the national body of Baptists over the issue of southern slavery, Southern Baptists have since been identifiable from Northern Baptists by their continuing attachment to prevailing notions concerning race in the South. Historically a rural church, the SBC is notable also for its non-ecclesiastic and democratic organizational structure. Often characterized as a captive of southern culture, the SBC has consequently often been studied for its usefulness as a mirror of social settings in the South.[1]

Southern Baptists in North Louisiana abandoned support for denominational schools other than colleges by the turn of the century, as Southern Baptist congregations proved unwilling to contribute funds for such schools, or to show much desire for their existence. Localities in North Louisiana, where white evangelical Protestants were predominant, had featured private, and ostensibly non-denominational, schools run by Protestant ministers during the nineteenth century. These were increasingly replaced by public schools, as the public school system grew during the twentieth century. Local support for education in Protestant North Louisiana remained minimal by 1900, a fact that reflected both the poverty and the minimal educational desires of the mostly rural or small-town people who resided in the northern parishes.

In South Louisiana, Southern Baptists deviated from their normal pattern of reliance on revivalism for religious aggrandizement. Concern over the dearth of white Baptist congregations in the southern parishes caused the Louisiana Baptist Convention (LBC) to sponsor schools in South Louisiana. The establishment of the Baptist Bible Institute in New Orleans and Acadia Baptist Academy in Acadia Parish reflected the belief of Louisiana Baptists that ministers who were natives of South Louisiana, trained in Baptist schools, might be effective in gaining converts where Baptist missionaries had failed during the nineteenth century and during the first two decades of the twentieth century.

South Louisiana's white population was overwhelmingly Catholic and the traditions and influences of Catholic culture, as well as the partial survival of the French language, made it difficult for Protestant missionaries to establish congregations in rural southern Louisiana. The purpose of Baptist schools in South Louisiana was to attract the children of South Louisiana natives who could be trained as Baptist ministers and who could gain converts through the better rapport that a native French-speaker was believed to possess among South Louisiana natives.

In the northern part of the state, Baptist educational efforts came to be characterized by an emphasis on Sunday Schools—as the religious supplement to Baptist reliance on public schools for the secular education of children. In areas where evangelical Protestants predominated, the expansion of both public shcools and denominational systems of Sunday Schools proceeded slowly after the turn of the century. By 1900, public school attendance in areas where Baptists predominated, were above average for the state but far below the state average in the lengths of terms public schools stayed open each year. Underfunding on the local level of government created this problem since local and parish governments were responsible for the majority of funds for public school construction and operation under Louisiana's public system of education until the 1930s.[2]

After 1898, the state government required local governments to increase the amount of tax funds raised for the purpose of public education and the state also increased its apportionments to local school boards during the first three decades of the twentieth century. Public school expansion resulted from increased funding required by state legislators during Louisiana's Progressive Era, but inequities in the system favored urban and black-belt areas over the rural and largely white parishes where evangelical Protestants were the dominant religious group.

To a great extent, class and urban-rural conflict are responsible for the pattern of educational expansion in the state. Religious affiliations, however, tended to reflect class differences and to contribute to the prolongation of educational deficiency in the rural areas of Protestant North

Louisiana. To the extent that class differences reflected educational disparities in Catholic South Louisiana as well, the cultural boundary served to accentuate the problem by aligning the rural populations of both sections of the state against each other, religiously and politically, to the advantage of urban and black-belt economic elites.

On the subject of southern racial relations, scholars have analyzed Southern Baptists as though, by defining the Southern Baptist "attitude" toward race, the mind of the evangelical, Anglo-Saxon Protestant South might thereby be uncovered and laid bare. A problem with such an approach to the study of Southern Baptists is that, like all religious denominations, the Southern Baptist Convention represents a large and diverse cross-section of people whose common "attitudes" are not easy (if not impossible) to pin down.[3] Consequently, when it is argued that Southern Baptists are at fault for having collectively failed to adopt and implement a specific church program for improvement of racial relations, the underlying assumption is that broad agreement on the matter, among the body of Southern Baptists, was possible.[4]

That agreement on the question of racial policy did not manifest is a reason why the Social Service Commission of the SBC failed to take any clear stand on racial relations after its inception in 1947. Despite apparent sympathy for the Civil Rights movement, the Commission abandoned any pretenses of speaking for the mass of Southern Baptists in 1964 by leaving the support or non-support for Civil Rights up to individual congregations to decide for themselves.[5]

On the subject of education, Baptists in Louisiana demonstrated a similar lack of consensus. Baptist leaders in the state convention generally expressed support for an ambitious Baptist educational program, but had difficulty raising funds from rural Baptists for educational purposes. A growing penchant for progressive social action and improved coordination and organization of denominational activities became evident in the years after 1910. While white Baptists failed to mobilize a consensus in favor of denominational schools, except for the mission schools in South Louisiana, a movement to expand, improve, and standardize Sunday Schools gained impetus after 1910. By World War II, Sunday Schools, as a religious supplement to public education, had become the primary components of a coherent Louisiana Baptist educational program—meant to facilitate a widening Baptist consensus on religious belief as well as to spread awareness of Baptist doctrines and gain converts to the faith.

The Education Commission of the Louisiana Baptist Convention reasoned in 1914 that, because the state had assumed control of education, but could not teach religion, then "the church must enter the field of [religious] education in the interest of the state." Continuing in this vein:

> The denomination which neglects the field of education or turns over the education of its young men and womanhood to secularism, the State or some other religious denomination will soon be relegated to the rear of the world's life and finally thrown on the trash heap of denominationalism as a castaway.

Its melodramatic tone notwithstanding, the preceding statement was clearly a plea for greater involvement in education by Louisiana's Baptists. In a thinly veiled reference to South Louisiana Catholicism, the commission declared that "a sacramental religion flourishes where ignorance abounds but a spiritual religion demands intelligent worshippers." However, since separation of church and state, leading to the development of secular public schools, was viewed as necessary for the continuing autonomy of Baptist congregations, secular public education came to be tolerated as a necessary evil. Consequently, the LBC's Education Commission became primarily interested in promoting Sunday Schools as a religious supplement to public education and in increasing financial support for the denominational college recently opened in Pineville, near Alexandria.[6]

In developing advocacy for a better Baptist educational program, the LBC Education commission of 1914 had to confront the reality that most of Louisiana's white Baptists had historically been unwilling to financially support denominational programs of education. Baptist congregations were widely scattered, rural, and largely uninterested in other than local matters of concern. Consequently, the commission's interest in expanding programs for Sunday Schools and in enlarging Louisiana College, became a hard sell.[7]

Found mostly in areas with poor educational opportunities and low educational attainment, congregations of Baptists could not be expected to place an exceptionally high value on educational expansion beyond the perceived needs of the locality. These needs, Baptists felt competent to supply without interference from outside agencies of the church or sometimes, even of the state. In short, rural Baptists, who were often farmers or small-town businessmen, craftsmen, or tradesmen, had little reason to place a high value on education beyond the attainment of literacy and the ability to perform simple arithmetic. Furthermore, as the overwhelming majority of the members of the Southern Baptist church, rural people tended to resent requests for contributions to fund such programs as progressive, elite Baptists of the cities thought desirable for the improvement of southern society. Aspirations and outlooks of the majority of Baptists were different from those of the elite, educated minority who represented Baptists at the annual conventions and who made up the members of the convention boards and agencies.

In perceptive commentary, Daniel Dennett described the people of North Louisiana in the 1870s as mostly Protestant of English, Irish and Scotch descent, most having come to Louisiana from Georgia, Virginia, the Carolinas, and Alabama. Dennett characterized them as a "thrifty, energetic, enterprising people," living on land not as fertile as in other areas of the state, "who know that they must work it to make a living from it," and who "do so with a will, and with commendable perseverance." Different from South Louisiana, where there were "immense plantations and few towns," North Louisiana had "much greater numbers of small farms, and numerous thriving villages, each with its two or three churches, 'male' and 'female' schools, masonic lodges, and perhaps a factory of some kind on a small scale."[8]

Dennett was not referring to the plantation areas of North Louisiana along the Mississippi, Red, and Ouachita rivers, but rather to what he termed the "piny [sic] woods" and "good uplands" parishes that covered much of North Louisiana in contrast to the marshes, wooded swamps, and prairies of the southern part of the state. Concerning the "good uplands" parishes of northwestern and northeastern Louisiana, plus parts of the Florida parishes, Dennett noted the similarity of this topographical portion of the state to "a large part of all the States lying east" of Louisiana. "It has its exact counterpart in the central parts of Mississippi, Alabama, and Georgia." Evidently, many North Louisiana people who had moved to Louisiana from these states had few geographical adjustments to make and very likely simply transplanted an entire way of life to a different location with a similar environment.[9]

Many of these people were poor, especially those in the pine woods parishes, whom Dennett characterized as "proverbially poor." At the turn of the century, the public educational system of Louisiana depended largely for funding on property tax collections at the local level of government. As Minns Sledge Robertson observed, this "tested the desire of the people of the parishes" to provide education—since they were the ones paying for it. Under the system, the largest problem school officials faced was the inability to keep existing schools in operation for a full term, due to lack of funds. Largely because of poverty, it took time for Protestant North Louisiana to embrace a comprehensive system of public education. Too preoccupied with the business of attempting to make a living from the soil, North Louisiana Protestants seemed reluctant to depart from their nineteenth century pattern of small farms, villages, and small, church-sponsored schools. Consequently, at the turn of the century, North Louisiana's public school system suffered from under-funding and from school terms far shorter in length than in southern Louisiana—an indication of the educational disinterest and/or financial disadvantages of North Louisiana Protestants.[10]

The average term for public schools in Louisiana in 1903, five years after important educational reforms in 1898, was six and one-half months.

The parishes in the state with the shortest terms (three to four and one-half months) were Bienville, Catahoula, Claiborne, West Carroll, Jackson, Livingston, Lincoln, Ouachita, Rapides, Sabine, Union, Washington, and Winn. With the exceptions of Claiborne, West Carroll, and Rapides, which had black majorities, these were precisely the areas of the state where white populations exceeded the black and where Southern Baptists were the dominant religious group. In fact, in only ten of the thirty-four North Louisiana parishes did the school term equal or exceed the state average. By contrast, ten of the fourteen parishes maintaining full nine month terms in 1903 were in Catholic South Louisiana. If a Southern Baptist consensus on the desirability of public educational expansion existed, it was a phenomenon not shared by most Southern Baptists in the pine woods and uplands of North Louisiana during the first years of the twentieth century.[11]

By the end of the nineteenth century, North Louisiana's parishes constituted a cultural area largely characterized by evangelical Protestantism. As time advanced during the twentieth century, Southern Baptists increased their percentage of the white religious population, just as North Louisiana's Negro Baptists did among the black religious. By 1940, all North Louisiana parishes were majority Protestant and by 1970, all North Louisiana parishes, except East Baton Rouge, were majority Baptist.[12]

Because of the nature of Louisiana politics between Reconstruction and World War II, North Louisiana political interests usually prevailed whenever they conflicted with interests identified with the southern parishes. In this situation, religious differences across the cultural boundary often became tied to political issues. The political combination of North Louisiana black-belt elites and urban Orleans Parish, with its largely independent political and economic concerns, tended to dictate what public educational policy would be in the state. The presence of the Catholic Church's expanding parochial school system in South Louisiana served to motivate North Louisiana politicians toward seeking control of public schools, while agreeing to a measure of local educational autonomy by Orleans Parish—whose political machine held the balance of political power between the two largely rural sections of the state.

Protestant control of the state's educational system had the effect of insuring that public schools would not threaten or disturb the cultural influence of Protestantism in North Louisiana. On the other hand, many South Louisiana Catholics tended to regard public schools as agents of Protestant, Anglo-American cultural influence. The effect was a tightening of religious tension and competition between Catholics and Baptists, especially, in the rural parishes—where South Louisiana Catholics responded to Protestant influence on public education with expansion of their parochial school system in the twentieth century. V. O. Key's observation that political elites from the black-belt and Orleans held power by dividing rural Baptists and Catholics across the cultural boundary applies here to the nature of the educational system at the turn of the century.[13]

In North Louisiana, public educational expansion in the twentieth century resulted from progressive legislation, aided in part by Protestant/Catholic religious antipathy and in part by the political hegemony of a planter/industrialist economic elite that had come to embrace the idea of economic modernization through educational expansion. As public schools grew in numbers and quality, under Protestant control, elements within the leadership of the Louisiana Baptist Convention who favored sponsoring Baptist academies, in preference to public high schools, increasingly lost influence.[14]

Baptist acceptance of public education would cause the denomination problems during the 1920s, when lack of consensus over the matter of education would become apparent in controversies over the secular nature of education in the public high schools. Baptist leaders would be forced to defend public schools—usually by criticizing Catholic parochial schools—while some of the rank and file became alienated and turned to the fundamentalist sects, or else became representative of a fundamentalist element within the denomination.[15]

Although forced to accept public schools for primary and secondary level education, Louisiana Baptists undertook to sponsor a denominational college for the higher education of ministers and a church elite. Beginning with a proposal at the annual state Baptist convention by Edwin O. Ware in 1892, a movement to build Louisiana College picked up steam and reached its culmination with the opening of the college in Pineville, near Alexandria, in 1906. Ware was a long-time Louisiana Baptist educational leader. During his long association with the Louisiana Baptist Convention, he took part in the opening of two denominational colleges and served, for a time, as president of Louisiana College. Although his tenure as president was for only one year, 1907-08, Ware is credited with saving the school by mortgaging his own home to raise funds for it in 1908, at a time during the crucial early years of the college when denominational support was negligible.[16]

Prior to the opening of Louisiana College, two Baptist colleges had been in existence since 1857. Keatchie College, a girls' college until 1879, was located at Keatchie in DeSoto Parish, about thirty-five miles south of Shreveport. Mt. Lebanon University was at Mt. Lebanon in Bienville Parish, site of the convention marking the inauguration, in 1848, of the Louisiana Baptist Convention. Mt. Lebanon was a boys' school until 1887, when it became co-educational for a time after the LBC had relinquished its control over the school. Both Mt. Lebanon and Keatchie were small colleges and both remained so after the Civil War, when funding became an increasingly serious problem.[17]

The LBC dropped its formal affiliation and control over Mt. Lebanon in 1873 and over Keatchie in 1879 because of financial embarrassment and accumulating debts. Keatchie continued to be operated by a local Baptist association, as was the case with Mt. Lebanon. Both schools continued to struggle with financial problems until the Louisiana Baptist Convention assumed control of the schools again in 1899. This development resulted from a controversy over the proposed construction of Louisiana College within the LBC leadership. Ware and his supporters were unable to convince the LBC that a new college was necessary when two Baptist colleges, with long traditions, already existed in the state. However, by 1904, the inadequacy of the physical plants at Keatchie and Mt. Lebanon, along with the debts under which these colleges still operated, finally persuaded a majority of the LBC leadership to begin soliciting bids from Louisiana cities for the location and contruction of a new college.[18]

The traditional shortage of educated Baptist ministers in Louisiana seemed not to bother many Louisiana Baptists prior to 1900. Out of eighty Baptist ministers in North Louisiana in 1870, only four did not work at another job as their primary means of making a living. It is doubtful that many of these ministers had much education. During the 1880s, the LBC alternately recommended Mt. Lebanon University and Mississippi College for prospective students of the ministry. But few ministerial students from Louisiana attended either institution during the 1880s. Then, during the 1890s, a movement for the improvement of ministerial education, led by Edwin Ware, became increasingly prominent within the LBC. Ware was a graduate of the Southern Baptist Theological Seminary in Louisville, Kentucky, and became determined, upon moving to Louisiana, to address the problem, as he and others saw it, of a dearth of trained ministers in the state.[19]

With the opening of Louisiana College, Ware now had the denominational college that he hoped would become a first-rate institution of higher learning and a source of better trained ministers. As the Education Commission of the LBC became the Board of Trustees for Louisiana College in 1921, the bulk of the Commission's activities in later years centered on improving the physical plant and endowment of Louisiana College. Financial problems beset the institution, however, from its beginning.[20]

Ware's mortgage helped the college survive in 1908, but a fire destroyed the institution's only two permanent buildings in 1911, forcing a new beginning in 1912. An LBC campaign to raise $100,000 for the school succeeded, largely due to the philanthropy of W.C. Beall, a Baptist deacon and owner of a sawmill near Pineville. During the 1920s, Louisiana College received $450,000 from the Southern Baptist Convention's $75 million campaign for Baptist education. However, the college had been earmarked by the SBC to receive $1,075,000 as its share of funds from the educational campaign begun in 1919. This disappointment, coupled with continuing poor support from Louisiana Baptists, kept the college in a state of indebtedness throughout the depression years.[21]

All debts were finally liquidated in 1941, when Louisiana College was valued at $750,000, with an endowment of $325,000. The college had grown from fifty-one students in 1906 to 170 in 1915, although only forty-nine of these were college students. By 1934, the college had enrolled an all-time high of thirty-four ministerial students. In 1941, 546 students were enrolled. However, affiliation with the Southern Association of Colleges and Secondary Schools had not yet been achieved. In 1951, the college's faculty had only one Ph.D., when current standards for regional accreditation required that twenty-five per cent of a college faculty hold the doctorate.[22]

Louisiana's Baptists were not the only ones who could complain of mediocrity in education. Four of thirty-one senior colleges affiliated with the Southern Baptist Convention in 1927 held no accreditation. Ten of thirty-one junior colleges were also unaccredited, as were twenty-two of the forty-five academies. In 1929, the Education Board of the SBC was abolished and replaced with an Education Commission, whose first report lamented the lack of any good post-graduate institutions, such as those maintained by Southern Methodists at Emory and at Southern Methodist University.[23]

The major problems were a lack of funds from contributions and the tendency of local communities of Baptists to initiate educational endeavors on their own, and then plead for denominational support. The result was an overabundance of small, poorly funded colleges.[24] In advising against starting any more colleges or academies, the SBC Education Board proposed that, with cognizance of the lack of financial support available for educational enterprises, Baptists "might save much money, be spared much embarrassment, and escape much humiliation incident to inefficiency and mediocrity" in unnecessary educational enterprises. With subsequent worsening of financial conditions during the Great Depression, the Board's advice was largely heeded. By 1941, the SBC retained only twenty-six senior colleges, twenty-four junior colleges, and eleven academies.[25]

By World War II, the public educational systems of the southern states had become viable, as a result of increasing tax support at the state level. Public education would flower in the post-World War II South as educational budgets continued to increase, making successful competition by private denominational schools more and more difficult. Forced by financial realities and by organizational structure to rely on public high schools for secondary education at the turn of the century, Baptists in the post-World War II period would increasingly be forced to turn to the state for higher education as well.

Evangelism had always been the primary emphasis of Southern Baptists. Next to the priority placed by them on the saving of souls, the necessity for educational attainment suffered by comparison. However, a link has always existed between education and evangelism. So much so that George Kelsey was moved to write that "among Southern Baptists education has more than the usual social significance. It is a doctrine."[26]

Baptists in Louisiana were aware of the connection between education and evangelism from the inception of the Louisiana Baptist Convention in 1848. They were aware of the importance of education toward both the promulgation of their religious beliefs and of its utility in the warding off of rival doctrines. Reasons for embracing at least some education included the necessity of keeping children in the faith, and of being "articulate enough to thwart the faulty preaching of clever men like Daniel Parker and Alexander Campbell." These men were leaders of an anti-missionary movement among Baptists in the nineteenth century, resulting in the formation of sects like the Campbellites, or Hard-Shell Baptists.[27]

Unlike sections of other southern states, North Louisiana did not become thickly enough settled to have much religious organization until the 1840s. By this time, the anti-missionary movement had passed its peak and Louisiana Baptists, already attuned to an evangelical spirit, had few Campbellites among them. The 1890 religious census listed only 202 members, in the entire state, of the Disciples of Christ—the denomination that grew out of Campbell's movement.[28]

Consequently, evangelism continued to characterize the religious and educational practices of Louisiana's Baptists. To spread the Baptist gospel and to effect the conversion of others to that gospel is how evangelical Baptists believed that social reform could best be pursued, during both the nineteenth and twentieth centuries.[29] But as Baptists (and Methodists) began to relinquish their control of education to the state during the twentieth century, preservation of the faith remained an educational priority among Louisiana Protestants. In the northern United States, where public educational systems were extensive and secularized, by 1900, Sunday Schools became the means of providing the necessary religious education. From the North after 1870, this educational innovation spread to the South, but did not have great impact until the twentieth century.[30]

The Louisiana Baptist Convention first took up the issue of "Sabbath Schools," in 1859, declaring them to be a problem "in that there is little interest in them in the state." However, no campaign to improve the situation concerning religious education ensued until 1871, as war and reconstruction controlled events during the 1860s. The convention's first Sabbath School Board reported forty-one schools in five North Louisiana Baptist associations in 1876. Three years later, the number of Sunday Schools had grown to 130. Growth stopped at this point, as the Board reported only 97 schools in 1881. At the request of the Board, a "field agent," M.E. Shadduck, was hired to organize Sabbath Schools and to coordinate interest on a statewide basis. Having organized only twenty-two Sabbath Schools, Shadduck resigned in 1884 and interest in this form of religious education waned over the closing years of the century.[31]

One major reason for the lack of interest in Sunday Schools was their poor quality, a problem addressed by the Sunday School Board of Louisiana Baptists in 1911. Emphasizing the need for better quality to make Sunday Schools effective, the Board declared that it would "no longer allow persons because of their willingness to undertake teaching," in Sunday Schools, but would "insist they are capable of teaching, and know the Book before they are allowed to teach." John B. Mosely became Sunday School secretary in 1911 and instituted a training program for Sunday School teachers, issuing diplomas for the completion of various levels of attainment. In addition, a system of grading the quality of Sunday Schools was inititated. Under Mosely's leadership, the number of Sunday Schools doubled from 250 in 1910 to 500 in 1915.[32]

In 1920, Louisiana Baptists participated in a Southwide Rural Sunday School Campaign, sponsored and largely funded by the Southern Baptist Convention. Seventeen teacher-training courses were conducted in cities and rural areas of the state during the summer of 1920, with attendance by 510 prospective Sunday School teachers. From this point, Sunday Schools progressed both in numbers and outreach, as the religious education of adults, as well as of children, became the goal. By 1931, Louisiana Baptists operated over 700 Sunday Schools among a little over 800 churches.[33]

By the 1930s, progress had been substantial enough to initiate a drive for standardization of the schools. Upon Mosely's death in 1934, there were 785 Sunday Schools in operation and teacher-training courses were reaching seventy-five per cent of the churches in the state annually. From this point, Sunday Schools remained an integral part of the functioning of Southern Baptist churches in Louisiana. Initiated out of need for suitable outlets for evangelism, Sunday Schools became transformed into factories of evangelical spirit among Baptists. Serving not only the purpose of religious education, Sunday Schools have grown to become the most successful arm of Southern Baptist efforts to convert others to the faith.[34]

Growth of the Sunday School movement among Louisiana's Baptists provides a prime example of the kind of cooperative program of which

Southern Baptists were capable, once a favorable consensus was demonstrated to exist among them. Similar to Baptist programs for the maintenance of missionary endeavors, the Sunday School education program was characterized by a lack of controversy and a high degree of central direction toward the accomplishment of specific goals—formulated by centralized agencies cooperating on the local, state, and interstate levels of church organization.

Having failed to develop a consensus over the desirability of denominational schools—as Negro Baptists had done—white Baptists in Louisiana came increasingly to rely on the state for first, secondary education for their children and finally, by World War II, higher education as well, due to lack of support for Louisiana College. Early Baptist efforts to provide secondary schools during the nineteenth century met with failure in North Louisiana and no new efforts to build secondary academies arose once the public high school system became formally established in 1908.[35] After 1917, however, Southern Baptists built two schools in South Louisiana, both of which survived into the post World War II period and became showcases of Southern Baptist activities in education and evangelism within the French Triangle.

Except among Negroes, who managed their own associations and church activities, Baptists were a tiny and uninfluential minority in the southern part of the state. As a result, southern Louisiana became a prime target for Baptist evangelism after 1890. Up to World War I, Baptist missionaries managed to influence very few South Louisianians in either the rural areas dominated by French Catholics, or in the towns and urban New Orleans, dominated by Catholics and an established minority of other Protestant denominations. Having stretched itself to its cultural limits in the northern part of the state and in the Florida parishes, the white Baptist denomination could not effectively penetrate the cultural barrier confronting it at the boundaries of the French Triangle by the customary methods of revivalist evangelism and Sunday Schools. As the primary bars to Baptist expansion in South Louisiana were barriers of language, culture, and Catholic heritage, a new method of evangelism had to be introduced to overcome the institutional and cultural hegemony of Roman Catholicism. The method introduced in 1917 was that of Baptist denominational academies, creating an unorthodox Baptist emphasis on intellectual persuasion, rather than on emotional jarring of the spirit. It was one thing to convince people who had no religion that they were sinners and must seek salvation; it was another entirely to convince an established population with ingrained traditions that they were following the wrong religion.

In founding the Acadia Baptist Academy in 1917, white Baptists made a purposeful effort to break through South Louisiana's cultural barriers. A pamphlet explaining the purpose of the academy proclaimed:

> The customs and habits of [southern Louisianians] have been influenced very little by American progress. . . . The only way this large section of the country [South Louisiana] can be reached for Christ is by educating their own converts and teaching them the Bible so they can go back and give it to their own people in their own language. One French convert can do more than twenty English-speaking pastors to reach this people.[36]

When the academy opened in 1917 with four teachers and fifty-nine students, it became the spearhead of white Baptist missionary endeavors in the "Cajun country" of South and Southwest Louisiana. An LBC publication of 1929 provided numbers to demonstrate the school's influence. With fifteen churches and 1024 members in 1919, the Acadia Baptist Association—covering much of the same area as the Catholic Diocese of Lafayette—grew to twenty-six churches and 2705 members by 1929. While there were, in 1919, eight Baptist churches in the Association territory where sermons were delivered in French, there were fifteen such churches in 1929. Ministerial and mission students from the academy were primarily responsible for founding these new churches and for operating them with the needs of French-speaking congregations in mind.[37]

The Baptist Bible Institute (BBI), founded in New Orleans in 1918, had much the same purpose as Acadia Academy, except that this institution developed into the New Orleans Baptist Theological Seminary by 1946. Today, this seminary is one of six regional theological seminaries maintained by the Southern Baptist Convention in the United States, with an operating budget, in 1987, of over four million dollars. During the 1920s and 1930s, however, the school struggled to survive. A total of $500,000 had been expected for BBI, as its share of the $75 million campaign of the SBC from 1919-1924. Only $183,000 was realized and, in 1925, the LBC relinquished control of the school to the SBC. A subsequent drive to raise $70,000, needed to retire debts on the school, netted only $4,000 by 1928. With a payment of $38,000 on the bonded debt of the school due in 1929, and $110,000 more due in 1930, BBI was in danger of being closed. These payments represented less than half of the debt outstanding on the school. The SBC, however, kept the school going, eventually transforming it into a theological seminary.[38]

The Education Commission of the Louisiana Baptist Convention reported in 1931 on the evangelizing mission of Acadia Baptist Academy and the Baptist Bible Institute. Pointing out that "eighty per cent of the state population" had still not been reached by Baptist evangelism, the importance of the two Baptist schools in South Louisiana was emphasized:

> Since the opening of Acadia Academy eleven churches have been constituted in the territory of what is now the Acadia Association. Eight of these were the results of the work of the Academy students. This together with the fact that twelve churches have been constituted in New Orleans since the opening of the Bible Institution, is a strong argument for the work of our schools as missionary institutions, ...[39]

Rapid initial progress during the 1920s spawned optimism for the expansion of Baptist influence in South Louisiana that masked the presence of factors tending to inhibit further expansion. The churches established by mission students from Acadia and from BBI were barely self-sustaining, some requiring financial contributions from the state convention to keep operating. Despite approximate doubling of Baptists in the Acadia Association between 1919 and 1929, little further growth had taken place by 1940. With 3053 members in 1940, an increase of over one hundred per cent from 1919, the increase from 1929-1940 was only 12.9 per cent. Between 1890 and 1936, the percentage of Southern Baptists to the total religious population of the Triangle parishes grew from 1.0 per cent to 1.3 per cent. While this growth indicated significant expansion, particularly after 1917, Baptist expansion by 1940 had only resulted in the permanent establishment of a small religious minority—whose impact on South Louisiana culture remained minimal into the post-World War II years.[40]

In Orleans Parish, growth was from 0.6 per cent of the religious to 1.1 per cent. In both Orleans Parish and in the Triangle, as a whole, white Baptists were among the most poorly represented religious denominations organized in the state. White Baptists outnumbered only Lutherans in the southern parishes, and were outnumbered by all other denominations in Orleans Parish in 1890. By 1936, white Baptists had barely overtaken Presbyterians and Jews, in addition to Lutherans, inside the Triangle. However, in Orleans Parish, white Baptists remained the smallest denomination organized in the parish in 1936.[41]

Despite the commitment of the LBC and the SBC toward maintenance of denominational schools in southern Louisiana, the Triangle parishes could not be effectively penetrated by Baptist evangelism. While French-language usage in southern Louisiana was one barrier to Baptist evangelism, other barriers also existed. Baptist experiments with educational institutions as centers of evangelism failed to achieve their purpose of spreading the Baptist faith inside the Triangle. Unable to shake the traditional hold of the Catholic Church in the southern parishes, Baptist growth was small in the years between 1890 and 1936, when such French Baptist missionaries as

Osime Derouen and Lucien C. Smith were busy overcoming the language barrier that Louisiana Baptists assumed responsible for their small impact within the Triangle.[42]

Baptist education programs reflected the tendency of religion to assume a leading role in cultural persistence. Where Southern Baptists constituted the majority of the religious population—in North Louisiana—denominationally sponsored education other than Sunday Schools received little support, since the denomination's impact on culture was secure. Even the denominational college struggled to survive in the years up to 1940 as enthusiastic support for Louisiana College came principally from an elite, educated minority within the state convention.

In South Louisiana, where Baptists had little impact on culture, formal educational programs had greater importance as a tool used to pursue an evangelical mission of converting Catholics. The success of Baptist Bible Institute and of Acadia Academy in converting Catholics to the Baptist faith was minimal by 1940, an indication that South Louisiana culture—historically tied to Catholicism and to Catholic-influenced cultural traditions—had social power equal to that of North Louisiana's in its ability to persist amidst profound political and economic change and to continue to associate cultural traditions to a dominant religious institution.

Education, as a key element in the process of cultural and religious persistence, concerned Catholics at least as much as Baptists. Consequently, Catholic education constitutes another important chapter in the history of cultural persistence and cultural boundary maintenance in post-Reconstruction Louisiana. Unlike Protestant North Louisiana, Catholic South Louisiana experienced a cultural invasion by politically dominant Anglo Protestants after 1880. As a sub-cultural area within a broader, largely Protestant-influenced southern regional culture, Catholic South Louisiana developed a remarkably strong and socially influential denominational education system between 1880 and 1940—in its effort to ward off cultural invasion from beyond the cultural boundary.

VI

Catholic Education and Cultural Persistence in South Louisiana

The cultural boundary separating North from South Louisiana has always featured religion as the primary differentiator between the two cultural areas. Catholicism has been the religious component of South Louisiana culture since the eighteenth century, but the Catholic Church was not securely established, even in South Louisiana, until the twentieth century. Catholic churches and schools were too few in numbers, throughout the nineteenth century, to serve populations in South Louisiana that were Catholic in terms of heritage and tradition, though not in actual practice.

A scarcity of churches also largely characterized Protestant North Louisiana over much of the nineteenth century. In 1832, in all of Louisiana, there were only ten Protestant and six Catholic churches. By 1890, 2308 Protestant and 184 Catholic churches had been built to serve a much enlarged religious population.[1] However in 1890, as in the early decades of the nineteenth century, most Louisiana citizens were not communicants of any organized religious denominations, even though most Louisianians identified with either Catholic or Protestant religious traditions. According to the religious census of 1890, thirty-six per cent of Louisianians were active members of religious denominations. While that percentage is far higher than it could have been in 1832, it is much smaller than in 1936, when fifty-four per cent of Louisianians were active religious communicants.[2]

In the half-century before 1890, when the differing cultures of North and South Louisiana were being formed, the weakness of religious organization meant that factors other than religion were at least partly responsible for their formation. Geography, politics, economics, and social inter-action between many different groups of people were all involved in the process of cultural formation. But religion—and religious differences—were most fundamental to why the cultural boundary maintained itself once people on each side of the boundary had formed different subjective identities for themselves.

In South Louisiana, the identity in question was not that of the Cajuns, or of the Creoles—not of any such particular ethnic group. Rather, the identity in question was shared by all of the different groups of South Louisiana—because they all shared the same unique geographical space, the same economic circumstances (and hence had similar political assumptions), and they also mostly shared the same religious heritages, traditions, and customs. This identity of being different from those Protestants in the pine woods and on the cotton plantations (despite differences between themselves) is what unified South Louisianians into a separate cultural milieu, if not a unified culture.

The different groups in South Louisiana—Cajuns, New Orleans Creoles, Genteel Acadians,[3] descendants of Midwestern rice farmers, Anglo-Americans, and Afro-Americans—all had different cultural traits and customs, but all were mostly Catholic. It is this Catholicity that gave them points of cultural intersection through common spiritual beliefs, interaction in church, shared religious holidays and festivals, and, in general, a shared joie-de-vivre or gaiety in living that was not characteristic of Anglo-Protestant Louisiana.

Lewis W. Newton made this point in 1933 in an article on Anglo/French conflict in antebellum Louisiana. Newton wrote that ". . . the greater levity and indulgence in amusements among the French population was due to their Catholic religion." In writing this, Newton was aware that formal church organization was weak during the time period of his concern, prior to 1860. According to Newton, "the hard circumstances of western life [and Louisiana was western at the time] . . . contributed to lessen the dependence of the people upon the institutional church," making them "more inclined to follow the bent of their economic or social interests without regard to religious consideration." As this state of affairs related to Anglo-French conflict, Newton asserted that Anglo immigrants into South Louisiana during the nineteenth century "were so lacking in religious attitudes or else so easy-going as not only to manifest no antagonism to Catholicism but even, if it suited their convenience, to fall in with it."[4]

In view of the high percentages of Catholic Church membership among the religious population of South Louisiana in both 1890 and 1936, it can only be surmised that as the institutional Catholic Church grew and strengthened its organizational presence, many Anglo-Americans of Protestant heritage did indeed "fall in" religiously with the Catholic French of the southern parishes.[5] Once having done so, they helped to strengthen the force of Catholic cultural traditions and to strengthen the cultural impact of Catholic customs, rituals, holidays, and festivals.

Had this not been the case, the Anglo invasion of South Louisiana during the nineteenth and twentieth centuries should have prevented the Catholic Church from becoming and remaining the dominant religious influence on the culture of the French Triangle parishes. But as the Anglo-American population grew in South Lousiana between 1890 and 1940, the percentage of Catholics among the religious population increased rather than declined. The implication suggested by this fact is that despite tremendous social, political, and economic change in South Louisiana during the first four decades of the present century—and despite the Americanization program introduced by Anglo-Americans in control of politics and the burgeoning public school system—the Catholic Church retained its predominant religious influence over the culture of the Triangle parishes.

In doing so, the Church had to co-opt the impact upon culture exercised by the public schools and by Americanization and, apparently, it succeeded in preserving among the various peoples of South Louisiana a common identity of cultural "differentness" from the people residing outside of the Triangle. This is remarkable, considering the differences that existed between various groups of people who nevertheless became, or remained, Catholic in the years up to and beyond World War II.

Chapter four of this volume examined the way in which the Church overcame the cultural challenge of black Baptists, by submitting to segregation of church parishes and by co-opting both public and Protestant education for blacks. The rest of this chapter is concerned with the way that Catholic education helped to co-opt public education for whites and how this helped enable the Catholic Church to increase its cultural influence within the French Triangle among the white population.

The Catholic Church maintained denominational schools in Louisiana since the French colonial period. Up to the twentieth century, the majority were private schools, founded and operated by religious orders. Operation of schools were entirely the responsibility of the religious orders involved, who depended for their living on tuition fees. Different from parochial schools, which were maintained by collections from parish churches and which were often free of tuition, Catholic private schools tended to become the educational preserve of economic elites in the Catholic population. During the nineteenth century, private schools characterized Catholic education in Louisiana because most Catholics lived in rural areas or small towns that did not have churches, much less parochial schools.

In other parts of the country, nineteenth-century Catholic populations were usually foreign-born minorities who tended to concentrate into close-knit communities for mutual aid, protection, and assurance from cultural attack by the dominant, largely Protestant, American population. The Catholic Church and parochial school were social institutions necessary for survival of the traits, language, and customs of the sub-cultural ethnic group—whether it was an enclave of Irish, Germans, Poles, Italians, or of some other predominantly Catholic nationality.

Catholics in Louisiana exhibited a different pattern. The majority in the early nineteenth century were of French heritage, but were not foreign-born. Unlike Catholic immigrants in the northern United States, nineteenth-century French Catholics were the native cultural group in South

Louisiana. With only six Catholic churches functioning in Louisiana in 1835, the majority of South Louisiana Catholics were only nominally Catholic, however. Postbellum construction of new churches and the organization of new church parishes continued well into the twentieth century to occupy most of the attention of the Catholic clergy in Louisiana. The situation in nineteenth-century South Louisiana was unusual in the United States in that the culture aided survival of the religion and its institutions, not the other way around.

The informal nature of Catholicism in South Louisiana carried on into the postbellum period of church expansion, overseen and directed by an alien clergy recruited mainly from Belgium and France. Foreign priests dominated the clergy in Louisiana until after World War II and were often shocked by what William Faulkner Rushton termed the neo-paganism of South Louisiana Cajuns. This neo-paganism resulted from the New World isolation of French people in Acadia and by cultural exchange with American Indians before the eighteenth-century expulsion of Acadians from Canada. Acadian relocation in areas of South Louisiana where no established churches existed and where no Catholic priests were available resulted in new cultural exchanges with Louisiana's Indians and blacks, producing the nominal Catholicism Rushton alternatively called "Cajunism."[6]

As a cultural designation, Rushton's Cajunism was not confined to descendents of the original Acadians, as German, Irish, English, Spanish, and Italian settlers all became absorbed into Cajun culture. This culture was distinct, but interrelated with that of white and black Creoles, to produce in South Louisiana a cultural milieu that, collectively, was distinct from Anglo North Louisiana and confined within the French Triangle.[7]

Despite the absorptive quality of culture in South Louisiana, that cultural blend was not impervious to invasion by Anglo Protestants, an invasion that began in the early nineteenth century and continued into the postbellum period. By 1900, the process of Americanizing South Louisiana was already well under way. By bringing with it the challenge to Catholicism of Protestantism, Americanization spurred the Catholic Church to increase its efforts at expansion, to become more integral to the culture of South Louisiana, and to begin bringing that culture into line with more orthodox Catholic religious practice.[8]

That is, Catholic Church expansion aimed not at retaining the nominal Catholicism of South Louisiana's people and culture, but at supplying churches and priests to develop actual Catholic Church attendance as well as to build Catholic schools in order to provide instruction in orthodox Catholic rituals and practices. By 1918, when enough new church parishes had been organized to create the new Diocese of Lafayette out of part of the

New Orleans Archdiocese, the Catholic Church in South Louisiana was well-enough established, at least in cities and towns, to pursue a role as protector of the culture identified with it. Before World War I, rural isolation had been most responsible for survival of both the cultural distinctiveness and the nominal Catholicism of the region. But that isolation was never complete and began to disappear during the present century. Like northern immigrant populations, Louisiana French Catholics were culturally defensive and turned to the Catholic Church for support in maintaining cultural integrity where it was threatened, in towns and cities under the political control of Anglo Protestants. As in the northern United States, Catholic schools were important to this function of the Church.

The educational center of antebellum Catholic Louisiana was the village of Grand Coteau, in the Teche region. Comprising St. Landry Parish and parts of the parishes of Iberia, St. Martin, and Lafayette, the Teche country was an area of prime farm land as well as of beautiful forests of oaks. Jesuits (Society of Jesus) built St. Charles College here in 1837 and previously, the Religious of the Sacred Heart had opened the Sacred Heart Academy in 1821, which still exists as a private college preparatory school for girls. Secondary schools existed elsewhere only in New Orleans, where the Ursuline Nuns were active in maintaining schools.[9]

Expansion of Catholic Church activities was more rapid in the postbellum than the antebellum era, aided by population growth that made the construction of churches and schools a more urgently felt priority. In the late nineteenth century, Catholic Church expansion was beset by numerous problems. Financial paralysis, communications and transportation difficulties, and yellow fever epidemics that periodically thinned the already over-burdened ranks of the clergy and religious were among the most serious of these problems. Still, beginning with Archbishop Blanc's episcopacy in the antebellum period, expansion ensued—though haltingly—until the twentieth century brought solutions to most of the nineteenth century's problems. One problem that persisted well into the present century, however, was the foreign character of Louisiana's Catholic clergy and religious. Although often French-speaking, the clergy in Louisiana were usually cultural outsiders who did not always understand the nature of the culture they had joined and who sometimes alienated their parishioners.[10]

A good example of cultural clash between priests and the French Catholics of Louisiana is the ill will against four French priests in the Teche region resulting from the priests' attempt to effect commutation of a young black man's sentence, following his conviction for a shooting in 1911. The priests involved were pastors of the churches at Arnaudville, Cecilia, Breaux Bridge, and St. Martinville, all in St. Martin Parish. The priests were unsuccessful in their effort and church attendance, particularly among men, dropped off as a result of animosity against the priests for interfering in the sensitive area of parish racial relations.[11]

In other areas of the country, immigrant populations sometimes resisted pressures from the dominant native society, resisted their concepts of Americanization, and sought to preserve Old World traditions and customs. Wherever this happened, the Catholic Church and Catholic schools often became instrumental agents for the preservation of foreign social traditions and foreign languages. When the American Catholic hierarchy decreed in 1884 that all Catholic parishes must build and maintain a parochial school, a controversy over the nature of Catholic education ensued. Proponents of the perpetuation of foreign cultural expressions believed that such Old World cultural survival should be a primary purpose of Catholic schools. Others within the Catholic hierarchy recognized the hostility that Old World cultural maintenance engendered among the majority population of Anglo-Saxon Protestants.[12]

Louisiana's Catholics, particularly in South Louisiana, did not experience the same kind of pressures for Americanization that northern immigrant populations faced. There was no controversy over the role of parochial schools in society. For one thing, Louisiana Catholics had historically placed little emphasis on parochial schools, private schools sufficing to meet the educational demands of a wealthy minority of French Catholics. For another, the majority of rural French Catholics felt little need for social institutions for the purpose of language and culture preservation. Isolated in the countryside, rural Catholic culture remained secure until the twentieth century brought economic change, increased urbanization, and the growth of an Anglo Protestant-dominated public school system. In any case, the Archdiocese of New Orleans came near financial insolvency during Reconstruction and needed the contributions of church parishioners to pay off debts, precluding any program of parochial school expansion.[13]

A further reason the school controversy of the early 1890s had little impact in Louisiana was the influence of Protestants in the state government, enacting legislation to prevent Catholics from moving toward any attempt to seek cooperative ventures with the state in education. Bishop John Ireland of Minnesota proposed an Americanization plan for parochial schools involving rental of Catholic schools to the state for specified periods of time during weekdays. Since the state would incur much of the expense of operating the schools under Ireland's "Poughkeepsie," or "Faribault Plan," as it was known, the plan involved solicitation of public funds for Catholic-owned institutions. Before Ireland introduced his plan in Faribault, Minnesota, thereby initiating a controversy over church-state separation in 1891, Louisiana had been the only state in the Union whose laws forbade the use of any public money for support of any kind of private school, religious or otherwise.[14]

Not content with the existing law, Louisiana's legislature enacted a statute in 1894 to clarify the state's constitutional ban on aid to private schools, and to state explicitly that the ban applied to any cooperative ventures between the state and religious schools, such as proposed by Bishop Ireland:

> The parish boards of directors of the several parishes of the state are prohibited from entering into any contract, agreement, understanding, or combination, tacitly or expressly, directly or indirectly, with any church, monastery or other religious order or association of any religious sect or denomination whatsoever, or with representatives thereof, for the purpose of running or to defray the expenses of the running of any public school or schools of the state, together or in connection or in combination with any private or parochial school or other institution of learning which may be under the control, authority, supervision, administration or management of any church, monastery, or other religious order or association or any religious sect or denomination whatever.[15]

Whatever Louisiana's Catholics thought about the controversy over parochial schools raging in the North, Louisiana's Protestants intended to ensure that their tax funds would not go toward alleviating Catholic financial problems in Louisiana.

Faced with Protestant opposition to parochial schools, as well as inability to finance them, Catholics in Louisiana had little choice but to postpone parochial school expansion and to disregard the decrees of the Third Plenary Council. In the meantime, Catholic elites desiring formal education and who tended to view a public education as socially inferior, had Catholic private schools. The majority of Louisiana's Catholics, who largely eschewed public schools as well, remained largely unaffected by formal education of any kind. Mainly by force of cultural tradition, the nineteenth-century rural cultural pattern of low educational attainment persisted into the twentieth century in South Louisiana.[16]

Most Catholic schools in Louisiana during the nineteenth century were operated and maintained by religious orders of teaching Sisters. Their academies, or "Select Schools for Young Ladies," reflected the Catholic emphasis on education of girls in Louisiana. Since co-educational education was prohibited until the late 1880s, a dearth of teaching brotherhoods in Louisiana precluded the spread of boys' academies and resulted in a reliance on young elite women to spread Catholic influence within their families and communities. As purveyors of culture, Catholic women, educated in

Catholic academies, played an important role in the nineteenth century in keeping Catholic practices and church attendance going.[17]

Such schools for elite young ladies also often attracted non-Catholic girls and aided survival of the Catholic Church in the small Catholic communities of North Louisiana, as well as in South Louisiana. There were always shortages of teaching sisterhoods, however. As a result, the Catholic preference for schools staffed by religious orders—for the reason that these schools tended to be long-lived, stable, and largely financially self-supporting—placed severe limits on the expansion of Catholic education.[18] Meanwhile, Catholic education for "the masses" in Louisiana's rural areas and small towns would have to await the establishment of more church parishes and the financial ability to maintain parochial schools during the twentieth century.

Urban Orleans Parish was always an exception to the general rule in educational matters in South Louisiana. State Department of Education requirements for schools and school boards were usually amended with the phrase "Orleans Parish excepted." Orleans had numerous private schools of all kinds and a public system far in advance of the rest of the state. As the headquarters of the Archdiocese of New Orleans, New Orleans also had a disproportionate number of Catholic schools—both private and parochial. In addition, both Catholic universities in Louisiana were located in New Orleans.[19]

Expansion of both the public and the Catholic systems of education in South Louisiana occurred at roughly the same time. Financial recovery by the Catholic Church in Louisiana resulted in an increased number of Catholic schools after 1906, under the administration of Archbishop James Hubert Blenk. A number of new parishes were created as more churches were built, in the ongoing effort to restore the scattered Catholics of Louisiana to the sacraments of the church. Under Archbishop Blenk, the Church in Louisiana finally attempted, seriously, to comply with the Third Plenary Council instructions concerning parochial school construction in all Catholic parishes. Also, the creation of separate parishes for Negroes received more attention, ten such separate parishes being created in the archdiocese between 1906 and 1917.[20] One consequence of the rapidly growing movement for segregation was that white Catholics became more inclined to contribute to the construction of parochial schools, since now they had no reason to withhold contributions for fear that the money might go toward schools for Negroes.

In addition, compulsory attendance laws went into effect during Blenk's tenure as archbishop. In 1910, school attendance became required for children aged eight to fourteen, only in the city of New Orleans. In 1914, compulsory schooling was extended to all cities with a population of

25,000 or more, adding only Shreveport to the list. Finally, in 1916, school attendance for children aged seven to fourteen became required everywhere in the state for a session of 140 days, or about six and one-half months. As the only alternative in many places to public schools, Catholic school enrollments received a boost from the compulsory attendance law, although the law was rarely enforced anywhere in the state until the 1940s.[21]

State laws concerning education also had the effect of improving Catholic education, since under the compulsory attendance requirements, Catholic schools had to conform to public standards in order to qualify as an authorized alternative to public education. State inspectors began visiting all schools in the state (except in New Orleans, which had its own inspection system and separate standards), including Catholic schools, after 1919. As with the expansion of parochial school systems in other areas of the country, the Catholic system in Louisiana had already begun to be systematized and standardized.[22]

Archbishop Blenk appointed the first school board for Catholic schools in the archdiocese and the first superintendent of the Catholic school system after a survey of schools he conducted upon taking over as archbishop in 1906. His appointee, Monsignor Leslie J. Kavanagh, oversaw the implementation of standards and administrative procedures copied from the Catholic school system of Boston, Massachusetts, following a trip to the Northeast for that purpose in 1908. As a result of Archbishop Blenk's desire to provide secular, as well as religious education to Louisiana Catholics, there was no problem in conforming to state requirements and satisfying state inspectors after 1919.[23]

In adopting the bureaucratic procedures earlier developed in cities of the North, which contained large populations of Catholic immigrants, the Church in Louisiana had begun to acquiesce in the ongoing campaign to Americanize French Louisiana. When a new state constitution demanded exclusive use of the English language in public schools in 1921, it had little impact on Catholic schools since the church had already begun implementing this change. Whereas Americanization in Catholic education became a Catholic policy established first in the North, only after a raging controversy between Catholics and with Protestants, it occurred in Louisiana without much fuss and as the result of the Church's financial ability, for the first time, to pursue a policy of parochial school expansion. In doing so, after 1906, the Church adopted progressive reforms being initiated in the state system. As the organization of new church parishes continued, the Catholic Church became secure in its hold on the religious population of South Louisiana. Since the Church itself sought to alter the cultural and religious practices of Louisiana's French Catholics, little controversy with Protestants developed over parochial school expansion and Americanization.

Individual schools and teachers likely continued to tolerate, or even encourage, French-speaking among French children, but this was not the Church's policy.[24]

Much credit should be given Archbishop Blenk for changing the direction and emphases of Catholic education in Louisiana. Blenk became interested, during his tenure as Archbishop of New Orleans from 1906-1917, in the development of a native Louisiana clergy. Opposition to this idea was very strong among the clergy of Louisiana, many of whom had claimed for decades that Louisiana's natives were somehow not suited for training as priests. Continuing a struggle begun by his predecessor, Francis Janssens, Blenk began to break down this resistance during his tenure as archbishop. He built a preparatory seminary for boys at St. Benedict, Louisiana, and began planning for the construction of a major seminary for the archdiocese, so that native Louisianians would not have to attend seminaries in St. Louis or Baltimore in order to become Catholic priests. Blenk died before a major seminary could be built, construction of the Notre Dame Seminary in New Orleans taking place during the episcopacy of his successor, Archbishop John William Shaw. Finally, however, after 1924, Louisiana would begin to feature a native clergy, trained within the state—a development that did much in later years to eliminate anti-clericalism and to tie the Church more closely to the culture of the areas in Louisiana that it served.[25]

Blenk's major contribution to Catholic education in Louisiana, however, was his insistence on reorganizing, standardizing, and expanding the parochial school system. Upon becoming archbishop, Blenk wrote that the "parochial school system is in everyway defective. It has to be organized and crowned with an efficient Catholic High School."[26] His interest in this area and his ability to promote his ideas among lay Catholic organizations and Catholic philanthropists went far in producing support and financing for parochial school expansion. His willingness, also, to adopt the secular curricula employed by the public schools allowed parochial school expansion to proceed in succeeding decades without undue controversy.[27]

The Catholic population in North Louisiana, in contrast to the southern parishes, was a cultural and religious minority. In the Diocese of Natchitoches, covering twenty-nine civil parishes north of the thirty-first parallel, stretching from Bayou Anacoco to the junction of the Red and Mississippi Rivers, Catholic education was necessary in order to combat the encroachment of evangelical Protestantism. Here, as in the rest of the largely Protestant southern states, Catholics lived amidst a population whose culture and traditions were rooted in evangelical Protestantism. Only in the few places in North Louisiana where French and Spanish settlements pre-dated the arrival of Anglo-Saxon immigrants in the nineteenth century, did the Catholic Church have much influence.

The Diocese of Natchitoches became the Diocese of Alexandria when Bishop Cornelius Van de Ven moved the diocesan headquarters from Natchitoches to Alexandria in 1910. This move reflected the fact that most Catholics in the diocese were located in the southern parts of the diocese, closest to Louisiana's cultural boundary. In fact, over half of the Catholic population of the diocese could be found in one civil parish of Louisiana. This was Avoyelles Parish, which is within the French Triangle and is culturally, part of South Louisiana. Outside of the southern parts of the diocese, Catholic enclaves existed in Natchitoches Parish and in the North Louisiana cities of Shreveport and Monroe. Except for these places, there were few Catholic schools, because there were few or no Catholics, few churches, and only scattered mission chapels.[28]

Urban concentration characterized the Catholic population of the Florida Parishes, north of Lake Pontchartrain and east of the Mississippi River, which were contained within the Catholic Archdiocese of New Orleans, before creation of the Diocese of Baton Rouge during the 1960s. These eight parishes constitute a second section of "North" Louisiana, as a cultural area, because of geographical similarities to the northern part of the state, as well as for its predominantly Anglo-Saxon Protestant population. As noted earlier, in Chapter Two, St. Tammany Parish belongs statistically within the French Triangle, because of its proximity to New Orleans and because of the cultural bonds between New Orleans and the southernmost portions of St. Tammany. If included among the Florida parishes, St. Tammany Parish, plus the city of Baton Rouge, contained seventy per cent of the Catholics in eight Florida parishes in 1890 and sixty-one per cent in 1936. Here, and in towns such as Ponchatoula in the southernmost parts of Tangipahoa and Livingston parishes, is where Catholics built parochial schools during the period of expansion after 1906, and where the majority of Catholics in the Florida parishes continued to reside.[29]

As in the Diocese of Alexandria, Catholic growth in Baton Rouge and in parts of other Florida parishes did not represent a breakdown of the cultural boundary. Catholic schools in Louisiana never had this kind of effect on the religious conversion of non-Catholics. Rather, these places were locations of already-existing Catholic populations that grew and became suitable locations for Catholic schools. Once established, Catholic schools in St. Tammany and in Baton Rouge served to strengthen and solidify the Catholic presence in those places.

Within the Triangle is where most Catholic school expansion took place after 1906. In New Orleans, the Catholic school system grew so strong as to nearly overshadow the public system. In 1960, Catholic schools in Orleans Parish enrolled approximately one-third of all children in school from kindergarten through high school. The same held true for Jefferson Parish, with its population concentration in suburban Metairie. With the location in New Orleans of the Catholic Xavier University and Loyola University of the South it became possible for New Orleans residents to remain in Catholic schools from kindergarten to attainment of the law degree, or of the Ph. D.[30]

Parochial school expansion in the Diocese of Lafayette began as part of the expansion program initiated by Archbishop Blenk after 1906. Expansion continued under Bishop Jules Jeanmard, after the diocese was created in 1918 by splitting off the area of the archdiocese west of the Atchafalaya River. The land area of the Diocese of Lafayette comprised thirteen civil parishes representing the area of settlement of the Acadians, or Cajuns, during the eighteenth century. Long distinguished elsewhere in the state by French-speaking and by aversion to formal education, the Acadian people of southwestern Louisiana were nearly all Catholic and were the people at which the Americanization programs of the public school system were most aimed. Southwestern Louisiana was the area of the state where rates of illiteracy continued to be highest into the 1950s.[31]

Daniel Dennett, an agricultural columnist for the New Orleans *Picayune* during the 1870s and 1880s, wrote critically of the Acadian people and their cultural traits. After praising the climate and soil fertility of the land on which Cajuns lived, Dennett concluded that they were "not a thrifty people":

> With the means around them of living well, they fare no better than the people who live on poor lands. Their educational advantages are poor, but they all learn to ride and to use a shotgun expertly about as soon as they learn to walk. . . . They are kind, hospitable and sociable among themselves, but shy and suspicious of a stranger, especially if, . . . he speaks no French.

Rural isolation characterized Dennett's Acadians and would continue to do so into the twentieth century.[32]

Only after 1900 did the rural isolation of southwestern Louisiana's people begin to break down. Both the public and Catholic school systems began to expand, especially after 1920, as towns in the region began to expand and to become urban areas. By 1925, such towns as Lake Charles, Lafayette, New Iberia, and Opelousas had Catholic high schools and parochial primary schools had proliferated in numerous smaller towns of the region. By 1944, there were fifty-five Catholic elementary schools and twenty-seven Catholic high schools in nine civil parishes in the Diocese of Lafayette, most having been built since 1910. By 1947, Catholic school enrollment in the thirteen parishes of the diocese represented twenty-three per cent of the total school enrollment in those parishes.[33]

The public system also expanded in the years after 1910. The attendance rate in public schools was just over thirty-four per cent of the educable youth (ages six to eighteen) of the state in 1903. In the parishes of the Diocese of Lafayette, the public school attendance rate was thirty per cent. However, excluding Calcasieu Parish, which had an unusually high attendance rate of fifty-nine per cent, the attendance rate of the remaining parishes was twenty-five per cent, in keeping with the alleged educational aversion of the Acadian people.[34]

By 1930, school attendance of the children of the state was over sixty-three per cent and the gap between Louisiana's school attendance rate, compared to the national average, had narrowed from almost nineteen per cent in 1910 to six per cent.[35] Still, illiteracy rates were highest in the Triangle parishes. In 1920, Louisiana's illiteracy rate of 21.9 per cent for people ten years of age and older, was the highest in the country. Twelve North Louisiana parishes had illiteracy rates higher than twenty-five per cent, in contrast to the Triangle, where illiteracy above twenty-five per cent characterized twenty-four of twenty-seven parishes. Following an adult education campaign during the 1920s, the state's illiteracy rate dropped to 13.5 per cent—still far above the national average of 4.3 per cent. In 1930, all thirteen of the state's parishes still reporting illiteracy rates above twenty-five per cent were in the Triangle.[36]

Continuing high rates of black illiteracy before World War II is one explanation for the high rates of illiteracy in Louisiana. However, if only the white population of the state in 1930 is considered, illiteracy was still far above the national average, at 7.3 per cent, and was again worse in South Louisiana. None of the North Louisiana parishes had native white illiteracy above ten per cent and all but three parishes reported rates below five per cent. By contrast, six Triangle parishes had white illiteracy rates above twenty-five per cent. Twelve more parishes had white illiteracy exceeding ten per cent, while only two, Orleans and West Baton Rouge, were below five per cent. Black illiteracy rates were also higher in South Louisiana than elsewhere.[37]

High illiteracy rates in South Louisiana prompted T. Lynn Smith and Homer L. Hitt, writing in 1952, to state:

> There is a definite association between the population of French language and French culture, and low educational status. Moreover, the educational standing of the population is lowest in those particular parts of the French section in which the Acadian influence has been the greatest.

Smith and Hitt pointed out that high illiteracy rates are generally characteristic of places, as in most of the pre-World War II South, where rural farm populations predominated. Concerning Louisiana, the gap between farm educational levels and those of towns and cities was larger than elsewhere, causing the high illiteracy rates. Further, the existence of a gap between the educational attainments of rural and urban people was most pronounced in the south-central part of the state, precisely where the cultural influence of the Acadian people was greatest.[38]

Although cultural conditions were different in southern Louisiana than in other parts of the South, especially in that most people living in southern Louisiana were Catholics, dating back to the eighteenth century, the Church began to operate in South Louisiana much as it did elsewhere in the country during the twentieth century. Catholic schools tended to be built only in the cities and larger towns, a pattern befitting the urban character of church organization elsewhere. In rural areas of North Louisiana, as in the rest of the Protestant South, the Church could never gain the initial foothold, through conversion, that it needed in order to sustain itself and to grow. Planting schools in rural areas would have been pointless, since the schools could not have survived due to a dearth of Catholic children to attend them. In rural areas of South Louisiana, there had been no need to plant schools for the purpose of conversion and financial problems had precluded the establishment of Catholic rural schools until after 1906 anyway. As a consequence, Catholic education did not reach most Catholics in the rural areas of mostly rural South Louisiana. Since public schools had also largely failed to reach those same people, cultural traditions among South Louisiana Cajuns had little or no emphasis on formal educational attainment.[39]

As it had for the entire nineteenth century, the Catholic Church in Louisiana continued, in the twentieth century, to follow the dominant social and political lead of the Anglo-Saxon Protestant South. When progressive reforms, including those educational reforms oriented toward a nativist concern for Americanization, came to Louisiana just before and following World War I, the Catholic Church participated in their implementation and furtherance. Except for the religious education provided, there was no difference in the curriculum of Catholic parochial schools as opposed to public schools. In the post-World War II era, the period of greatest public school expansion and modernization, the Catholic educational system followed suit with its own greatest period of educational outlays. That French Catholics in South Louisiana continued to lag behind other sections in terms of school attendance was the result of cultural traditions rooted in the values of an agricultural society.[40]

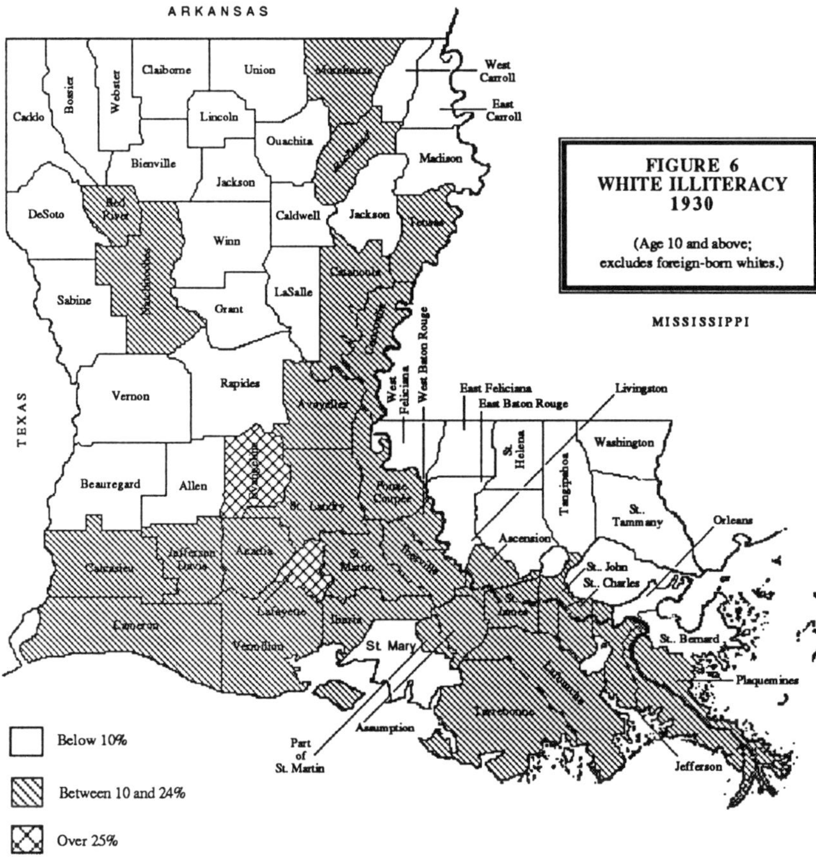

FIGURE 6
WHITE ILLITERACY
1930

(Age 10 and above; excludes foreign-born whites.)

Below 10%

Between 10 and 24%

Over 25%

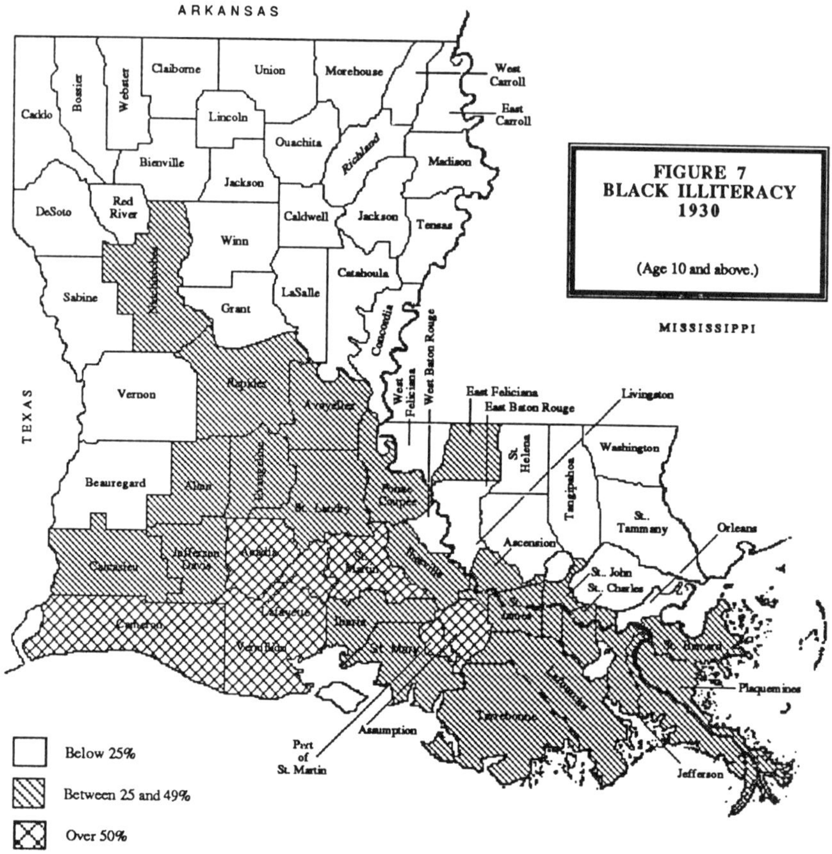

FIGURE 7
BLACK ILLITERACY
1930

(Age 10 and above.)

Edwin L. Stephens, former president of Southwestern Louisiana Institute (SLI, now the University of Southwestern Louisiana), the state teacher's college in southwestern Louisiana, pointed out in 1935 that "the Acadians have always been and still are in the main a pastoral people." Stephens considered it understandable that English-language educational expansion in the Cajun parishes had been retarded by the persistence of French-speaking among Cajuns. Addressing himself to the cause of high illiteracy rates in the French parishes, Stephens pointed additionally to the slow development of his own institution, SLI, as both cause and effect of the retarded development of both public and Catholic schools in the Acadian region. As a result of the lack of both primary and secondary schools in the region, SLI had to begin, in 1898, as an institution which admitted "students of very low academic achievement during the first years of its existence." In turn, as long as SLI functioned as a primary and secondary school, the development of public and Catholic schools in the surrounding areas suffered. Once SLI dropped its pre-college curricula in 1921, it began to upgrade its standards and to produce better-trained teachers, which had an eventual effect of improving the quality of schools in the whole area from which SLI drew its students. From this point, the education of Cajuns became a matter of school proliferation and of increased enrollments. For both the public and Catholic schools, the financing for expansion was not adequate to meeting the needs of the region until after World War II.[41]

The Catholic school system that developed in southern Louisiana, and especially in New Orleans, could not be characterized as deficient in comparison to the state system. Public school officials realized the urgent need for educational expansion and welcomed the Catholic educational system as a beneficial supplement to the growing, but still inadequate, pre-World War II public system. State Superintendent of Education Thomas H. Harris, a Methodist, applauded the Catholic school system and regretted that Protestants did not likewise build more denominational schools in the northern part of the state. Had it not been for the Catholic system, formal education would likely have eluded more South Louisiana Cajuns, for a longer period of time, than proved to be the actual case.[42]

In time, as South Louisiana urbanized, increasing numbers of French Catholics came under the influence of Catholic schools. Before 1940, as rural isolation continued to be prevalent in South Louisiana, the nominal Catholicism that had characterized South Louisiana's nineteenth-century population continued to characterize an isolated population of rural Catholics in South Louisiana. As long as this situation obtained, educational levels in the southern part of the state remained low, since rural people often ignored the compulsory attendance law or else allowed children to withdraw from school at the minimum age of fourteen.

Catholic schools in towns and cities had little effect on the pattern of religious affiliation in the southern part of the state. They did, however, begin to reverse the nineteenth-century pattern of nominal Catholicism and led, eventually, to an increased role by the Church in South Louisiana's cultural evolution—as formal religious practice became more prevalent. Eventually, Catholic schools also had the effect of cultivating a native clergy, which has largely ended the dominance of foreign priests in the years after World War II.

Members of Louisiana's Catholic hierarchy, such as Archbishops Blenk and Shaw, as well as Bishop Jeanmard of the Diocese of Lafayette, had begun to realize that if the Catholic Church was to become more integral to the culture of South Louisiana, it would have to recruit and train native South Louisiana priests, both black and white. Prior to 1940, accomplishment of that goal had not yet been realized, though Catholic school expansion and rapidly increasing urbanization had already begun to increase the Church's influence over South Louisiana society.[43]

During the period from 1880 to 1940, as rural isolation and nominal Catholicism began to break down in South Louisiana and as Americanization assumed greater social impact, rapid social change began to take place. By 1940, South Louisiana was no longer the foreign country within a country that it had been at Louisiana's statehood in 1812. The traditional rural pattern of life was apparently becoming a thing of the past. Still, the distinctiveness of South Louisiana culture persisted even as distinctions between the Cajun and French Creole cultural traditions became blurred and as black Creoles became increasingly segregated within South Louisiana's complex cultural and ethnic mix.

More predominantly Catholic in 1936 than in 1890, South Louisiana and its Catholic-sponsored holidays, festivals, and opposition to Prohibition continued to feature cultural expressions clearly distinct from those of Protestant North Louisiana. The contribution of Catholic schools toward the persistence of South Louisiana's cultural separateness was their impact in enlarging the role and influence of the Catholic Church on South Louisiana's social and cultural development after 1880. The enlarged social function assumed by institutions of the Church after 1880 helped to create social stability that prevented the loss of South Louisiana's separate cultural identity as political, economic, and educational developments changed the face of Louisiana during the twentieth century.

VII

Methodists, Other Denominations, Public Educational Development, and the Cultural Boundary

While Catholics and Baptists built the majority of denominational schools in Louisiana before World War II, Methodists, Presbyterians, Episcopalians, Lutherans, and Jews all became involved, at one time or another, in educational ventures. Most schools built by religious groups other than Methodists did not survive the Reconstruction period. In general, these minority religious groups had their greatest impact on education through the activities of individuals who were members of their faiths.

Following the state's 1845 legislation creating a public educational system, little progress ensued toward the construction of public schools. As a result, antebellum education was largely handled through the agency of private schools, although a public system did emerge in the city of New Orleans before the war. Most of the private schools in the state were small non-denominational schools opened by individuals who ran them for profit. Since many of the state's educated Protestant ministers had small financial support from their congregations, ministers often taught in the small private schools as a means of supplementing their income.[1]

Many antebellum planters in the sugar parishes of Louisiana were Catholic and made use of Catholic private schools for their children. Even in the southern parishes, planters were well-represented in the ranks of the state's Episcopalian, Presbyterian, and Methodist populations, although the first two denominations were always concentrated most heavily in New Orleans before World War II. An influential political group, both Catholic and Protestant planters usually did not support the public educational system. They reasoned "with some justification," as noted by Joe Gray Taylor, "that they would have to pay for them," if the public schools were allowed to proliferate into a truly extensive state system. As a result, planter opposition to public schools retarded the growth of the state system into the twentieth century and allowed private denominational and non-denominational schools to flourish.[2]

For a brief time between 1868 and 1877, the state did try to expand the public system. In demonstrating concern for the educational disparity among freedmen following the war, the state's Reconstruction government attempted to racially integrate the public schools. Encountering massive resistance in the rural parishes, the state government made no attempt to enforce integration, except in Orleans Parish.[3]

Although Louisiana's black population outnumbered the white in 1860 and would continue to do so until the 1900 census, blacks made up only eight per cent of the population of New Orleans in 1860 and were still outnumbered nearly three to one by whites in 1890. As the capital of the state during Reconstruction, the only metropolitan center, and the home of the majority of the state's former "gens de couleur libre," New Orleans became the testing ground for the experiment in school integration. Despite assurances that a majority white population would mean no cases in which blacks outnumbered whites in the public schools, white flight from public schools occurred after 1868.[4]

There were ten private schools in New Orleans in 1868. One year later, there were thirty. In 1870, the number increased to seventy-three. By 1875, there were over one hundred. About half of these were Catholic schools, which had increased in number from eight to forty-nine between 1868 and 1875. Much of this Catholic school construction represented a Catholic attempt to assume dominance of education in New Orleans. Unfortunately, the attempt proved costly in later years, as indebtedness caused by the rapid school construction of the 1870s precluded further Catholic educational expansion until 1906.[5]

With seventy-six public schools in 1874, New Orleans had 67,272 educable children, youths of both races aged six to twenty-one. Highest public school enrollment during Reconstruction was 17,194 in 1874. This figure represented enrollment of twenty-five per cent of the educable youth—a low figure even for the pre-1920s period of generally low enrollments. Public school enrollment in 1874 should have been higher (over thirty per cent), but were low because of protest against the integration of approximately five hundred Negro children in the schools. The accompanying increased attendance in private schools was a consequence of those protestations.[6]

Besides the Catholics, German immigrant denominations in the city opened parochial schools after 1870. Between them, German Evangelical Lutherans, German Evangelical Protestants, and German Presbyterians opened seven schools by 1877. Southern Methodists opened a high school in the city, four Episcopalian parochial schools appeared, and Presbyterians built six grammar schools, plus a boys' and a girls' high school. Presbyterians even organized their own school board and hired the former superintendent of city schools, William O. Rogers, to head it. The majority of these schools were discontinued when Democrats assumed control of the state government in 1877 and ended the experiment with school integration. Some of the Protestant schools that survived Reconstruction, such as the Presbyterian girls' high school, were forced to close during the 1880s.[7]

With the return to power of Bourbon Democrats in 1877, the school system was reorganized. Throughout the state, however, public schools continued to be too few, poorly equipped, and lacking in adequate monetary support from local governments. State Superintendent of Education William G. Brown recognized in 1874 that, "unless local authorities tax themselves, present schools only can be maintained." Because of restrictions on the power of local authorities to tax themselves for educational purposes—written into the 1879 Constitution—public schools continued, for the rest of the century, to rely on state appropriations that were too small to effectively augment the funds provided by local property taxes.[8]

Indications were that local authorities in many parishes were not interested in educational expansion. Prior to 1877, the State Board of Education received little cooperation from local governments. An extreme example of educational indifference occurred in St. Bernard Parish, where the state school appropriation, small as it was, was partly "appropriated" by school officials. One public "school" was operated in a mule stable with children having to endure the smell from a stall just six feet from them. White Leaguers in Red River Parish murdered the parish school board treasurer after forcing him to open the safe containing the parish school funds. The parish treasurer in Plaquemines Parish got caught embezzling $8000 from the state school appropriation in 1874 and was subsequently aquitted by a sympathetic jury. After the "Radical Republican" regime disappeared in 1877, interest in public educational expansion continued to flag.[9]

In the meantime, until the 1898 state constitution allowed parishes to collect special taxes for school construction and maintenance, small, private, and non-denominational—albeit Protestant—schools continued to handle much local educational need. In the years before Catholic expansion of parochial schools after 1906, small non-denominational schools flourished even in the southern Catholic parishes. Varying in quality, even bad schools still required tuition and were consequently beyond the reach of poorer citizens. As the net result of educational neglect in the state—by government officials, by religious denominations, and by the public in its apathetic acceptance of the absence of educational opportunities—illiteracy soared. William Ivy Hair aptly concluded that, among southern states, Louisiana "climbed from fifth to first place in ignorance between 1880 and 1890," with a rate of illiteracy of over seventy per cent for blacks and over twenty per cent for native whites.[10]

Negro denominations did what they could to alleviate the disadvantaged educational condition of blacks in the state, but could provide educational opportunities—of the kind not geared toward agricultural or vocational pursuits—only to a miniscule fraction of the black population. The seventeen Negro Baptist associations in Louisiana, affiliated with the National Baptist Convention, were most involved with construction of black denominational schools. In 1916, they owned sixteen of the eighteen black denominational secondary schools not affiliated with northern white missionary agencies. Negro Methodists maintained the other two—Homer College, in Claiborne Parish, and the Lampton Literary Institute, in Rapides Parish.[11]

Negro Methodist denominations, as offshoots of the white-dominated Methodist Episcopal Church, or of the Methodist Episcopal Church, South, continued into the 1870s to be dominated by the episcopal structures of the white denominations. Lacking the autonomy of the Negro Baptists, the Negro Methodist denominations attracted fewer converts than the Baptists prior to the 1870s and never attained the large memberships of the Negro Baptists in Louisiana. Despite declaring education an avowed priority of Negro Methodist church activities, Negro Methodist denominations could never develop the educational organizations and financial support for schools that Negro Baptists, through sheer numbers, could muster. Where Negro Methodists were numerous, as in Alabama, Georgia, and the Carolinas, they built more schools and pursued a stronger educational mission than in Louisiana.[12]

Although never as strong an educational force as other northern missionary agencies, the Lutheran Board of Colored Missions established nine schools for Negroes in the South in 1879. Eight of those schools, all primary parochial schools, were in New Orleans. Still operating in 1916, these Lutheran schools had a collective monetary value of $25,500, employed twenty teachers, and enrolled 1037 black elementary students. All were one-room schools in mission chapels or in rented buildings. The evangelistic impact of these schools on the black population of New Orleans appears to have been at least as strong as that of the Northern Methodist schools—Gilbert Academy and New Orleans University. It is probable that the majority of Lutherans in New Orleans were blacks and Lutherans did outnumber Negro Methodists in the city by 1936. Elsewhere in the state, the numerical strength of Negro denominations was also strongest where schools maintained by those denominations were located.[13]

In 1890, St. Mary Parish ranked second only to Orleans in the size of its Negro Methodist population, among twenty-seven southern Catholic parishes. The black Methodist Gilbert Academy located in St. Mary moved to New Orleans in 1919. Afterwards, St. Mary's Negro Methodist population declined, ranking only seventh among the Triangle parishes by 1936. Claiborne Parish, the site of Homer College, maintained by the Colored Methodist Episcopal Church, contained the second largest Negro

Methodist population of the thirty-five northern parishes in 1890. By 1936, Claiborne had the largest Negro Methodist population in the state, followed by Orleans, with its two black Methodist institutions.[14]

Rapides Parish, site of the only other black Methodist academy, was a slight exception to the rule. Seventh among the northern parishes in 1890 in numbers of Negro Methodists, Rapides ranked only ninth in 1936. Still, in both 1890 and 1936, Rapides contained the largest number of Negro Methodists of any parish in the central part of the state.[15]

With white denominations, the pattern of numerical strength correlated less obviously to the existence of denominational schools, partly because only Catholics erected white denominational schools in any great numbers. Also, white Protestants favored either non-denominational private schools—most numerous during the nineteenth century—or public schools, as the Protestant-dominated public school system expanded in the twentieth century.

One white Protestant denomination that never fully accommodated its position on education to reliance on public schools was the Protestant Episcopal Church. Every year from 1865 to 1886 resolutions were introduced at the Episcopalian General Convention calling for the establishment of parochial schools. Many Episcopalians disliked public schools, both for their secular nature and for their generally poor quality, as common schools for the masses. Although Episcopalians did build parochial schools in the North, they did not do so in Louisiana until after World War II.[16]

A good explanation for the failure of Episcopalians to establish schools in Louisiana is found in the religious statistics of Louisiana before World War II. There were only 5162 Episcopalians in the entire state in 1890, nearly three thousand in New Orleans alone, where they constituted all of three per cent of the religious population. By 1936, the number of Episcopalians had grown to over 17,000, nearly half still in New Orleans. Over the years since 1936, Episcopalian growth in the state has made Episcopalian schools feasible.[17]

Presbyterians were even less numerous in Louisiana than Episcopalians. The Presbyterian population grew from just under 4000 in 1890 to just under 14,000 in 1936. Over half resided in the urban areas of New Orleans, Baton Rouge, and Shreveport. The remainder were scattered throughout the state in much smaller groups. Few parishes had more than one Presbyterian church before World War II and the congregation in Lafayette, first organized in 1875, was probably typical of Presbyterian congregations in most of the state. In 1920, the pastor in Lafayette complained that only about half of the church members attended service regularly. Those who did attend did no evangelistic work outside the church.

He concluded that "worldly conformity is too prevalent for the Church's good." Four years later, the same pastor commented: "Our people here generally are like the people in most places and try out almost every fad."[18]

Concluding, probably correctly, that such behavior among Church members was the result of a lack of proper religious indoctrination, the Louisiana Synod created a Department of Religious Education in 1924 that began operating in 1927. As with other Protestant groups in Louisiana, the Presbyterian Educational Department placed a great deal of emphasis on the improvement of Sunday Schools. These had been deficient in teacher quality, in lesson materials, and in enrollments. With the onset of the Depression, Presbyterian Sunday Schools continued to struggle, until increased affluence and population growth after the war brought improvements in all phases of Church activity—especially in the area of physical plants.[19]

Neither Northern nor Southern Presbyterians operated denominational schools other than colleges after the 1870s. Since then, Presbyterian absence in the private school field has been characteristic of the denomination. In formal recognition of long-established practice, the Northern Presbyterian General Assembly adopted a strong statement in 1957 declaring its "support of public education and its role in the United States." That statement might also have applied to the educational stance of the Southern Presbyterians as well.[20]

White Southern Methodists, with larger numbers of religious communicants, showed greater educational ambitions than either Presbyterians or Episcopalians before World War II. With an educational outlook similar to that of Southern Baptists and equal organizational capabilities, Southern Methodists evolved a program of educational activity nearly identical to that of Southern Baptists.

With the founding of Centenary College at Jackson, East Feliciana Parish, in 1825, Methodist interest in higher education manifested earlier than that of Baptists in Louisiana.[21] Three more colleges were built during the 1850s. Homer College, in Claiborne Parish, came under the control of the Colored Methodists, who splintered from the white Southern Methodist Church in 1870. Pierce and Payne College, in DeSoto Parish, did not survive the Civil War and Reconstruction. However, Centenary and the Mansfield Female College, in DeSoto Parish, did survive into the twentieth century, as counterparts to the Baptist Mt. Lebanon University for men, and Keatchie College for women.[22]

Like the Baptist colleges, Centenary and Mansfield entered the new century with old and inadequate physical plants. Two years after Baptists established Louisiana College, near Alexandria, to replace Mt. Lebanon, the Methodists moved Centenary to a new urban location in Shreveport, where the school has since remained. Both female colleges, Keatchie and Mansfield, were eventually abandoned by their denominations—Keatchie by the Baptists in 1912, and Mansfield by the Methodists in 1930.[23]

As did Baptists, Methodists established academies in various parts of the state that were abandoned when public high schools came into existence about the turn of the century. Evergreen Institute, established in Avoyelles Parish in 1856, was one of the largest Methodist denominational schools of the nineteenth century. Also like Baptists, the Methodist college and Sunday Schools became the educational priorities of the Annual Conference by 1919.[24]

In 1919, as the Southern Baptist Convention was launching its $75,000,000 Campaign ($20,000,000 for education), the Southern Methodist General Conference launched a similar drive to raise $23,000,000 for denominational education. Like the Baptist campaign, the Methodist funding drive fell far below its goal, collecting only about $8,000,000 by 1928. As a result, improvements made on Centenary College created serious indebtedness on the school, a problem similar to that of the Baptist Louisiana College during the Depression years. In further similarity to Baptist education, a Sunday School teacher training program brought better quality and higher enrollments to Methodist Sunday Schools after 1920.[25]

One difference between Methodist and Baptist education in Louisiana was that Methodists supported their denominational college with better funding than Baptists gave Louisiana College. Instead of retiring debts on Centenary College during the 1930s as Baptists did with Louisiana College, Methodists increased their debts in order to upgrade their school. In 1939, the conference Board of Education reported that Centenary had qualified for accreditation by the Southern Association of colleges and Secondary Schools—an important measure of commitment to meeting educational standards that Baptists failed to display with Louisiana College.[26]

In addition, Louisiana's Southern Methodists began requiring a minimum of two years of college work by its ministers in 1926. In 1945, a Southern Baptist minister could still lament the lack of education on the part of Southern Baptist ministers: "Ignorance is one of the greatest sins of the church. . . . Many of our ministers are 100 years behind the times." With improvements at Centenary and better educational standards, Methodist ministers in Louisiana did not have to bear such criticism. While Louisiana College, in 1951, had one Ph. D. on its faculty, forty per cent of Centenary's faculty held doctorates by 1953. Further, Centenary was in sound standing with the Southern Association, both academically and financially, as Louisiana College was not.[27]

One other important religious group existed in Louisiana before World War II. This was the small minority of Louisianians who were Jewish, of both the Reformed and Orthodox faiths. According to Leo Shpall, the first Jewish congregation in Louisiana was founded in 1828, in New Orleans. By 1842, there were about 2000 Jews living in New Orleans. From this point, little growth occurred in the Jewish population for the remainder of the century, as the 1890 census reported 2750 Jews in Orleans Parish and 3374 in the entire state. By 1936, Jews numbered over 13,000 (8700 in New Orleans) and were about as numerous in the state as Presbyterians.[28]

Partly because of the effects of the Civil War, in drawing whites closer together, Jews experienced little discrimination in Louisiana of the kind Jews endured in other parts of the country. Small numbers, business acumen, and social philanthropy on the part of Louisiana's Jews are other reasons, as well as the fact that, in Louisiana, Reform Jews predominated—creating less divergence from Christian religious practices than would have been true if the majority were Orthodox.[29]

The Jews of New Orleans organized the Hebrew Educational Society in 1866, which opened a school available to Jews and non-Jews alike. This institution gave way in 1910 to the New Orleans Hebrew School. Already in existence, since 1896, was the library, gymnasium, and lecture facilities built by the Young Men's Hebrew Association and the Young Women's Hebrew Association. However, the private philanthropy of Jewish individuals had broader significance to education in Louisiana than the activities of Jewish organizations.[30]

One such individual was the New Orleans businessman, Isidore Newman. The Isidore Newman Manual Training School, which Newman founded in New Orleans in 1903, reflected its benefactor's interest in promoting the training of skilled workers. By the 1930s, however, the Isidore Newman School had become the state's model secondary school. Educational innovations, proven successful there, were sometimes copied by the state's public schools. To the present day, the Newman School is still considered by many to be the finest academic secondary school in Louisiana.[31]

Jews in Louisiana had little problem with the cultural boundaries existing in the state. As a distinctive and highly successful minority, Jews were as culturally alien to North Louisiana Protestants as they were to South Louisiana Catholics. They posed no danger to the dominant cultures of either section and avoided clashes with the politically dominant Protestants through a shared outlook on church-state separation as best for the health of both religion and government.

A Jewish lawyer from Shreveport, Sidney L. Herold, built a reputation after 1912 for involvement in legal cases concerning the separation of church and state. He brought suit against the Caddo Parish School Board in 1913 for the Board's approval of Bible-reading in public schools, winning his case against Bible-reading in 1915 on the grounds that this practice violated the separation of church and state. Jews subsequently became members of the Caddo Parish School Board in the 1920s and two Shreveport high school principals in the 1920s were Jewish. In 1928, following Protestant protest against Louisiana's new Free Textbook Program, which distributed free books to church schools and became the first such program in the country to be justified by the child-benefit theory in state aid to education, Herold brought suit against the state on the grounds of violation of separation of church and state. Herold took the case to the Supreme Court, where his suit was denied in 1930, a decision hailed as a victory for the cause of Catholic education in the United States. Herold's action in both suits demonstrated a consistent position by the Jewish minority in cases concerning separation of church and state—a position necessary for a religious minority seeking guarantees against religious discrimination.[32]

Episcopalians and Presbyterians also had little trouble with the cultural boundary, for they too were minorities in both sections of Louisiana. Although these Protestant religious groups should have felt at home in Protestant North Louisiana, few lived there. The 1890 religious census revealed that all but 7110 of 115,808 Protestants in North Louisiana belonged to the major Baptist and Methodist denominations. About half of those who were not members of the major religious groups belonged to sectarian offshoots of those groups, such as the Primitive Baptists or the Methodist Protestant Church. Out of the remaining 3570, 2969 were either Presbyterians or Episcopalians. There were 1257 Presbyterians and Episcopalians out of a Protestant population of 40,320 in twenty-four South Louisiana parishes (excluding Orleans), almost exactly the same percentage of Presbyterians and Episcopalians, among Protestants, as in the northern parishes (3.11 per cent to 3.06 per cent).[33]

Perhaps the rural nature of Louisiana throughout the nineteenth century best explains the establishment of the boundary by 1890 between Catholic populations on one side and Baptists and Methodists on the other. Walter Brownlow Posey made the observation that Episcopalians had been content during the first half of the nineteenth century to leave the field of evangelism on the frontier to Methodists, Baptists, and Presbyterians. In Louisiana, with large areas of sparsely settled territory little removed from frontier conditions, Presbyterians as well as Episcopalians abandoned the field of evangelism during the nineteenth century. It made little difference to Presbyterians and Episcopalians in the towns and cities, or on the plantations, whether the country people were Baptists, Methodists, or Catholics.[34]

Minority religious groups were most represented in urban areas and in the black-belt parishes, where their adherents were often among the most prominent and influential leaders in economic and political affairs. From positions of power in local and state government, individual Presbyterians and Episcopalians exerted great influence over public educational development. Such influence reflected upper-class interests that conflicted with the best educational interests of the majority of rural Baptists, Methodists, and Catholics on both sides of the cultural boundary. After 1898, upper-class influence in government became evident in that educational reforms tended to benefit black-belt and urban parishes to the exclusion of areas where rural Baptist or Catholic religious influence was greatest.

In 1888, the Louisiana legislature passed a General Public School Act that required parishes to collect at least a one and one-half mill tax, based on property assessments, for public schools. This provision was nearly identical to one in the 1898 Constitution that allowed parishes to tax beyond a one and one-quarter mill requirement, if they wished. Collection of such taxes was hailed as a new beginning for the public school system after 1898. Few parishes, for some years beyond 1898, collected more than the required one and one-quarter mill. However, collection of the minimum requirement represented improved funding for schools since the 1888 Act had been ignored by most parishes. In commenting on the change in support of public education from 1888 to 1898, Rodney Cline referred to the "time-honored principle that laws enacted upon an unwilling or an unready populace are likely to be ineffective." However, Cline did not explain what made Louisiana's population seem more receptive to public educational expansion in 1898.[35]

Perhaps the most important provision of the 1898 Constitution was the disfranchisement of Negroes. For the public educational system the important provision was that state funds for public schools were to be apportioned to parishes on the basis of the total number of educable children in the parishes of the state, aged six to eighteen. What this meant to the Bourbon Democrats in charge of school boards and police juries was that, since Negroes were disfranchised, there could be no opposition to counting the children of both races, receiving the state appropriations, and then spending a disproportionate share of the school funds on schools for white children. Unfortunately for the predominantly white, hill-country parishes, they had few blacks to count as educables and the system worked to increase their educational disparity with the urban and black-belt parishes.[36]

Such disparity contributed to a situation in which there were two large groups of whites in the state who were educationally disadvantaged: rural Baptists and Methodists in the North Louisiana pine woods and uplands parishes, and rural South Louisiana French Catholics. Other religious denominations with largely urban memberships had better access to both public and private educational facilities. As the most educationally disadvantaged group, Negroes used their religious organizations to found schools in an attempt to overcome educational disadvantages. Rural white Protestants and Catholics, with traditions of low educational attainment, suffered from the lack of public educational development in their parishes at a time when their religious denominations were either abandoning denominational schools or facing financial barriers to educational expansion.

As a truly silent majority, Louisiana's rural white population got left out when the urban and plantation whites finally decided to support an expanded public system. With the educational reforms of the 1898 constitution, it was not the religious minorities of the state who were disadvantaged. Quite to the contrary, it was the religious majority of Negro Baptists and Methodists, rural white Southern Baptists and Methodists, and rural white and Negro Catholics.

The cultural, religious, and economic practices of these rural people were rooted in their eighteenth and nineteenth century origins. Social and cultural change was much less evident among them than among others in the cities and towns. They were the people most responsible for the presence and persistence of the cultural boundary, for they also constituted the majority of people in the state.

For the state's religious minorities, found mainly in urban places or on plantations, the cultural boundary was less meaningful. Represented in the state's economic, political, and intellectual elite out of proportion to their small numbers, Presbyterians, Episcopalians, and Jews were, in the main, a more prosperous group of people than the majority of Baptists, Methodists, and Catholics. They conducted their activities without regard for the religious prejudices and cultural heritages of the major religious groups. Insulated by economic status, along with the Baptist and Catholic elite, they represented the vanguard of progressivism in Louisiana. By World War II, changes in society introduced by progressives indicated a greater interest in protection of economic status than in sponsoring widespread social reform. Despite Huey P. Long's introduction of social reform on an unprecedented scale after 1928, the cultural boundary remained intact by World War II as Louisiana's religious majority remained largely unrepresented in the state's political and economic power structure.[37]

Up to World War II, the political and economic processes that produce social and cultural change had not greatly affected the older process of religious continuity and cultural persistence in large areas of the state. An emerging "civil religion," characterized by materialism and nationalism, was not yet strong enough in Louisiana to challenge, or to share the loyalty that Louisianians gave to their conventional religions. As rural values reinforced by conventional religious tradition persisted, educational expansion failed to subsume provincialism. Common class interests of rural white and black Baptists and Catholics remained buried beneath disunity caused by racial and cultural antagonisms between themselves. Unbound by these cultural antagonisms and having economic interests to protect, planter and industrial elites, in league with the growing middle-class of the towns and cities, exploited the political and cultural disunity of the rural population to retain political and economic hegemony in Louisiana.[38]

Leaders of the major denominations, less bound than most members of religious groups to nineteenth century rural values and traditions, recognized a need for social uplifting on the part of their denominational activities. Although in different ways, all the major denominations turned to education as key to the process of social uplift. The years between about 1910 and 1940 witnessed a transformation in the educational values of the religious majority, as the educational influence of the minority of religious leaders slowly bore fruit. While urban/rural, black-belt/pine woods, and black/white educational disparities were partially a result of the class differences that religions reflected, these disparities were not caused exclusively by political and economic exploitation. To a great extent, educational disparities were the result of educational disinterest on the part of adherents of the major religious groups, although this was less true of black religion.

To the extent that religious antipathy and cultural boundary maintenance between Baptists and Catholics politically divided rural whites between the two sections of the state, class exploitation emerged as a plausible cause of educational disparities. However, that explanation implies that Huey Long, who managed to politically unite North and South Louisiana after 1928 and to institute educational reforms and expansion, somehow accomplished the feat through educating rural whites to sudden awareness of their exploitation and became the cause for increased public interest in educational expansion and reform during the 1930s.

A better explanation is one that accounts for change in the educational attitude of the religious majority by 1928 so that an astute politician like Long could take advantage of an existing social reality. While Louisiana religions were socially conservative and promoted the persistence of traditional values and cultural expressions, they also came to embrace an educational ideal calling for the social advancement of their adherents within the two sections of the state. The expansion of their educational programs after 1910 attest to the existence of that ideal—as did Long's political interest in educational reforms after 1934.

After 1898, as rural Baptists and Catholics of both races experienced fewer benefits from public educational reform than other groups, religious education programs began to expand, reflecting spread of the progressive, organizational reform spirit to these groups. Catholic parochial schools in South Louisiana copied administrative and curricular trends in the public school system, serving to supplement that system and to increase its benefits for greater numbers of poor blacks and whites. Black Baptists in North Louisiana attempted to maintain denominational schools until public school expansion began to reach poor rural blacks in the 1930s. White Baptists abandoned denominational schools, except for colleges, after 1898 but significantly expanded their system of Sunday Schools. Centralized organization, standardization, and direction of that system after 1910 transcended the otherwise independent, isolated character of locally autonomous Baptist congregations. Over time, Sunday School expansion and operation resulted in development of stronger educational desires and ideals by Louisiana Baptists.

When Long introduced a plan to equalize funding for public schools in all areas of the state in 1934, rural Baptists and Catholics in both sections of the state enthusiastically supported this reform. By the 1930s, both Catholics and Baptists had become committed to strong educational programs adapted to co-existence with the public educational system. The result was less political tension across the cultural boundary, greater educational opportunities for adherents of the major religious denominations, and no threat to the continuing religious dominance of Baptists and Catholics on either side of the cultural boundary.

VIII

Conclusion

The impact of religion on society is a prime factor in the histories of world civilizations. Any college student recognizes the important role of Hinduism on Indian culture, of Christianity on Roman and European history, of Islam on the history of North Africa and the Middle East, or of Puritanism as the established religion of the Massachussetts Bay Colony. However, with the establishment of church/state separation as a lasting principle in American history following the Revolution, historians have tended to ignore or to downplay the role of religions on American society.

That generalization is less true in the case of the history of the American South. In this particular case, historians have often been concerned with southern Protestantism as an example of the cultural distinctiveness of the American South. Writers like H. L. Mencken and Ernest Kurtz have pointed to the presence of a southern "Bible Belt" as being debilitory to southern cultural and economic development.[1] Others, like Wilbur J. Cash, have described conservative Protestantism as part of the collective "mind of the South."[2] Still others, like Kenneth K. Bailey or Samuel S. Hill, have been concerned to trace the histories of Protestant denominations in the South, or to define their impact on southern politics.[3] But few historians have attempted to examine the role that religions have played in the cultural education of society's members, except to recognize in vague terms that it has such a role.[4] An emphasis of this study is that such an ommission ignores the central importance of religion's educational functions and consequently, causes the failure to recognize religion's impact on cultural evolution.

In Louisiana, people from both sections of the state have historically shown strong attachments to a southern regional identity as well as to American nationalism. French political autonomy disappeared in South Louisiana as early as 1850 and cultural differences have not posed any problem to the regional and national loyalties of people in either section of the state. While predominant usage of the French language and French political culture both disappeared in South Louisiana, Catholicism remained and grew stronger over time. Religious affiliation became linked to cultural expression and to the survival of cultural differences between the northern and southern sections of the state.

Rural isolation was also an important factor in the survival of cultural differences. Public education, as a secular influence on society, was resisted most strongly in the rural areas of both Protestant and Catholic Louisiana. Once the state began to assume the largest proportion of educational funding in the 1930s, public schools began to have a greater impact on the relatively poor rural areas of the state. The accusations of William Ivy Hair and V.O. Key that Louisiana's political elites attempted to retain political hegemony prior to the 1930s through conscious denial of adequate educational opportunities—to both black and white rural citizens—were apparently valid.[5] The question raised by Key is why these political elites were relatively more successful in depriving rural people of educational opportunities than their counterparts in other southern states.

The answer lies partly in the reinforcement of educational apathy among Louisiana's rural people by their religious affiliations. In the case of South Louisiana Catholics, particularly among the Cajun population, such apathy is more easily understood in terms of a desire to have withstood persistent pressures for Americanization. Avoidance of outsiders and of English-speaking neighbors partly characterized their attempts to resist change. Constant accusations of backwardness and ignorance, for being different, created a sense of inferiority among Cajuns and black Creoles that reinforced a tendency to avoid association with public schools and their Protestant teachers, principals, and administrators. To some degree, the Catholic Church reinforced that avoidance by its advocacy of Catholic education—while being financially unable until about 1910 to provide free parochial schools, particularly on the level of secondary education.[6] Consequently, rural French Catholics continued into the twentieth century to regard education as the province of the church, while remaining unable to afford tuition expenses at Catholic private schools in the towns and cities.

Explaining the educational apathy of rural white Baptists and Methodists in the northern sections of the state is not as easy. Attachment to politically and socially conservative congregations had much to do with the persistence of rural cultural patterns in North Louisiana. Churches acted as social institutions imparting moral education to reinforce rural values that conflicted with the secular orientation of public schools. Consequently, they contributed to reinforcing a world-view that was narrow in outlook, averse to social and economic change, and that conflicted with modernist or scientific teachings in the public schools.

The failure of the state to provide educational funds, where property valuations were too low for local governments to adequately fund educational expansion, also contributed to educational disadvantages—especially in the pine woods parishes, where evangelical Baptists and Methodists predominated. The social conservatism instilled by the evangelical rural churches incited little motivation, on the part of their congregations, to seek political solutions to the problem of educational disadvantage. As a result, evangelical religious conservatism played into the hands of the planter and industrial elites who desired to avoid having to pay for the equal distribution of educational advantages in Louisiana.

Educational advantages under Louisiana's educational system, prior to the 1930s, accrued to urban areas with adequate funding from property taxes and with a stronger public perception of the economic benefits of education. Advantages also accrued, after 1898, to Black-belt parishes where the planter elites were to be found. Despite the low property valuations of these largely rural parishes, educational funding was less a problem for whites in Black-belt parishes than in parishes where few blacks were present because state educational apportionments were based on the total number of educable children of both races. Following disfranchisement, it became the practice in Black-belt parishes to spend a disproportionate percentage of the state apportionment on schools for the white minority, and to ignore the improvement of educational facilities for the black majority.

The non-urban and non-Black-belt areas of the state, where religious affiliations most tended to reinforce rural isolation, were the areas of the state with the least political clout and the worst public school systems. Since the cultural boundary in Louisiana acted to socially and economically separate groups of rural whites along lines of a Protestant/Catholic antipathy, it also acted to prevent the political cooperation necessary to offset the planter/industrialist/urban political coalition seeking to preserve its hegemony. It took the extraordinary political genius of Huey P. Long to tap the political potential present in a union of rural populations of North and South Louisiana.

V.O. Key, Jr. once explained that Long, the political dictator, appeared in Louisiana and not in some other southern state because problems traceable to the Civil War were more pronounced in Louisiana than in other southern states. Therefore, according to Key, those problems required harsher remedies. Long, the reformer, helped to provide remedies to social and economic problems, but Louisiana then had to live with a new (and just as corrupt) political system put in place by Long, the political power broker.[7] A reason for the pronounced condition of Louisiana was its cultural boundary. The boundary, outlined by the isopleths of the French Triangle, acted to separate and limit communication between two groups of people vastly different from each other, yet sharing common problems. Religiously, and in the end, politically, it served to pit evangelical Protestants against French Catholics, allowing economic elites in both sections of Louisiana to benefit from the cultural division of the more numerous rural whites.

George D. Kelsey summarized the elements that made Catholic culture incompatible with one dominated by Protestants, and by Southern Baptists in particular, in concluding that Baptists clearly oppose Catholics "on every important issue of Christian doctrine." Yet, as Kelsey also notes, Baptist opposition to Catholicism rests primarily on social and political grounds, and only secondarily on theological or other grounds of religious practice.[8]

Protestant opposition to Catholicism was pronounced in some areas of North Louisiana. From 1916-18, Catholic missionary priests attempted to convert North Louisiana Protestants to Catholicism by traveling through the northern part of the state on a railroad car furbished as a mobile chapel. But these "journeys of St. Paul," as Catholic priests referred to the chapel car missions, were unsuccessful in their purpose and often provoked hostility from Protestants. Survivors of these missions complained of "the most aggressive bigotry" aimed against them, which were sometimes "so rife and so wild, that the protection of parish officials had to be sought." Attempts to administer church services to small numbers of Catholics in the Protestant parishes sometimes met with disturbances designed to disrupt proceedings and, on numerous occasions, the priest could not obtain food or provisions from locals who refused to sell anything to a Catholic missionary.[9]

For their own part, rural French Catholics were also socially and culturally defensive up to World War II, seeking to prolong cultural isolation for as long as possible. In this set of cultural conditions, reconciliation between Catholics and Protestants had to occur before educational opportunities could effectively extend to larger numbers of rural and small town Louisianians.

The political genius of Huey Long lay in his ability, at least temporarily, to have overcome the religious antipathies that aligned rural Protestants against rural Catholics and to unite them politically along lines of class interest.[10] Joe L. Green has suggested that Long accomplished this remarkable feat by a process of educating rural whites to desire more material comfort and to believe that the economic greed of the old political elite was responsible for material comforts being denied them.[11]

By educating rural whites to desire automobiles and washing machines and by teaching them that they deserved such material possessions, Long introduced rural Louisiana into the twentieth century. The enormous appeal of Long's Share the Wealth philosophy did not whet the growing appetites for worldly comfort among rural Louisianians, but it did increase that appetite and helped to create a social climate in which education as a means to more prosperity was better received than before.[12]

It was also Long's policies that resulted in the assumption by the state of the largest responsibility for funding public educational expansion. Glen Jeansonne pointed out that Louisiana, in 1980, ranked "near the bottom nationally in literacy, per capita income, and education—approximately the same position it occupied in Long's day. . .," casting "doubt upon the 'realism' of those who believe Long brought lasting institutional change to his state." Jeansonne correctly argued that Long did nothing to alter Louisiana's tradition of corruption in politics. It is true as well, as Allan P. Sindler related, that much of Louisiana's increased educational budget under Long went to Louisiana State University, and that Long's heavy-handed involvement with Louisiana education caused the Southern Association of Colleges and Secondary Schools to withdraw accreditation from Louisiana schools. Although probably partly for reasons of personal power, it still remains a fact that Long placed the power for educational policy-making in the hands of state government for the first time—a progressive and much-needed reform. That the state government of Louisiana has often abused this power is the flip-side of Long's historical legacy in education.[13]

Long's repeal of the poll tax in 1934 was also politically significant. This device of disfranchisement had previously been an important source of revenue for the state's educational apportionments, at the same time that it helped perpetuate rural people's educational disadvantages by serving to discourage participation in politics. While Long's anti-corporate stance and his preference for replacing poll tax revenues with money from oil and gas severence taxes for education might have discouraged industrial relocations to Louisiana, it also served to politically unite rural Louisianians along lines of class interest.[14]

Contrary to the assertion by Lawrence Goodwyn that Populism represented the last gasp of grassroots democracy in the United States and in the South, Louisiana society was never more democratic than in the years after World War I, when both cultural sections cooperated in overthrowing the coalition that had ruled the state since Reconstruction.[15] Rural Louisiana society had never been more united than with its democratic consensus demanding the economic means to improve rural living and to gain accessibility to popular entertainments and consumer products. Over the power of these societal aspirations, southern religions became powerless to prevent shared loyalties to such prophets of material prosperity as Henry Ford—or Huey P. Long.

This fundamental difference between Louisianians of the nineteenth and twentieth centuries—that material comforts are an American birthright—created new orthodoxies and altered the meaning of social and religious conservatism. It also tended to provide greater societal sanctioning of increased secularism in churches, as well as in schools. This transformation assumed greater significance after World War II than before, because of relatively greater economic prosperity following the Second World War, but has its origins in the years after about 1910.

Up to World War II, Louisiana retained high illiteracy, disfranchisement, rural poverty and isolation, a largely agricultural economy, and religious conservatism. The continued presence of all of these factors indicated that, despite social and economic changes between 1880 and 1940, provincial outlooks survived among many Louisianians, causing cultural differences on each side of the cultural boundary to persist into the post-war years. Despite urbanization, industrialization, expansion of educational opportunities, erasure of the legal color bar, more liberal religious attitudes, and greater economic integration between sections of the state, cultural differences and the cultural boundary continue to persist in the post-war era. In fact, the cultural boundary defined by religious affiliations on either side has grown stronger since World War II.[16]

In conformity to a national pattern, evident in the North by the late nineteenth century but not in the South until after World War I, Louisiana's religious denominations began to adapt their theologies and social outlooks toward accommodation with the modern, technological, and increasingly urban world confronting them. Influences from the secular world of radio, public education, literature, and the press began to pervade society in Louisiana and in the rest of the South.

The clearest evidence that outlooks toward society, among religious groups, have converged into greater social harmony and less theological discord, is the proliferation of fundamentalist sects in the years following World War II. The growth of these sects suggests that the most conservative of religious people became dissatisfied with the increasingly modernist social posture of Protestant denominations and of the Catholic Church.[17] Relatively unimportant in Louisiana in the years before World War II, fundamentalist sects, as offshoots of the denominations, represent people in the state who could not accept increasing denominational accommodation to the secular world of material prosperity. Their presence ironically affirms the growth of an ecumenical spirit among the denominations that has resulted in denominational mergers and a greater spirit of cooperation among Protestant and Catholic clergymen in more recent times.[18]

Studies of religion have identified correlation between fundamentalist sects and social deprivation. In the case of Louisiana before World War II, it is clear that the most conservative denominations were those with memberships that were mostly rural and poor. Since World War II, greater economic prosperity has softened the once hard-line fundamentalist posture of Louisiana's Baptists and Methodists. If "church-sect theory," developed by Max Weber, H. Richard Niebuhr, and Charles Y. Glock, is valid, then sectarianism in Louisiana represents the minority of Protestants and Catholics who have broken away from their denominations because they could not compromise with the secular world.

Socially deprived, either of economic status or else of some other form of social status or sense of belonging, sectarians seek to replace their feelings of social deprivation with feelings of religious purity and superiority. Once characteristic of the rural, evangelical Protestant churches, the relationship between economic deprivation and religious purity among Baptists and Methodists has given way to a new relationship characterized by social and economic integration into the societal mainstream and less religious purity and emotional fervor. Those who remained socially deprived in some way, or else who simply could not divide their loyalty between conservative religious belief and the emerging national civil religion, became members of the new sects. These are the people who continue to adhere to puritanical theologies, religious emotionalism, and social conservatism that is so extreme it can be perceived as radicalism by others more expansive in their outlooks.[19]

While it is true that Louisiana's religions accommodated to political, economic, and social change by World War II, their effect on educational development in the state before that time was largely one of impeding the rapid progress of public educational expansion. Seen from the viewpoint of public educational proponents, this was a regrettable consequence of the continuing influence of religion and of the cultural boundary within the state. However, there is more to be explained about religions and the cultural boundary in Louisiana than their role in retarding educational progress. After all, education is a wider process of socialization and adjustment to change that is not entirely within the scope of the public school system to successfully guide and accomplish. Religion plays a major role in the process of educating society's members.

In South Louisiana, as well as elsewhere in the country, the Catholic Church pursued denominational activities such as Catholic education most effectively in urban environments. Consequently, the rural patterns of life that continued to prevail over large portions of the southern section of the state served to hinder the educational effectiveness of the Catholic Church. The Church's program of racial segregation and its progressive educational reforms, aimed at Americanization and the secularization of school curricula, demonstrated willingness to conform to regional and national efforts to produce a modern, progressive society.

In fact, because of the urban nature of the Catholic Church and the perception that urban growth was rapidly coming to characterize the "New South" by World War II, the National Catholic Social Action Congress (NCSAC) of 1939 became encouraged to believe that the Catholic Church might become able to assume a leadership role in supplying moral direction for southern economic progress. In 1939, the Committee on the South of the NCSAC expressed its perception that disagreements among southern Protestants over accommodation to urban, industrial change had produced serious rifts within Protestant groups, serving to cast doubt upon the continuing existence of any Protestant consensus in southern society.

Guided by this perception, the NCSAC came to believe that economic progress in the South was being led by men without adherence to moral and religious principles. To the mind of the members of the NCSAC Committee on the South, the persistence of economic problems in the South was being exacerbated by a failure on the part of southern economic leaders to see the "connection between economics and moral principles." In agreeing that economic backwardness was a result of inattention to social betterment through the process of improving social justice, the committee concluded that: "With the disintegration of old line Protestantism it appears now that only a meeting of Catholic southerners can supply this key."[20]

The NCSAC, however, was off-base in its assumption that southern Protestantism had disintegrated. Quite to the contrary, Protestantism continued to be the dominant religious influence on southern culture, and still is. Only in South Louisiana was Catholicism dominant over Protestantism—and there, in the years prior to World War II, many Catholics were rural people that the urban-centered Catholic Church had difficulty reaching with its educational program.

In North Louisiana, Protestant evangelical churches were better able to influence rural people because the nature of organization of these churches reflected their frontier origins in the eighteenth and nineteenth centuries. They had always been, and remained, predominantly rural churches. Unlike the Catholic Church, Southern Baptists and Southern Methodists resisted the encroachment of secular, civil influences upon their educational ideals. Strongly democratic in orientation, the evangelical churches were also strongly anti-intellectual and largely retentive of fundamentalist theological belief in the years prior to World War II. As a consequence, North Louisiana evangelicals were passive participants, at best, in the southern progressive movement—and in educational reform.

Cynical and mistrustful of economic elites, who were the leaders of the progressive movement in the South, North Louisiana's rural evangelicals did not share the economic motivations that produced the educational expansion taking place in Louisiana's towns and cities. Seeking to preserve the pattern of rural life prevalent at the turn of the century, rural evangelicals remained committed to political and religious organization that was concerned with matters of local interest. Consequently, the retention of provincial outlooks toward education did not manifest into social consensus demanding extensive change in the existing system of public education. The movement to standardize public education, characteristic of progressivism on the state level of government, continued to have small impact on the rural countryside as long as local governments continued to be responsible for collecting and allocating revenues for the operation of public schools.

As matters stood during Louisiana's Progressive Era, extensive change would not occur until after the Depression made even the minimal support for education provided by local governments impossible. Only during the mid-1930s did local governments begin to share control of education with the state. Consequently, it was only after the Depression that extensive educational expansion took place, since even the state had to await recovery of the severely depressed state and national economy. The cultural boundary, for its part in the preservation of separate provincial outlooks, served to strengthen the effects of localism on education in the state. Differing outlooks toward education by Catholics and by North Louisiana's evangelical Protestants caused slow educational expansion to characterize Louisiana on both sides of the cultural boundary before World War II.

Though willing to embrace progressive educational expansion in South Louisiana through its Catholic school system, the Catholic Church proved as unable as the state to effectively counter the self-imposed cultural isolation of the rural population. In North Louisiana, where rural people were the vast majority of the evangelical Protestant denominations, progressive ideals of educational reform were largely confined to Sunday School expansion and improvement.

Self-imposed isolation partly characterized the religious adherents on both sides of the cultural boundary, and for the same reason. Both rural French Catholics in the southern section and rural evangelical Protestants in the northern section of the state sought to preserve their own cultural traditions. On the one hand, rural Catholics preferred backwardness to the Americanization policy inherent in both the Catholic and public school systems. On the other, rural Protestants preferred slow educational expansion, under their own control, to the more rapid expansion that could be realized under a progressive, state-controlled system.

A reason why educational expansion was resisted was the perception that a state-controlled system would require greater secular standardization and would be geared toward inculcation of loyalties to non-local religious and civil organizations. Both rural Catholics and rural Protestants resisted rapid educational reform because the idea of outsiders, beyond their local religious and political arenas, having influence on the way their children thought about the world—and of their places in it—did not appeal to them.

As Louisiana's cultural boundary demonstrates, wherever religious pluralism is outweighed by the successful aggrandizement of one particular religious tradition, external influences meet resistance. As in the case of the Catholic Church in South Louisiana, the socializing effects of the Church met resistance when it sought to incorporate external influences as part of its socialization program. The Church persisted, however, and the force of loyalty to the Church eventually prevailed over the survival of outmoded cultural attachments. The process was slow and difficult and comprised, essentially, the educational function of the Church—to guide the cultural accommodation of its adherents to change.

Significant, widespread social change came to Catholic South Louisiana during the early part of the nineteenth century when the former French and Spanish colony became an American state. Large areas of rural South Louisiana continued to be characterized by cultural isolation well into the twentieth century. Affiliation with the Catholic Church was only one component of the cultural baggage that South Louisianians sought to preserve and to protect from cultural and political encroachment by Anglo-Saxon Protestants. The Catholic Church realized the necessity of compromising with the politically dominant and numerically superior population of Protestants in the southern region of which Louisiana was a part. The Church aquiesced in sanctioning racial segregation and adopted the curricula and organization of the Protestant-dominated public educational system in its own schools. The Catholic Church resisted the institution of a native South Louisiana clergy until the process of accommodation with the larger southern region had been accomplished, through the Americanization of French Catholics. This process did not reach fulfillment until the post-World War II era, approximately by the 1960s. That the process required more than a century to complete attests to the resistance of French Catholics to the programs of their own churches, as well as to those sponsored by Protestants. In the end, the Catholic Church accomplished the accommodation it desired and retained dominion over the religious affiliation of South Louisianians.

Evangelical Protestant churches came to face a similar problem of accommodation to external influences following the conclusion of the Civil War. In their case, the congregational autonomy of churches prevented southern evangelical denominations from formulating and instituting effective programs of cultural accommodation with external influences on either an intra-denominational or an inter-denominational level. Consequently, the religious predominance of evangelical denominations in the South contributed to the persistence of southern regional isolation from the rest of the country well into the present century.

Denominational elites, however, could accept many of the ideas of the northern Social Gospel during the Progressive Era, and worked within southern denominations to influence the social outlook of the majority of southern evangelicals. Facing a problem of resistance similar to that of the Catholic hierarchy in South Louisiana, Protestant denominational elites were the only southern evangelicals interested in state-wide and regional communication and organization. Through the state and regional conventions and conferences of the southern denominations, which church elites came to control and to use to communicate with each other, denominational educational goals came into being. Unattached to the provincialism that characterized the rural congregations, denominational elites were the ones who struggled to accommodate southern religions to northern and national perceptions of the social function of religion.

Their first, and still their most successful venture in this direction was the institution and proliferation of denominational Sunday Schools. Though introduced in the nineteenth century, Sunday Schools that were standardized under a centrally directed denominational system did not come about in Louisiana until the years after about 1910. After that time, denominational conventions and conferences assumed much greater influence over the activities of local congregations than before. Sunday Schools became the Protestant educational equivalent of the Catholic parochial school. Within evangelical denominations, the institution came to aquire the function of intra-denominationally accommodating religious belief and cultural attachments to social changes introduced by the secular environment. Like Catholic parochial schools, Protestant Sunday Schools served to guide a slow, difficult process of cultural adjustment—a process that southern Protestants have been undergoing since the Civil War.

A major significance of Louisiana's cultural boundary is that religious affiliations define its location. Within the distinctive cultural or ethnic groups, largely characterized by the influence of particular religious traditions, religion assumes the educational function of culturally accommodating communicants to secular cultural influences. Because of the connection between religion and the process of cultural change, religion has suffered criticism by members of society impatient, in the past, to see rapid and unimpeded educational progress made.

By their nature as social institutions, religious denominations are conservative, because they face the formidable task of creating a moral and social consensus within their denominations. Key to the process of developing consensus among church members, religious education is slow in socializing church members, for there is always religious debate over the formulation and expression of theologies, or of what activities in the social setting constitute evil. In the case of evangelical Protestant denominations such as the Southern Baptists, whose organization is democratic, changing the denominational consensus is necessarily a careful, deliberate process, since there is always the risk of alienating and losing members to the more conservative Protestant sects.

In theory, the Catholic hierarchical system of organization is better able to impose doctrine from above. However, the Catholic hierarchy has never, by any means, demonstrated complete consensus within its own ranks. As an international denomination, the Catholic Church competes for religious authority under widely varying circumstances of cultural and political reality on all of the world's inhabited continents—and cannot enforce international consensus on all matters of church doctrine and policy. Similarly, different cultural conditions across the United States make consensus among American Catholics impossible. In the case of Louisiana between 1880 and 1940, the clergy was largely foreign-born and often had difficulty asserting authority over the church laity. The consequences for Catholic educational policies in Louisiana were therefore similar to those of Baptists. Policies had to be adapted to the cultural setting and to the desires of the population. Consequently, the socialization function of the Catholic Church in Louisiana was slow as well.

That religious educational processes in Louisiana were slow in accommodating to social and economic change does not detract from their social utility. It does not suffice to criticize religion for being conservative, as scholars and non-religious commentators sometimes do. A far better analysis of the past relationship between religion and the educational process is one that credits religions for having accommodated to change in the past—and that recognizes the importance of religion's educational functions, rather than emphasizing the slowness with which religions perform them.

The continuing existence of Louisiana's cultural boundary points to another facet of the educational and socializing functions of Louisiana religions—their willingness to sanction cultural traits and identities, of which religious affiliations are a prime component. Unlike civil government—especially when in the form of a centralized federal or state system—largely concerned with the economic and political competition for power between competing groups in a plural society, religions could not function without enough consensus to maintain the membership of their adherents. For this reason, the socialization function of churches was slow because they had to respect the subjective cultural identities of church members. That is, Louisiana's churches did not sponsor programs that would result in rapid and perhaps chaotic social discontinuities with the past. Instead, churches were concerned with social and cultural stability. In the absence of religious pluralism in Louisiana society, cultures identified with religious traditions persisted in the face of much political and economic change between 1880 and 1940. As the continued integrity of the cultural boundary since World War II suggests, religions were largely successful in accommodating change without uprooting the cultures of people in the state.

Although atypical of the South in many respects, Louisiana has always been part of the region. In Louisiana, as well as in the rest of the southern region, religion and education must be taken into account in order to understand cultural evolution and cultural distinctiveness on either side of cultural boundaries. The case of cultural boundary maintenance in Louisiana serves to demonstrate, in microcosm, how different religious traditions preserved distinct cultural identities within a larger society. It also explains more than the integral impact of religion on the history of Louisiana. It suggests that religion's educational impact on the larger southern region and on other areas of the country deserve closer examination than has been attempted in the past. Awareness of the centrality of religion to cultural boundary formation and maintenance can aid us in determining the location of cultural boundaries in the United States and elsewhere, not only in the present, but in the historical past as well. The value of studies that trace the histories of cultural boundaries is obvious in that they would improve understanding of our cultural past and, therefore, would be useful in helping us to make better sense of our circumstances at present. Surely, this is to be encouraged for the tolerance and good will that understanding of differences can create.

Notes

Chapter I

[1]*Louisiana: A Guide to the State; Compiled by Workers of the Writers' Program of the Work Projects Administration in the State of Louisiana* (New York, 1941); hereafter cited as WPA, *Louisiana: A Guide to the State*), 190-195.

[2]Ibid.

[3]Ibid., 225-226.

[4]Christopher Hallowell, *People of the Bayou: Cajun Life in Lost America* (New York, 1979), 113.

[5]WPA, *Louisiana: A Guide to the State*, 3, 95-96.

[6]Ibid., 97.

[7]Hallowell, *People of the Bayou*, 88. The term "coon-ass" is of unclear origin, but is a pejorative term widely adopted by South Louisianians, who ignore the pejorative connotation.

[8]The rise of a technological, secularized culture is a prominent topic in all standard textbook accounts of twentieth century American history. It is also evident in the titles of such books as John Kenneth Galbraith, *The Affluent Society* (Boston, 1958); or Gabriel Vahanian, *The Death of God: The Culture of Our Post-Christian Era* (New York, 1961).

[9]Robert N. Bellah, "Civil Religion," *Daedalus*, 96 (1967): 1-26; Martin E. Marty, "Two Kinds of Two Kinds of Civil Religion," in Russell E. Richey and Donald G. Jones, eds., *American Civil Religion* (New York, 1974), 139-157.

[10]Ibid.; Robert Michaelson questions usage of the term "religion" in reference to civil religion, preferring his own designation, "American faith." Robert Michaelson, *Piety in the Public School: Trends and Issues in the Relationship Between Religion and the Public School in the United States* (New York, 1970), 4-5.

[11]Marty, "Two Kinds of Two Kinds," 145-146.

[12]George Brown Tindall, *The Emergence of the New South, 1913-1945* (Baton Rouge, La., 1967), 254, 284; Sister Raymond McLaughlin, *A History of State Legislation Affecting Private Elementary and Secondary Schools in the United States, 1870-1945* (Washington, D.C., 1946), 31-32; Minns Sledge Robertson, *Public Education in Louisiana After 1898* (Baton Rouge, La., 1952), 3-9.

[13]Henry Allen Bullock calls the dual educational system that developed in the South, "The Great Detour," in that it circumvented the sincere desire of Southern blacks to improve educational attainments—by its emphasis on the provision of vocational education, as well as by its inadequate funding of black schools and the resultant poor quality of black education. Henry Allen Bullock, *A History of Negro Education in the South; From 1619 to the Present* (Cambridge, Mass., 1967), 85-88, 123, 148; Tindall, *The Emergence of the New South*, 254.

[14]Louis R. Harlan, *Separate and Unequal: Public School Campaigns and Racism in the Southern Seaboard States, 1901-1915* (Chapel Hill, N. C., 1958), 12-20; Bullock, *A History of Negro Education*, 123; Woodward, *Origins of the New South*, 406. The topic of black education and religion in Louisiana is the focus of Chapters Three and Four.

[15]William Hicks, *History of Louisiana Negro Baptists: 1804-1914* (Nashville, Tenn., 1914), 31; Labbé, *Jim Crow Comes to Church*, 21; John W. Storey, "The Negro in Southern Baptist Thought, 1865-1900" (Ph. D. dissertation, University of Kentucky, 1968), 91; L. M. Hagood, *The Colored Man in the Methodist Episcopal Church* (Westport, Conn., 1970), 84-88, 142-147.

[16]Dolores Egger Labbé, *Jim Crow Comes to Church: The Establishment of Segregated Catholic Parishes in South Louisiana* (Lafayette, La., 1971), 24-25, 38-40, 58-64.

[17]Bertram Wyatt-Brown, *Yankee Saints and Southern Sinners* (Baton Rouge, La., 1985), 158-160; Orlando Patterson, *Slavery and Social Death: A Comparative Study* (Cambridge, Mass., 1982), 35, 73; Albert J. Raboteau, *Slave Religion: The "Invisible Institution" in the Antebellum South* (Oxford and New York, 1978), 165, 212, 219-220, 317-318.

[18]John Dollard, *Caste and Class in a Southern Town*, 3rd ed. (Garden City, N.Y., 1957), 224, 248.

[19]Labbé, *Jim Crow Comes to Church*, 49-50, 55, 64.

[20]In calling for more parochial schools for blacks, a New Orleans Catholic priest complained in 1889 that the children of black Catholic families who attended public schools "wound up by joining the Baptist and Methodist churches." Una Roberts Lawrence Resource Files, 2:4, Southern Baptist Historical Library and Archives, Nashville, Tenn.

[21]Roger Baudier, *The Catholic Church in Louisiana* (New Orleans, 1939), 406; Labbé, *Jim Crow Comes to Church*, 23; U. S. Bureau of the Census, *Report on Statistics of Churches in the United States at the Eleventh Census: 1890* (Washington, D.C., 1894); hereafter cited as *Religious Census*, 1890. See explanation for derivation and use of black religious statistics in Chapter Two and in Chapter Four.

[22]Baudier, *The Catholic Church*, 507-508; U. S. Bureau of Education, *Negro Education: A Study of the Private and Higher Schools for Colored People in the United States*, Vol. one, by Thomas Jesse Jones (Washington, D.C., 1916), 123.

[23]In 1916, the bulk of educational activity for Louisiana blacks was still in the area of primary education. Of 60,654 black students, approximately 700 were doing secondary level work and only twenty-four were involved with college-level work. U. S. Bureau of Education, ibid., Vol. two, 287.

[24]Baudier, *The Catholic Church*, 519; Sister Mary Josephine Kenney, "Contributions of the Sisters of the Blessed Sacrament for Indians and Colored People to Catholic Negro Education in the State of Louisiana" (M.A. thesis, Catholic University of America, 1942), 36.

[25]The Archbishop of New Orleans decreed in 1949 that "Negroes must be allowed to worship in whatever church they please and must not be asked to sit in specially designated pews." The Commission on Human Rights of the Catholic Committee of the South began concentrating its endeavors for the civil rights of blacks, during the 1950s, in Louisiana. The commission reported in 1950 that it would seek "the ultimate removal of the color-bar from our Catholic universities, colleges, seminaries, academies, high schools and elementary schools." Catholic Committee of the South, "Commission on Human Rights of the Catholic Committee of the South: Its Principles, Objectives and Achievements," Catholic Committee of the South, *Records, 1939-1956*, File 20, Amistad Research Center, Tulane University, New Orleans, Louisiana. Desegregation of Catholic schools in New Orleans took place in 1962. *New Catholic Encyclopedia* (New York, 1967), 8:1026.

[26]Charles Barthelemy Rousseve, *The Negro in Louisiana: Aspects of His History and His Literature* (New Orleans, 1937), 42.

[27]Fredrik Barth, "Introduction," in Fredrik Barth, ed., *Ethnic Groups and Boundaries: The Social Organization of Culture Difference* (Boston, 1969), 19, 37-38; Leonard Broom, Bernard J. Siegel, Evon Z. Vogt, and James B. Watson, "Acculturation: An Exploratory Formulation," in Paul Bohannon and Fred Plog, eds., *Beyond the Frontier: Social Process and Cultural Change* (Garden City, N.Y., 1967), 257.

[28]Leo A. Despres, "Introduction," in Leo A. Despres, ed., *Ethnicity and Resource Competition in Plural Societies* (The Hague and Paris, 1975), 2-3; Harmannus Hoetink, "Resource Competition, Monopoly, and Socioracial Diversity," in ibid., 21.

[29]Daniel Dennett, *Louisiana, As It Is: Its Topography and Material Resources . . . and People of the State* (New Orleans, 1876), 30, 35.

[30]Lewis William Newton, *The Americanization of French Louisiana: A Study of the Process of Adjustment Between the French and the Anglo-American Populations of Louisiana, 1803-1860* (New York, 1980), 192-193. Having lost numerical superiority in the state during the middle of the nineteenth century, French Louisianians next lost political control of parish and town governments in South Louisiana during the early part of the twentieth century—as people of French background remained dominant majorities only in rural areas of South Louisiana. Lawrence E. Estaville, Jr., "Changeless Cajuns: Nineteenth-Century Reality or Myth?" *Louisiana History*, 28 (1987): 133-136.

[31]Slavery and plantations existed in Louisiana prior to the introduction of sugar production in 1753. Indigo was the major staple crop until the 1790s, when the revolution in Santo Domingo disrupted French colonial production of sugar in the West Indies. J. Carlyle Sitterson, *Sugar Country: The Cane Sugar Industry in the South, 1753-1950* (Lexington, Ky., 1953), 4-12.

[32]Matthew J. Schott, "Class Conflict in Louisiana Voting Since 1877: Some New Perspectives," in Glenn R. Conrad, ed., *Readings in Louisiana History* (New Orleans, 1978), 270, 272.

[33]Schott, "Class Conflict in Louisiana Voting," 270, 272; William Ivy Hair, *Bourbonism and Agrarian Protest: Louisiana Politics, 1877-1900* (Baton Rouge, La., 1969), 18-24, 59.

[34]Hair, *Bourbonism and Agrarian Protest*, 18-24, 59; Matthew J. Schott, "Progressives Against Democracy: Electoral Reform in Louisiana, 1894-1921," *Louisiana History*, 20 (1979): 249-251.

[35]V.O. Key, Jr., *Southern Politics in State and Nation* (Knoxville, Tenn., 1984), 159-160.

[36]Rosan A. Jordan, "Folklore and Ethnicity: Some Theoretical Considerations," in Nicholas R. Spitzer, ed., *Louisiana Folklife: A Guide to the State* (Baton Rouge, La., 1985), 51. Economic differences between North and South Lousisana, caused by differences in their agricultural systems up to World War II, exacerbated religious antipathy between the sections, causing North-South religious difference to have often over-shadowed rural-urban and planter-poor white conflicts in state politics. Schott, "Class Conflict in Louisiana Voting," 272; T. Lynn Smith and Homer L. Hitt, *The People of Louisiana* (Baton Rouge, La., 1952), 128, 134-136.

[37]Joe Gray Taylor, *Louisiana: A Bicentennial History* (New York, 1976), 81-82; Charles William Dabney, *Universal Education in the South*, Vol. I (New York, 1969), 27-31, 47-50, 361.

[38]By 1893, New Orleans had three white public high schools and the construction of another in Shreveport had been approved by the State Board of Education. By 1902, there were thirty semi-public high schools, partly funded by private contributors, across the state. Public high schools for blacks did not appear in Louisiana until the 1920s. Louisiana State Board of Education, *Official Proceedings, 1869-1925*, Minutes of August 18, 1892, May 24, 1893, April 29, 1902, Louisiana State University Library, Baton Rouge, Lousiana; Minns Sledge Robertson, *Public Education in Louisiana After 1898* (Baton Rouge, La., 1952), 55-58, 82.

[39]Louisiana conducted its first census to determine the number of educables (children aged 6-18) in the state. Of the 404, 757 counted, only 185,355 were in attendance in public schools. For white children, the attendance rate was 55.3, and for blacks, 36.9 per cent. Over 75 per cent of educational funds came from either local taxes or local contributions from private citizens. Robertson, *Public Education in Louisiana*, 9, 188. The state reported the existence of over 400 private schools in 1899, many in North Louisiana parishes where no Catholics resided. Louisiana Department of Education, *Biennial Report of the State Superintendent of Public Education, 1898-99* (Baton Rouge, La., 1900), 33.

[40]Even following the removal of Bible-reading in public schools, the placement of teachers in the public school system continued to be an educational priority of South Louisiana's white Baptists. Louisiana Baptist Convention, *Acadia Baptist Academy: A Denominational Asset; Some Facts You Would Like to Know About Your School* (Alexandria, La., 1929), 9; Louisiana Baptist Convention, *Annual*, 1941, 27-29.

[41]Taylor, *Louisiana*, 81.

[42]For detailed treatment of the national debate over public aid for parochial schools, see Daniel F. Reilly, *The School Controversy, 1891-1893* (Washington, D.C., 1943); Sister Raymond McLaughlin, *A History of State Legislation Affecting Private Elementary and Secondary Schools in the United States, 1870-1945* (Washington, D.C., 1946).

[43]Leo Shpall, *The Jews in Louisiana* (New Orleans, 1936), 15-17; *Herold v. Parish Board of School Directors* 136 La. 1034, 68 So. 116 (1913).

[44]Louisiana's Superintendent of Public Education from 1908-1940, Thomas H. Harris, had argued for state control of educational funding for twenty years before he found a state Governor, in Huey P. Long, sympathetic to the idea. As soon as the state assumed the majority responsibility for collecting and apportioning educational funds, Harris began to argue for increased federal funding. (T.H. Harris Papers, 1:A,Q,R, 3:N,R, 4:D,O, Southwestern Archives, University of Southwestern Louisiana).

[45]Smith and Hitt, *The People of Louisiana*, 88-90, 102-105; Walter J. Primeaux, "The Small Louisiana Farmer, A Vanishing Breed," *Louisiana Studies*, 8 (1969): 185-193.

[46]Expansion of denominational education in Louisiana became part of a national religious education movement, begun in 1903, which sought "to inspire the educational forces of our country with the religious ideal," and "to inspire the religious forces of our country with the educational ideal," so as to advance, within the public mind, "the sense of its [education] need and value." Arlo A. Brown, *A History of Religious Education in Recent Times* (New York, 1923), 177-178. Educational programs of the two major white denominations in Louisiana are the focus of Chapters Five and Six.

[47]Key, *Southern Politics*, 160.

[48]Charles Reagan Wilson, *Baptized in Blood: The Religion of the Lost Cause, 1865-1920* (Athens, 1980), 34.

[49]Robert Wuthnow, "Religious Movements and Counter-Movements in North America," in James A. Beckford, ed., *New Religious Movements and Rapid Social Change* (London, 1986), 1-3.

[50]Except for the catechism taught at the beginning of each school day, Catholic school curricula were the same as in public schools. Catholic schools also used many of the same texts as the public schools, and had been doing so before the introduction of state laws imposing educational standards on private schools during the 1910s. Diocese of Lafayette, *Course of Studies for the Elementary Grades of the Parochial Schools of the Diocese of Lafayette* (Lafayette, La., 1920), contained at Archives of the Diocese of Lafayette; Louisiana State Board of Education, *Official Proceedings*, Minutes of March 17, 1909.

[51]Self-ascribed in-group cultural traits, derived from symbolic association with such cultural features as language, food, music, or religion, provide the basis for cultural stereotyping that links the members of a culture into a common identity and that provides the means for acculturating outsiders into the culture. Through symbolic social mechanisms, members of cultures can accommodate to rapid and profound changes in the socio-political and economic arenas of daily life without losing the subjective idea of cultural distinctiveness. Fredrik Barth, "Introduction," 9-17, 37-38; Rosan A. Jordan, "Folklore and Ethnicity," 51.

Chapter II

[1]Matthew J. Schott, "Class Conflict in Louisiana Voting Since 1877: Some New Perspectives," in Glenn R. Conrad, ed., *Readings in Louisiana History* (New Orleans, 1978), 272.

[2]Professor Schott has taken issue with the class conflict theme, which writers like Roger W. Shugg and Allen P. Sindler have used to describe Louisiana politics in line with the planter-

hill farmer dualism of other Southern states. In contrast to Shugg's class conflict of the nineteenth century, accepted by Sindler to show continuity with the Huey Long era, Schott argues convincingly "that a more common opposition [than that of planter against poor white], as revealed by parish voting data, existed between whites on opposite sides of a line delineating the predominantly Catholic and predominantly Protestant parishes." Ibid.

[3]A cultural boundary, formed by the existence of different social systems on either side of it, derives its origins, according to anthropologists, from economic factors. For example, Leo A. Despres explained that, "explicit in much of" the work of anthropologists involved in the identification of cultural and ethnic boundaries, "is the view that the genesis and persistence of ethnic boundaries, the incorporation of ethnic populations, and the organization of inter-ethnic relations are generally related to factors affecting the competition for environmental resources." Leo A. Despres, "Introduction," to Leo A. Despres, ed., *Ethnicity and Resource Competition in Plural Societies* (The Hague and Paris, 1975), 1-3; Leo A. Despres, "Toward a Theory of Ethnic Phenomena," in Despres, ed., *Ethnicity and Resource Competition*, 196, 200.

[4]Much of anthropological research involving the delineation of cultural and ethnic boundaries consists of studies of primitive cultures and their interactions with others. However, the applicability of the concept of cultural boundaries is not limited to primitive, homogeneous societies. The concept is also useful in describing human relations in modern poly-ethnic societies, such as in Louisiana. Fredrik Barth defined a poly-ethnic social system as one that is "integrated in the market place, under the control of a state system dominated by one of the groups, but leaving large areas of cultural diversity in the religious and domestic sectors of society." Fredrik Barth, "Introduction," to Fredrik Barth, ed., *Ethnic Groups and Boundaries: The Social Organization of Culture Difference* (Boston, 1969), 12-19.

[5]A good description and analysis of the cultural boundary, with historical and modern information, can be found in Nicholas R. Spitzer, ed., *Louisiana Folklife: A Guide to the State* (Baton Rouge, La., 1985). See especially, Rosan A. Jordan, "Folklore and Ethnicity: Some Theoretical Considerations," in ibid., 51.

[6]T. Lynn Smith and Homer L. Hitt, *The People of Louisiana* (Baton Rouge, La., 1952), 48-49; Harnett T. Kane, *The Bayous of Louisiana* (New York: William Morrow and Co., 1944), 330-331; Sue L. Eakin, *Avoyelles Parish . . . Crossroads of Louisiana Where All Cultures Meet* (Baton Rouge, La., 1981), 3-4; Fred B. Kniffen and Sam Bowers Hilliard, *Louisiana: Its Land and People*, revised edition (Baton Rouge, La., 1988), 124, 131, 165.

[7]Some would argue that the cultural boundary disintegrated by the turn of the century. Lawrence E. Estaville, Jr., in particular, in a recent article, pointed out that the geographical isolation of Cajuns from other groups of people is a myth, since the opportunities Cajuns possessed for water travel were better than in most areas of the country during the nineteenth century. Further, such innovations as telephone communications, electric lights, and improved agricultural techniques were also adopted by nineteenth century Cajuns. Estaville concludes that the invasion of Anglo-Saxon culture and the intercommunication that existed between Cajuns and other people had broken down Cajun isolation by the turn of the century. Lawrence E. Estaville, Jr., "Changeless Cajuns: Nineteenth-Century Reality or Myth?" *Louisiana History*, 28 (1987): 129-135, 139. While what Estaville has written about the Americanization of French Louisiana is certainly partially true, he has ignored the other side of the coin: the Gallicization and Catholic conversion of Anglos in Southern Louisiana.

[8]Kniffen and Hilliard, *Louisiana*, 171-177. The story of how the oil industry got started in Louisiana after the turn of the century has been vividly related by Christopher Hallowell, in *People of the Bayou: Cajun Life in Lost America* (New York, 1979), 53-66. Anthropologists have observed that "material culture forms are more generally amenable to change than are symbolic culture forms." That is, material prosperity will be accepted by cultures, despite the changes it introduces. However, cultural traits maintained by such symbolic boundary-maintaining mechanisms as bi-lingualism, religion, music, holiday rituals, etc., are not as easily broken down. These symbolic mechanisms of culture maintenance persist, and tend to acculturate outsiders into the self-aware "in-group." See: Leonard Broom, Bernard J. Siegel, Evon Z. Vogt, and James B. Watson, "Acculturation: An Exploratory Formulation," in Paul

Bohannon and Fred Plog, eds., *Beyond the Frontier: Social Processes and Cultural Change* (Garden City, N.Y., 1967), 257-270.

[9]U. S. Bureau of the Census, *Report on Statistics of Churches in the United States at the Eleventh Census: 1890* (Washington, D.C., 1894), hereafter cited as *Religious Census*, 1890; U. S. Bureau of the Census, *Religious Bodies: 1936*, 2 vols. (Washington, D.C., 1941), hereafter cited as *Religious Census*, 1936.

[10]*Religious Census*, 1890; *Religious Census*, 1936.

[11]Joe Gray Taylor, *Louisiana: A Bicentennial History* (New York, 1977), 8; *Religious Census*, 1890.

[11]Baudier Papers, 6:22, Archdiocesan Archives, New Orleans, Louisiana (AANO). Kniffen and Hilliard, *Louisiana*, 147. To a lesser extent than St. Tammany, the parishes of Livingston and Tangipahoa also display the characteristics of the French Triangle, as a result of the proximity of their Southernmost portions to the Orleans and Jefferson Parish metropolitan area.

[12]*Religious Census*, 1890; *Religious Census*, 1936; Roger Baudier, *The Catholic Church in Louisiana* (New Orleans, 1939), 503.

[13]*Religious Census*, 1936; Norval D. Glenn and Ruth Hyland, in "Religious Preference and Worldly Success: Some Evidence from National Surveys," *American Sociological Review*, 32 (February, 1967): 75-77, state that "in the non-Southern regions, most Catholics live in cities . . . ." Their statistics must evidently have given them a distorted view of Southern Catholicism because of the large number of rural Catholics in their survey from Southern Louisiana. The Catholic Church in northern Louisiana, and in the Southern region at large, does not deviate from the national pattern of urban concentration (where Catholic schools are most often available). Consider, for example, a report of the Catholic Committee of the South, from 1952: "Speaking of statistics—outside of Louisiana and a few scattered counties elsewhere in the Southeast, the Catholic Church in the South is urban." Catholic Committee of the South, *Records, 1939-1956*, File 20, "Miscellaneous Reports," Amistad Research Center, Tulane University, New Orleans, Louisiana.

[14]Charles Shanabruch, "The Louisiana Immigration Movement, 1891-1907: An Analysis of Efforts, Attitudes, and Opportunities," *Louisiana History*, 18 (Spring 1977): 203, 212-213, 225; William Francis Lawrence, "European Immigration Trends of Northeast Louisiana, 1880-1900," *Louisiana History*, 26 (1985): 46-49.

[15]U. S. Bureau of the Census, *Fifteenth Census of the United States: 1930; Population* (Washington, D.C., 1932), 3:972; hereafter cited as *Population Census*, 1930.

[16]Shanabruch, "The Louisiana Immigration Movement," 203-210, 225-226; Donald J. Millet, "Town Development in Southwest Louisiana, 1865-1900," *Louisiana History*, 13 (1972): 156-165, 168. A book, endorsed by the Louisiana State Grange "as the most reliable means of imparting correct information to immigrants, and to people of all sections and countries who desire to become acquainted [sic] with the hidden wealth of our State," was circulated widely in the 1870s and 80s. Daniel Dennett, *Louisiana, As It Is: Its Topography and Material Resources . . . and People of the State* (New Orleans, 1876), iv; Rodney Cline, "The Life and Work of Seaman A. Knapp" (M.A. Thesis, Louisiana State University, 1936), 32-35.

[17]*Religious Census*, 1890; *Religious Census*, 1936. Knapp, incidentally, was Methodist. Cline, "The Life and Work," 15.

[18]*Religious Census*, 1890.

[19]*Religious Census*, 1890; *Religious Census*, 1936.

[20]*Religious Census*, 1890.

[21]*Religious Census*, 1890; *Religious Census*, 1936. From the beginning of its settlement, West Feliciana Parish had strong ties to the southwestern counties of Mississippi. William Darby,

an early traveler through the region, noted in 1817 that "unlike those on the alluvial borders of the rivers, the settlements in [Feliciana] are scattered over the country as in the Mississippi Territory." With the completion of a rail line between St. Francisville, the principal West Feliciana town and Woodville, Mississippi, during the 1840s, the difficulty of transportation to Baton Rouge or New Orleans resulted in continuation of the parish ties with Mississippi. Darby referred to West Feliciana and the southwestern Mississippi counties as "one of the richest economic sections south of the Mason and Dixon line." West Feliciana became the first parish in Louisiana, outside of New Orleans, to establish an Episcopal church, largely because of the presence of Episcopalians from Mississippi. Edwin Adams Davis, *Plantation Life in the Florida Parishes of Louisiana, 1836-1846: As Reflected in the Diary of Bennet H. Barrow* (New York, 1943), 5, 9; Richard Oliver Gerow, Bishop of Natchez, comp., *Catholicity in Mississippi* (Natchez, 1939), 426; Ginny Garrard, "A History of the Protestant Episcopal Church in Shreveport, Louisiana, 1839-1916," *North Louisiana Historical Association Journal*, 9 (1978): 193.

[22]*Religious Census*, 1890; *Religious Census*, 1936.

[23]*Religious Census*, 1890; *Religious Census*, 1936; J. Carlyle Sitterson, *Sugar Country: The Cane Sugar Industry in the South, 1753-1950* (Lexington, 1953), 86-87.

[24]*Religious Census*, 1890; *Religious Census*, 1936.

[25]Ibid.

[26]Baptists represented 49.9 per cent of the religious population of the thirty-four northern parishes in 1890. By 1936, with northern Louisiana now comprised of thirty-seven parishes, Baptists were 55.1 per cent of the religious. Methodists, meanwhile, declined from 29.9 to 20.1 per cent. Ibid.

[27]See map of religious demography within flap on back cover of Edwin S. Gaustad, *Historical Atlas of Religion in America* (New York, 1976).

[28]John T. Gillard, *Colored Catholics in the United States* (Baltimore, 1941), 19-20.

[29]Loretta M. Butler, "A History of Catholic Elementary Education for Negroes in the Diocese of Lafayette, Louisiana" (Ph.D. dissertation, The Catholic University of America, 1963), 123.

[30]George Eaton Simpson, *Black Religions in the New World* (New York, 1978), 228.

[31]Blacks made up 51.4 percent of Louisiana's population of 940,000 in 1880. By 1940, the total population had grown to 2,364,000 but the black percentage had decreased to 35.9 percent. U. S. Bureau of the Census, *Historical Statistics of the United States, Colonial Times to 1970* (Washington D.C., 1975), Part I, 28.

Chapter III

[1]Albert J. Raboteau, *Slave Religion: The "Invisible Institution" in the Antebellum South* (Oxford and New York, 1978), 204.

[2]Una Roberts Lawrence Resource Files Series of the Home Mission Board Records, 3:6, Southern Baptist Historical Library and Archives, Nashville, Tenn. (hereafter cited as Lawrence Files).

[3]Lawrence Files, 3:6; U. S. Bureau of the Census, *Report on Statistics of Churches at the Eleventh Census: 1890* (Washington, D.C., 1894), hereafter cited as *Religious Census, 1890*; Inez Moore Parker, *The Rise and Decline of the Program of Education for Black Presbyterians of the United Presbyterian Church U. S.A., 1865-1970* (San Antonio, 1977), 34-36, 42-44, 49, 54-55.

[4]Lawrence Files, 3:6.

[5]Sue L. Eakin, "The Black Struggle for Education in Louisiana, 1877-1930s" (Ph.D. dissertation, University of Southwestern Louisiana, 1980), 66-67, 71-72, 173, 180; Sister Mary David Young, "A History of the Development of Catholic Education for the Negro in Louisiana" (M.A. thesis, Department of Education, Louisiana State University, 1944), 83, 84.

[6]Eakin, "The Black Struggle," 153, 180, 241.

[7]Letter, Reverend Walter S. Alexander to M. E. Strieby, May 13, 1876 (American Missionary Association Archives, New Orleans, Louisiana, Amistad Research Center, Tilton Hall, Tulane University), hereafter cited as AMA Records.

[8]Letter, J. A. Adams to M. E. Strieby, February 7, 1877, AMA Records.

[9]Letter, J. A. Adams to M. E. Strieby, January 20, 1876; ibid., May 8, 1877, AMA Records. Straight was the favored choice of the city's black Catholics, who had no such school in New Orleans of their own.

[10]Letter, J. A. Adams to M. E. Strieby, December 9, 1876, AMA Records.

[11]Felton G. Clark, text of speech, "Wings Over Jordan: The Program of the Negro Land-Grant Colleges," Lawrence Files, 5:5. What Clark did not say was that, in 1915, there were only twenty-four Negro college students in Louisiana, and none of them attended Southern University. U. S. Bureau of Education, *Negro Education: A Study of the Private and Higher Schools for Colored People in the United States*, Volume Two, by Thomas Jesse Jones (Washington, D. C., 1917), 287.

[12]Clark, "Wings Over Jordan," Lawrence Files, 5:5.

[13]Eakin, "The Black Struggle," 173.

[14]The *Annual* of the Consolidated American Baptist Missionary Convention (Negro Baptists) for 1877 reported 45,000 Negro Baptists in Louisiana. This total far exceeds the 27,736 Southern Baptists (white Baptists), the largest white Protestant denomination in Louisiana, reported by the 1890 census. Consolidated American Baptist Missionary Convention *Annual*, 1877, 35; *Religious Census*, 1890; *Religious Census*, 1936.

[15]Catholic influence on blacks and black education in Louisiana is the topic of Chapter Four.

[16]In 1890, over fifty-four per cent of Louisiana's black religious were Baptist. By 1936, over sixty-six per cent were Baptist, *Religious Census*, 1890; *Religious Census*, 1936. White Baptist involvement with black Baptist education in Louisiana began with the hiring of an evangelist in 1889, whose job was to attend meetings of the black associations and to "instruct them in the right principles of theology, church polity and practical religion." In 1886, the Louisiana Baptist Convention appointed a five-man committee to oversee the denomination's work among the colored people of Louisiana. In its report of 1887, the committee stated: "Your Committee would state that we find that the Convention has no work among the colored people, and therefore we have nothing upon which to base a report." Louisiana Baptist Convention, *Annual*, 1886, 18; ibid., 1887, 22; ibid., 1889, 27.

[17]*Annual* of the National Baptist Educational Convention, 1892, 5.

[18]*Annual* of the National Baptist Convention (hereafter cited as NBC *Annual*), 1898, 3, 53-54.

[19]NBC, *Annual*, 1900, 32, 111.

[20]Ibid., 111.

[21]Ibid.; Ibid., 1899, 20.

[22]Ibid., 43; Ibid., 1898, 21, 53.

[23]Ibid., 1900, 32.

[24]Ibid., 1901, 97-98; Lawrence Files, 3:6. Each district association of the state convention of Louisiana Negro Baptists sponsored academies. William B. Hicks, *History of Louisiana Negro Baptists, From 1804 to 1914* (Nashville, Tenn., 1914), 78-79.

[25]NBC, *Annual*, 1901, 97-98.

[26]Ibid., 98, 165.

[27]*Annual* of the Louisiana Conference of the Methodist Episcopal Church, South, 1920, 8, 20; Ibid., 1923, 48, 62.

[28]C. Penrose St. Amant, *A Short History of Louisiana Baptists* (Nashville, Tenn., 1948), 67-68.

[29]NBC, *Annual*, 1903, 119.

[30]Ibid., 1907, 66.

[31]R. W. Perkins, "Leland University, New Orleans, Louisiana," Lawrence Files, 2:12.

[32]Ibid.

[33]U. S. Bureau of the Census, *Historical Statistics of the United States, Colonial Times to 1970* (Washington, D.C., 1975), Part I, 28. In 1900, the national percentage of the population, aged 5-20 years, who were enrolled in school, was 50.5 per cent. The percentage for whites was 54.9 per cent, and for blacks, 31 per cent. In Louisiana in 1900, 38.1 per cent of whites, aged 5-20, were enrolled in school, but for blacks, the percentage was only 18.5. By 1910, the white percentage had risen to 51.7 (comparable to the national average of 59.2), as the result of the system of high schools for whites opened during the first decade of the century. The black percentage in 1910, however, had risen to only 27.2. The percentage of Louisiana blacks aged 5-20 would not rise above fifty per cent until 1930, as the result of the appearance of a public system of high schools for blacks, beginning with the opening of four black public high schools in 1923. Minns Sledge Robertson, *Public Education in Louisiana After 1898* (Baton Rouge, La., 1952), 56-58, 82, 183. Figures quoted from: U. S. Office of Education, *Statistics of the State School Systems*, Circular No. 255 (Washington, D.C., 1946-1947).

[34]Lawrence Files, 2:12.

[35]Edwin R. Embree, "Every Tenth Pupil," *Survey Graphic*, 23 (1934): 538-541.

[36]Thomas H. Harris Papers, Memoirs, 1:S, Southwestern Archives, University of Southwestern Louisiana.

[37]Ibid.

[38]Ibid., 1:C; Robertson, *Public Education*, 192.

[39]Robertson, *Public Education*, 192.

[40]Lawrence Files, 2:25; Bullock, *A History of Negro Education*, 124, 148-152; Eakin, "The Black Struggle," 161.

[41]Bullock, *A History of Negro Education*, 88, 120-124.

Chapter IV

[1]White religious groups involved with Negro education had difficulty operating freely because of native white sentiment against other whites involved in aid of any kind to Negroes. A carryover from the Reconstruction period and Southern white hatred for "carpetbaggers" and "scalawags," white antipathy to educational aid for Negroes continued into the twentieth century. Letter, Rev. Walter Alexander to J.A. Strieby, May 29, 1876,

American Missionary Association Archives, Amistad Research Center, Tulane University, New Orleans, Louisiana.

[2]Although Negro Methodist denominations had split from the predominantly white Northern and Southern Methodist denominations by 1870, Negro Methodists in Louisiana did not sponsor their own schools to the extent that Negro Baptists did, relying more than Baptists on public primary and northern Protestant secondary schools. L.M. Hagood, *The Colored Man in the Methodist Episcopal Church* (Westport, Conn., 1970), 88, 142-147, 299, 306; Thomas Jesse Jones, *Negro Education: A Study of the Private and Higher Schools for Colored People in the United States* (Washington, D.C., 1917), 1:345, 374-375.

[3]U. S. Bureau of the Census, *Report on Statistics of Churches in the United States at the Eleventh Census: 1890* (Washington, D.C., 1894), hereafter cited as *Religious Census*, 1890; U. S. Bureau of the Census, *Religious Bodies: 1936* (Washington, D.C., 1941); hereafter cited as *Religious Census*, 1936.

[4]In a manuscript entitled "Our Native Clergy," Monsignor Francis Leo Gassler wrote in 1936 of "Archbishop Perche's well-known lack of financial ability having brought the diocese to the verge of imminent disaster," causing other problems as well, such as the necessity of closing the archdiocesan seminary in 1883. (Roger Baudier Papers, 9:10, Archdiocesan Archives, New Orleans, Louisiana); hereafter cited as Baudier Papers, AANO.

[5]*Religious Census*, 1890.

[6]Una Roberts Lawrence Resource Files, Series of the Home Mission Board Records, 2:4, (Southern Baptist Historical Library and Archives, Nashville, Tenn.); hereafter cited as Lawrence Files.

[7]Sister Mary David Young, "A History of the Development of Catholic Education for Negroes in Louisiana" (M.A. Thesis, Louisiana State University, 1944), 57, 61-62; Roger Baudier, *The Catholic Church in Louisiana* (New Orleans, 1939); hereafter cited as Baudier, *The Catholic Church*), 461, 489; Roger Baudier, *One Hundred Years of the Upper Teche* (Arnaudville, La., 1953), 47-49.

[8]Roger A. Fischer, *The Segregation Struggle in Louisiana, 1862-77* (Urbana, Ill., 1974), 90-99, 115-116; Baudier, *The Catholic Church*, 461, 501, 507-508; Charles E. Nolan, "Carmelite Dreams, Creole Perspectives: The Sisters of Mt. Carmel of Louisiana (1833-1903)," (Ph.D. dissertation, the Pontifical Gregorian University, Rome, Italy, 1970), 213. While there were only 15 Catholic schools in Louisiana in 1860, Archbishop Perche reported "more than a hundred parochial schools in the State" in 1872. Circular Letter to the Clergy of the Diocese of New Orleans, October 3, 1872, AANO.

[9]Concerning state non-support for black public schools, the former State Superintendent of Education for Louisiana (1908-1940), Thomas H. Harris, stated simply (in 1940) that "Negro schools have always been neglected, and still are." T.H. Harris Papers, 1:S, Southwestern Archives, University of Southwestern Louisiana.

[10]In a letter from historian Paul A. Kunkel to Roger Baudier (Chronicler of the Archdiocese of New Orleans), dated May 11, 1959, Kunkel pointed out a conclusion of some of his research: "namely, that the French-Spanish, ultimately religious (Catholic), legal influence, did much to mitigate the harshness of slavery in Louisiana before the Civil War." Baudier Papers, 10:9C, AANO. See also Paul A. Kunkel, "Modifications in Louisiana Negro Legal Status under Louisiana Constitutions, 1812-1957," *Journal of Negro History*, 44 (1959): 3-7.

[11]To whites, "all Africans who were not of pure blood were gens de couleur," colored people, who "were always a class apart, separated from and superior to the Negroes, ennobled were it only by one drop of white blood in their veins." Alice Dunbar-Nelson, "People of Color in Louisiana," part one, *Journal of Negro History*, 1 (1916): 361; ibid., 2 (1917): Part II, 52, 63; Rodolphe Lucien Desdunes, *Our People and Our History*, translated from French by Sister Dorothea Olga McCants (Baton Rouge, La., 1973), 97; Joe Gray Taylor, *Louisiana: A Bicentennial History* (New York, 1977), 26-27, 42-43, 49, 75-77; Charles Barthelemy Rousseve, *The Negro in Louisiana: Aspects of His History and His*

Literature (New Orleans, 1937), 42; Gary B. Mills, *The Forgotten People: Cane River's Creoles of Color* (Baton Rouge, La., 1977), xxix.

[12]Rousseve, *The Negro in Louisiana*, 43, 46; Taylor, *Louisiana*, 85; Dolores Egger Labbé, *Jim Crow Comes to Church: The Establishment of Segregated Catholic Parishes in South Louisiana* (Lafayette, La., 1971), 12-13; Loretta M. Butler, "A History of Catholic Elementary Education for Negroes in the Diocese of Lafayette, Louisiana" (Ph.D. dissertation, The Catholic University of America, 1963), 12; John T. Gillard, *Colored Catholics in the United States* (Baltimore, 1941), 56.

[13]Baudier Papers, 10:16, AANO. Desdunes, *Our People and Our History*, 99; Young, "A History of Negro Education in Louisiana," 29-30, 37, 44, 47-49; Diocese of Lafayette, *Initial Report of the Lafayette Diocesan Schools, 1943-44* (Lafayette, La., 1944), 9; The Holy Family Sisters were operating twenty-one schools, altogether, in Louisiana in 1944. Butler, "A History of Catholic Elementary Education in the Diocese of Lafayette," 172.

[14]Young, "A History of Education for Negroes in Louisiana," 57, 61-62; Baudier, *The Catholic Church*, 433-434; Roger Baudier, *One Hundred Years of the Upper Teche* (Arnaudville, La., 1953), 47-49, 57.

[15]Ibid., 47; Young, "A History of Education for Negroes in Louisiana," 82. Besides the school in Arnaudville, the Drexel Foundation helped fund small black Catholic schools in St. James, Breaux Bridge, Crowley, Oubre, and New Orleans in the years prior to 1915. Baudier Papers, 9:15, AANO.

[16]Madeleine H. Rice, *American Catholic Opinion in the Slavery Controversy* (New York, 1944), 159-160; Francis P. Cassidy, "Catholic Education in the Third Plenary Council of Baltimore," part one, *Catholic Historical Review*, 34 (October, 1948): 266, 293-294, 300; John Whitney Evans, "Catholics and the Blair Education Bill," *Catholic Historical Review*, 46 (October, 1960): 286-287. As Roger Baudier related in a memorandum of 1956 to Robert Guste, little educational work for black Catholics was undertaken until ". . . Archbishop Blenk appeared in 1906. Then Negro work really got under way–schools, institutions, organizations, catechital work. But it was still very late." Baudier Papers, 10:9E, AANO.

[17]Labbé, *Jim Crow Comes to Church*, 23; Baudier, *The Catholic Church*, 400, 461-466.

[18]*Louisiana: A Guide to the State; Compiled by Workers of the Writers' Program of the Work Projects Administration in the State of Louisiana* (New York, 1941), 3, 95-96.

[19]William Faulkner Rushton, *The Cajuns: From Acadia to Louisiana* (New York, 1979), 11-12.

[20]Deviant religious practice was also common among whites in South Louisiana, particularly among Acadians (Cajuns), whose cultural exchanges with Indians and blacks resulted in informal religious observance and a form of neo-paganism that William Faulkner Rushton has termed "Cajunism." Rushton, *The Cajuns*, 6-9. Cajun men commonly considered religious observances to be something women did, giving rise to the old Acadian saying that " a man saw the inside of a church for his first communion, his marriage, his daughter's wedding and his funeral." Roger Baudier and Millard F. Everett, *Knights of Columbus in Louisiana, 1902-1962* (New Orleans, 1965), 13-14.

[21]Baudier, *The Catholic Church*, 507-521.

[22]Labbé, *Jim Crow Comes to Church*, 4, 17-20, 24-25; Sue L. Eakin, "The Black Struggle for Education in Louisiana, 1877-1930s" (Ph.D. dissertation, University of Southwestern Louisiana, 1980), 66-67, 71-72.

[23]Baudier, *The Catholic Church*, 461, 489.

[24]Ibid., 461, 489, 519.

[25]Ibid., 94-95, 111. The state requirement of a four-year Normal degree had been in force for white teachers since 1923, reflecting the disparity that existed in the expansion of the

white and black systems of education in Louisiana. Further, the four-year Normal requirement for black elementary teachers was not installed until 1947, before which time teachers continued to come from the County Training Schools. Robertson, *Public Education*, 72, 137.

[26]Young, "A History of Catholic Education for Negroes in Louisiana," 110, 113. By 1942, the number of rural schools in Louisiana staffed by Xavier graduates had grown to twenty-two. There were forty-six teachers and 2416 pupils in these schools. Sister Mary Josephine Kenney, "Contributions of the Sisters of the Blessed Sacrament for Indians and Colored People to Catholic Negro Education in the State of Louisiana" (M.A. Thesis, The Catholic University of America, 1942), 36.

[27]Church segregation became even more pronounced in the years after 1918, with 12 new black parishes in the Archdiocese of New Orleans and 7 in the Diocese of Lafayette between 1918 and 1934. By 1960, there would be 114 separate black parishes in the state. Baudier, *The Catholic Church*, 489, 494-495, 507-521, 524, 539-540; Labbé, *Jim Crow Comes to Church*, 64-68; *New Catholic Encyclopedia*, 8 (1967): 1025.

[28]Baudier, *The Catholic Church*, 489; Labbé, *Jim Crow Comes to Church*, 24-25.

[29]Letter from James Hubert Blenck to Rev. Thomas O. Finney, July 1906, research file in possession of Charles E. Nolan, AANO.

[30]By 1916, there were twenty black parochial schools in South Louisiana according to a U. S. Government survey of black schools. Jones, *Negro Education: A Study of the Private and Higher Schools for Colored People in the United States*, 1:312. Catholic sources, however, reported thirty-nine black parochial schools in the archdiocese in 1918 and eleven more in the Diocese of Lafayette by 1920. New Orleans, *The Morning Star*, 51 (April 6, 1918): 12; Butler, "A History of Catholic Elementary Education for Negroes in the Diocese of Lafayette, Louisiana," 12.

[31]James D. Anderson, *The Education of Blacks in the South, 1860-1935* (Chapel Hill, N. C., 1988), 31-32, 86-90; Henry Allen Bullock, *A History of Negro Education in the South; From 1619 to the Present* (Cambridge, Mass., 1967), 88, 120-124.

[32]Lawrence Files, 2:12; National Baptist Convention, *Annual*, 1903, 19; Anderson, *The Education of Blacks in the South*, 238-241.

[33]A published statement by the Catholic Committee of the South maintained that segregation had never been "a recognized policy of the Catholic Church anywhere." Instead, it was "the unhappy product of regional prejudice and traditions which the Church merely tolerated at one time because it was felt that conflicts and tensions might otherwise arise." Catholic Committee of the South, *Commission on Human Rights of the Catholic Committee of the South: Its Principles, Objectives and Achievements* (New Orleans: Committee of the South, 1950), pamphlet contained in Records of the Catholic Committee of the South, 1939-1956, File 20 (Amistad Research Center, Tulane University, New Orleans, Louisiana); hereafter cited as C.C.S., *Commission on Human Rights*, Amistad Center.

[34]*Herold v Parish Board of School Directors*, 136 La. 1034, 68 So. 116 (1913); Taylor, *Louisiana: A Bicentennial History*, 81.

[35]Gillard, *Colored Catholics in the United States*, 19-21.

[36]*Religious Census*, 1890. The figure of 20,000 black Catholics in South Louisiana also results from subtracting the 40,000 black Protestants in South Louisiana (plus 3,000 black Catholics in North Louisiana) in 1890 from the total of 63,000 black Catholics reported in the state in 1865—a date preceding the mass defections from Catholic to Protestant churches by South Louisiana blacks. George Eaton Simpson, *Black Religions in the New World* (New York, 1978), 228; Gillard, *Colored Catholics in the United States*, 94-95.

[37]John T. Gillard, *The Catholic Church and the American Negro* (Baltimore, 1929); John T. Gillard, *Colored Catholics in the United States* (Baltimore, 1941).

[38]Gillard, *Colored Catholics in the United States*, 20, 25.

[39]*Catholic Action of the South* (official journal of the Diocese of Lafayette, Louisiana), 21 (April, 1953): 47; *New Catholic Encyclopedia*, 8 (New York, 1967), 1025.

[40]Gillard, *The Catholic Church and the American Negro*, 46-60; Gillard, *Colored Catholics in the United States*, 16-17, 20, 25.

[41]Gillard, *Colored Catholics in the United States*, 20, 25.

[42]*Catholic Action of the South* (Diocese of Lafayette), 12 (December, 1943): 38.

[43]Letter, Rev. Harold L. Cooper to Emile A. Wagner, Feb. 28, 1956, Baudier Papers, 10:9E, AANO.

[44]C.C.S., *Commission on Human Rights*, Amistad Center.

[45]Ibid.; *New Catholic Encyclopedia*, 8 (1967), 1026.

[46]Randall M. Miller, *Catholics in the Old South: Some Speculations on Catholic Identities* (Notre Dame, Ind., 1981), 3-4. Similar conclusions concerning Southern Protestantism were drawn by John Lee Eighmy in *Churches in Cultural Captivity: A History of the Social Attitudes of Southern Baptists* (Knoxville, Tenn., 1972).

[47]Baudier Papers, 10:10D, AANO.

Chapter V

[1]An influential book on Southern Baptists and Southern culture that exemplifies much of the scholarly work done on the subject is John Lee Eighmy, Jr., *Churches in Cultural Captivity: A History of the Social Attitudes of Southern Baptists* (Knoxville, Tenn., 1972). Another social analysis of Southern Baptists is George D. Kelsey, *Social Ethics Among Southern Baptists, 1917-1969* (Metuchen, N.J., 1972). For a similar analysis of Southern Baptists in the antebellum South, see Walter Brownlow Posey, *The Baptist Church in the Lower Mississippi Valley, 1776-1845* (Lexington, 1957). Some other influential books have an expanded coverage to include Southern Methodists, Presbyterians, and Episcopalians in addition to Baptists. Kenneth K. Bailey, *Southern White Protestantism in the Twentieth Century* (Gloucester, Mass., 1968); Samuel S. Hill, Jr., *Religion and the Solid South* (Nashville, Tenn., 1972).

[2]Louisiana Department of Education, *Biennial Report, 1902-03* (Baton Rouge, La., 1904), 54-57, 66; Louisiana State Board of Education, *Official Proceedings, 1869-1925*, Minutes of August 11, 1903, Louisiana State University Library.

[3]J. Wayne Flynt, "One in the Spirit, Many in the Flesh: Southern Evangelicals," in David Edwin Harrell, Jr., ed., *Varieties of Southern Evangelicalism* (Macon, Ga., 1981), 36.

[4]Samuel S. Hill, Jr., for example, made this charge in writing that "not until legislative and legal requirements made it all but mandatory did the Southern Baptists exert much leadership in implementing humane treatment of those blacks who share the same geographical space." Hill, "Epilogue," in Eighmy, *Churches in Cultural Captivity*, 207-208.

[5]John Lee Eighmy raised this point about the SBC leadership's fear of alienating constituent congregations. Eighmy, *Churches in Cultural Captivity*, 179-182.

[6]Louisiana Baptist Convention, *Annual*, 1914, 35-37.

[7]In nineteenth century Louisiana, Southern Baptists were almost exclusively rural, having weak organization even in small towns. William A. Poe, "Religion and Education in North Louisiana, 1800-1865," in B.H. Gilley, ed., *North Louisiana: Essays on the Region and Its History, Volume one, To 1865* (Ruston, La., 1984), 120. In the 1920s, "ninety-two per cent of the Southern Baptist churches were either in open country or in towns of less than 2500

population." Even those congregations in cities were usually made up of people who came from the country and still adhered to rural values. James M. Thompson, Jr., *Tried as by Fire: Southern Baptists and the Religious Controversies of the 1920s* (Macon, Ga., 1982), 36. Before Louisiana Baptists built the Baptist Bible Institute in 1918, Southern Baptists were so unrepresented in urban New Orleans that "most of the people of the city thought all Baptists were Negroes, many had never heard the name before, ..." J.W. Newbrough, "New Orleans: The Heart of the Home Mission Field," unpublished paper, 1927, J.W. Newbrough, Biographical Data, Articles, Correspondence, 1932-36, Southern Baptist Historical Library and Archives, Nashville, Tenn..

[8]Daniel Dennett, *Louisiana, As It Is: Its Topography and Material Resources . . . and People of the State* (New Orleans, 1876), 30.

[9]Ibid., 17, 32, 35. Pine woods areas include all or portions of the parishes of Calcasieu, Catahoula, Grant, Livingston, Natchitoches, Rapides, St. Helena, St. Tammany, Tangipahoa, Vernon, Washington, and Winn, although Calcasieu has a large area of prairie and other of these parishes have alluvial strips where the Red, Ouachita, Black, and Pearl Rivers flow through them. The uplands areas include all or portions of Bienville, Bossier, Caddo, Caldwell, Claiborne, DeSoto, East Feliciana, East Baton Rouge, Jackson, Morehouse, Ouachita, Red River, Sabine, Union, Webster, and West Feliciana. The only North Louisiana parishes not included in these two categories were the parishes of East and West Carroll, Concordia, Franklin, Madison, Richland, and Tensas, which were characterized by rich farmland resulting from alluvial deposits of the Mississippi River.

[10]Dennett, *Louisiana, As It Is*, 31; Minns Sledge Robertson, *Public Education in Louisiana After 1898* (Baton Rouge, La., 1952), 9.

[11]Louisiana State Board of Education, *Official Proceedings, 1869-1925*, Minutes of August 11, 1903; U. S. Bureau of the Census, *Report on Statistics of Churches in the United States at the Eleventh Census: 1890* (Washington, D.C., 1894); hereafter cited as *Religious Census*, 1890. South Louisiana, however, with its longer school terms, had difficulty in getting its educable children to attend schools. The problem of poor attendance rates was particularly pronounced among black children in the Southern parishes, probably because of the wage-labor system prevalent in the sugar parishes.

[12]*Religious Census*, 1890; U. S. Bureau of the Census, *Religious Bodies: 1936* (Washington, D.C., 1941); hereafter cited as *Religious Census*, 1936; Edwin S. Gaustad, *Historical Atlas of Religion in America* (New York, 1976).

[13]V.O. Key, Jr., *Southern Politics in State and Nation* (Knoxville, Tenn., 1984), 160.

[14]Anticipating funds from the Southern Baptist Convention's campaign, after 1919, to raise $75 million for Baptist education, an LBC committee in charge of planning fund allocation proposed the establishment, in North Louisiana, of three more academies–in addition to the two founded in South Louisiana in 1917. A vote of the 1919 state convention shelved the proposal. LBC, *Annual*, 1919, 23.

[15]James M. Thompson, Jr. described the evolution of the 1920s controversies over the teaching of evolution in public schools in two ways. First, progressive Southern Baptists were adherents of a Southern Social Gospel, which was, in essence, a "response to the challenge of modern industrial society." Since the majority of Southern Baptists had no contact with urban, industrial settings, they were not concerned with the social problems that Social Gospellers wished to ameliorate. As the seminal progressive reform, education became a subject on which Southern Baptists disagreed. Social Gospel adherents sought to defend and expand the public educational system, while conservative, fundamentalist Baptists preferred scrapping the system, if it became too secularized. Thompson also described the controversy as reflecting a difference in theology among Baptists. The fundamentalists adhered to a stricter, Calvinistic version of pre-millennial belief about the return of Christ. More liberal Baptists shared the post-millennial, less Calvinistic version predominant among Northern Baptists. Thompson, *Tried as by Fire*, 34-36, 132-133; Charles H. Hopkins, *The Rise of the Social Gospel in American Protestantism, 1865-1915* (New Haven, Conn., 1967), 318.

[16]John Pinckney Durham and John S. Ramond, compilers, *Baptist Builders in Louisiana* (Shreveport, 1934), 327; E.O. Ware not only first proposed the building of Louisiana College, but his resolution in 1893 resulted in the appointment of the first Education Committee of the LBC in 1893. LBC, *Annual*, 1893, 13; Glen Lee Greene, *House Upon a Rock: About Southern Baptists in Louisiana* (Alexandria, La., 1973), 260.

[17]Lela Beall Costello, "Mt. Lebanon University: A Brief History," *The Baptist Message*, December 19, 1957, 6-8; *The Baptist Message*, October 25, 1962, 14.

[18]Keatchie became a girls' college once again and Mt. Lebanon once more a boys' college. ibid.; C. Penrose St. Amant, *A Short History of Louisiana Baptists* (Nashville, Tenn., 1948), 62.

[19]Poe, "Religion and Education," 124; LBC, *Annual*, 1880, 15; ibid., 1881, 13; ibid., 1887, 3; Durham and Ramond, *Baptist Builders*, 327. Ware spoke at the annual convention on the subject of the need for better educated ministers in 1893. LBC, *Annual*, 1893, 14-15.

[20]St. Amant, *A Short History*, 64-66.

[21]Ibid., 64-67; Greene, *House Upon a Rock*, 262-264.

[22]Ibid., 264, 267; St. Amant, *A Short History*, 63,67; LBC, *Annual*, 1915, 11; ibid., 1934, 60; ibid., 1941, 33.

[23]Southern Baptist Convention, *Annual*, 1927, 486-488; ibid., 1929, 33, 35, 37.

[24]For example, in Louisiana, the M.E. Dodd Foundation was set up in 1921 in order to build Dodd College, a junior college for girls opened in Shreveport in 1927. The LBC raised money for the Dodd Foundation after 1924, but then withdrew support from the school in 1931. Dodd College managed to survive the depression years but finally closed in 1942. Money for this school might more profitably have been used during the depression to clear debts on Louisiana College. *The Baptist Message*, November 8, 1962, 22.

[25]SBC, *Annual*, 1927, 92; ibid., 1941, 85. Despite impassioned pleas for educational contributions by the Education Commission of the Louisiana Baptist Convention, contributions remained small. From $900 in 1910, contributions rose annually by sixty-five per cent up to 1915, when they totalled $5264. This was not adequate to meet the running expenses of Louisiana College, as the Education Commission complained both in 1915 and in 1917. In 1941, the LBC appointed a special committee to propose a program for improving Baptist education in Louisiana. Predictably, the committee's top priority in its list of proposals was the need for more money for Louisiana College—in order for it to meet the standards of the Southern Association of Colleges and Secondary Schools. LBC, *Annual*, 1909, 36; ibid., 1914, 7, 35-37; ibid., 1915, 5, 10; ibid., 1917, 45; ibid., 1941, 33.

[26]Kelsey went on to explain that the Baptist ideal of education is that of medieval scholasticism. Since man is a being of both intellect and spirit, education must be both intellectual and spiritual, founded upon religion. Kelsey, *Social Ethics Among Southern Baptists*, 41-42.

[27]Posey, *The Baptist Church in the Lower Mississippi Valley*, 99-114.

[28]Poe, "Religion and Education," 121-22, 127; *Religious Census*, 1890.

[29]John Lee Eighmy, "Religious Liberalism in the South During the Progressive Era," *Church History*, 38 (September, 1969): 368.

[30]St. Amant, *A Short History*, 121-125; J. Donald Butler, *Religious Education: The Foundations and Practice of Nurture* (New York, 1962), 65; Victor M. Lidz, "Secularization, Ethical Life, and Religion in Modern Societies," in Harry M. Johnson, ed., *Religious Change and Continuity* (San Francisco, 1979), 212-213.

[31]In 1886, the convention again exhorted Louisiana Baptists to organize more Sunday Schools. A total of 300 were reported in 1892. However, by 1904, the number had declined

again to 200. LBC, *Annual*, 1859, 17; ibid., 1871, 15-16; ibid., 1881, 11, 21; St. Amant, *A Short History*, 122-124.

[32]St. Amant, *A Short History*, 124; LBC, *Annual*, 1911, 44-45; ibid., 1915, 48.

[33]Ibid., 1920, 28, 36, 114; ibid., 1931, 62.

[34]Ibid., 1929, 13; ibid., 1931, 62; ibid., 1933, 48; St. Amant, *A Short History*, 125; The onset of the depression caused a temporary setback in the growth of Sunday Schools, especially in the area of standardization. However, by 1933, growth had resumed and has since apparently kept pace with growth of the numbers of churches and church members, as an inseparable component of functioning Baptist churches.

[3]*The Baptist Message*, October 25, 1962, 9,13.

[36]Louisiana Baptist Convention, *Acadia Baptist Academy: A Denominational Asset; Some Facts You Would Like to Know About Your School* (Alexandria, La., 1929).

[37]Ibid., 6-7.

[38]St. Amant, *A Short History*, 79; *Bulletin* of the Baptist Bible Institute, 1925-26, 10; Southern Baptist Convention, "The Baptist Bible Institute: What It Is and What It Does," pamphlet, 1929, Southern Baptist Historical Library and Archives.

[39]LBC, *Annual*, 1931, 18-19.

[40]Figures compiled from: LBC, *Acadia Baptist Academy*, 6; Acadia Baptist Association, *Annual*, 1940, 20; *Religious Census*, 1890; *Religious Census*, 1936.

[41]Ibid.

[42]Osime Derouen's chief claim to fame as a French missionary was his part in the conversion of L.C. Smith to the Baptist faith. Smith, the founder and long-time trustee of the Acadia Baptist Acdemy, is the best-known and most successful French Baptist missionary. As the Superintendent of French Missions for the Louisiana Baptist Convention, Smith and younger proteges from the Acadia Academy are credited with the growth that took place in the Acadia Association between 1924 and 1934, when fifteen new Baptist churches were organized in a seven-parish area of Southern Louisiana. Durham and Ramond, *Baptist Builders*, 391, 435; Carl E. Conrad, "Lucien C. Smith," unpublished biographical sketch, undated, availbable at Mae Lee Memorial Library, Louisiana Baptist Convention Archives, Alexandria, Louisiana, 4 pp.

Chapter VI

[1]Lewis W. Newton, "Creoles and Anglo-Americans in Old Louisiana–A Study in Culture Conflicts," *Southwestern Social Science Quarterly*, 14 (June, 1933): 40; U. S. Bureau of the Census, *Report on Statistics of Churches in the United States at the Eleventh Census: 1890* (Washington, D.C., 1894); hereafter cited as *Religious Census*, 1890.

[2]A frequent complaint by critics of the government religious censuses of 1890, 1906, 1916, 1926, and 1936 is that they undercounted the numbers of Protestants in North Louisiana. According to the 1890 census, 42% of South Louisianians were religious communicants, while only 28% of North Louisianians were. The 1936 religious census showed that only 40% of the North Louisiana population was religious compared to 72% for South Louisiana. This is most probably inaccurate, since it is doubtful that South Louisiana's people were more religious than North Louisiana's as the figures indicate. *Religious Census*, 1890; U. S. Bureau of the Census, *Religious Bodies: 1936* (Washington, D.C., 1941); hereafter cited as *Religious Census*, 1936.

[3]James H. Dormon makes the point that class differences among the Acadian population makes it necessary to recognize cultural difference between the majority of poorer Acadians (or Cajuns) and the wealthier, better educated elite among them (Dormon's Genteel

Acadians). Dormon, "The Cajuns: Ethnogenesis and the Shaping of Group Consciousness," in Glenn R. Conrad, ed., *The Cajuns: Essays on Their History and Culture* (Lafayette, La., 1978), 241.

[4]Newton, "Creoles and Anglo-Americans," 36.

[5]Catholics represented 73% of the religious population of the Triangle parishes in 1890 and 78% in 1936. As an Anglo-American presence has continued to increase in South Louisiana since World War II, the Catholic percentage among the religious population has grown even stronger. *Religious Census*, 1890; *Religious Census*, 1936; Edwin S. Gaustad, *Historical Atlas of Religion in America* (New York, 1976), 165. Lawrence E. Estaville, Jr. demonstrated through his sample of over 24,000 names in the 1900 census that Anglos represented 70% of the state population as well as significant percentages of the population in South Louisiana urban areas. Estaville was also able to demonstrate Anglo-American control of political offices in South Louisiana by 1900. Estaville, "Changeless Cajuns: Nineteenth-Century Reality or Myth?" *Louisiana History*, 28 (Spring 1987): 133-137.

[6]William Faulkner Rushton, *The Cajuns: From Acadia to Louisiana* (New York, 1979), 6-9. Before Catholic schools appeared in greater numbers in the twentieth century, private catechism teachers were common in South Louisiana. They were called the "montreur et montreuse de catechisme." These lay teachers prepared children at home for their first Communion and sometimes operated small private schools. Baudier Papers, 9:3, Archdiocesan Archives, New Orleans, Louisiana (AANO).

[7]Rushton, *The Cajuns*, 4, 9-10.

[8]For example, St. Martinville, an eighteenth century Acadian town on the Teche Bayou (and home of the Evangeline Oak, the fictional setting for Evangeline's awaiting of Gabriel in Longfellow's poem) did not have a permanent Catholic school until 1892. Charles E. Nolan, "Carmelite Dreams, Creole Perspectives: The Sisters of Mount Carmel of Louisiana (1833-1902)," (Ph.D. dissertation, The Pontifical Gregorian University, Rome, Italy, 1970), 203.

[9]Ibid., 394-402; Roger Baudier, *One Hundred Years of the Upper Teche* (Arnaudville, La., 1953), 9-13; *New Catholic Encyclopedia* (New York, 1967), 8:1026.

[10]Baudier, *The Catholic Church*, 476; Widespread anti-clericalism, particularly among men, was an unfortunate consequence of foreign domination of the priesthood. During the 1840s and 1850s, bitter disputes had arisen between the priesthood of the New Orleans Archdiocese and Catholic laymen over the ownership of Catholic church properties. Baudier Papers, 11:7, AANO.

[11]Baudier, *One Hundred Years of the Upper Teche*, 54.

[12]Robert Michaelson, *Piety in the Public School: Trends and Issues in the Relationship Between Religion and the Public School in the United States* (New York, 1970), 124-133; Francis P. Cassidy, "Catholic Education in the Third Plenary Council of Baltimore," *Catholic Historical Review*, part one, 34 (October, 1948): 259-260, 293-294; John J. Meng, "Cahenslyism: The Second Chapter, 1891-1910," *Catholic Historical Review*, 32 (October, 1946): 302-303, 314-315.

[13]Meng, "Cahenslyism," 313 317.

[14]Meng, "Cahenslyism," 313-317; Larson, *When Parochial Schools Close*, 327-329; McLaughlin, *A History of Legislation Affecting Private Schools*, 26. Despite laws against public aid for parochial schools, two South Louisiana Catholic schools did enter into an arrangement with local public school authorities before the turn of the century, under a plan similar to that of Bishop Ireland's in Minnesota. These schools, in Iota and Breaux Bridge, in the parishes of Acadia and St. Martin, respectively, were ordered by Archbishop Chapelle to discontinue the arrangement after its nature became known to him. Sister M. Andree Condon, "The Development of the Financial Procedures for the Establishment and Maintenance of Catholic Schools in the Archdiocese of New Orleans, 1727-1958" (Ph.D. dissertation, Louisiana State University, 1959), 128.

[15]Ibid., 53; Louisiana, *Revised Statutes*, 1915, Vol. I, Section 2528. "No funds raised for the support of the public schools of the state shall be appropriated to or used for the suport of any private or sectarian schools," is a clause contained in both the 1879 and 1898 state constitution. Constitution, 1879, Article 228m; Constitution, 1898, Article 253.

[16]Brasseaux, "Acadian Education," 213-214; Robertson, *Public Education*, 181, 83.

[17]Baudier Papers, 9:3, 4, AANO.

[18]Baudier Papers, 9:3, 4, AANO. A valuable source of information on the operation of girls' academies in North Louisiana and of the conditions under which teaching Sisters operated in Louisiana,in general, are two volumes of letters selected, translated from French, and edited by Sister Dorothea Olga McCants of the Daughters of the Cross, a religious order active in Catholic education in North Louisiana since the 1850s. McCants, *They Came to Louisiana: Letters of a Catholic Mission, 1854-1882* (Baton Rouge, La., 1970), and *With Valor They Serve: A Sequel to They Came to Louisiana* (Baton Rouge, La., 1975).

[19]Robertson, *Public Education*, 146-147.

[20]Expansion of the Catholic educational system became possible only after paralyzing debts, incurred during the 1870s, were finally retired in 1904, by Archbishop Louis Placide Chapelle. In order to accomplish retirement of the archdiocesan debts, Chapelle became forced to tax church congregations by apportioning the debt out to individual church parishes. These paid off the debt through payments representing twelve per cent of their annual income from contributions over a five-year period. Baudier, *The Catholic Church*, 494-495, 507-521.

[21]Robertson, *Public Education*, 178; U. S. Bureau of the Census, *Thirteenth Census of the United States: 1910*, Vol. II: *Population, Alabama-Montana* (Washington, D.C., 1913), 790.

[22]McLaughlin, *Legislation Affecting Private Schools*, 83; Robertson, *Public Education*, 7, 146-147.

[23]Kavanagh attended the 7th annual convention of the Federation of Catholic Societies in Boston and consulted with Father George A. Lyons, Superintendent of the Boston Catholic Schools. Baudier Papers, 9:4, AANO; Baudier, *The Catholic Church*, 507-508; The State Superintendent of Education from 1908-1940, Thomas H. Harris, recalled his relationship with Catholic school officials: "I found the [Catholic school] authorities anxious to have their schools meet the standards required of the public schools in such essentials as buildings, epuipment, libraries, laboratories, courses of study, and qualification of teachers. The Catholic colleges, elementary schools, and high schools were always open to the supervisors of the state department of education and all possible courtesies were extended to these officials. . . . Except that religious instruction was given, the work of these church-affiliated schools was similar to that in the public schools." T.H. Harris Papers, Memoirs, 3:3s, Southwestern Archives, University of Southwestern Louisiana.

[24]Baudier, *The Catholic Church*, 508; Dormon, *The People Called Cajuns*, 70; The restructuring of Catholic education under Archbishop Blenk was not without controversy altogether. Opposition from some of the clergy in Louisiana was aroused by a ten cent per year tax imposed on students in parochial schools in order to pay for the activities of the new Catholic School Board from 1910-13. Baudier Papers, 9:4, AANO.

[25]Baudier, *The Catholic Church*, 507, 521, 524. Considering the interest in seminaries shown by Archbishop Blenk and of Archbishop Francis Janssens before him, it is a coincidence that the Notre Dame Seminary did not become reality until the episcopate of Archbishop Shaw, the first native American Archbishop of New Orleans. Blenk had three main educational goals upon becoming archbishop: to establish preparatory seminaries, to establish a major seminary for native vocations, and thirdly, to revamp the parochial school system, to include Catholic high schools. He accomplished two of the three. "Archbishop Blenk," research file in possession of Charles E. Nolan, AANO.

[26]Letter, Archbishop James Hubert Blenk to Rev. Thomas O. Finney, July, 1906. Contained in "Archbishop Blenk," research file in possession of Charles E. Nolan, AANO.

[27]Baudier, *The Catholic Church*, 508, 521.

[28]Baudier, *The Catholic Church*, 468-472; U. S. Bureau of the Census, *Report on Statistics of Churches in the United States at the Eleventh Census: 1890* (Washington, D.C., 1894); hereafter cited as *Religious Census*, 1890. A census of all church parishes in the Diocese of Alexandria in 1915 revealed that out of a total Catholic population of 36,200, 19,665 (54%) resided in Avoyelles Parish. *Official Catholic Directory*, Diocese of Alexandria, 1915. In 1936, Avoyelles' percentage had declined to 45%, but 96% of the Catholics in the diocese could be found in Avoyelles, Rapides, Sabine, and Natchitoches parishes, in addition to the cities of Shreveport and Monroe. *Religious Census*, 1936.

[29]Growth of the Catholic population of Baton Rouge did not become pronounced until after 1900, when the city began the phenomenal growth that has characterized it during the twentieth century. By 1918, there were only two Catholic parishes in Baton Rouge, and two Catholic schools. By 1936, there were six Catholic parishes in the city and at least two more Catholic schools. Although Catholics were outnumbered in the city almost two to one by Protestants in 1936, Catholics had become the largest single denomination in the city. *Religious Census*, 1890; *Religious Census*, 1936; Baudier, *The Catholic Church*, 511, 513-514, 527-528.

[30]Loyola, established by Jesuits in 1904, gained university status in 1911. Xavier, established by the Sisters of the Blessed Sacrament, in 1915, gained university status in 1925. It was the only Catholic university for Negroes in the nation. U. S. Bureau of the Census, *Census of Population: 1960; Characteristics of the Population, Louisiana* (Washington, D.C., 1963), 1:Part 20, 195-196; Baudier, *The Catholic Church*, 498-499, 519.

[31]Baudier, *The Catholic Church*, 537; Brasseaux, "Acadian Education," 212-214, 216-218; T. Lynn Smith and Homer L. Hitt, *The People of Louisiana* (Baton Rouge, La., 1952), 103-107.

[32]Daniel Dennett, *Louisiana, As It Is: Its Topography and Material Resources . . . and People of the State* (New Orleans, 1876), 23. Dennett edited the *Planter's Banner*, in Franklin, St. Mary Parish, nearly continuously from 1847 to 1873. Although an outsider, who emigrated to Louisiana as a school-teacher, from Dubuque, Iowa in 1841, Dennett lived among the Cajun people for nearly thirty years and knew them well. *New York Times*, January 6, 1891; such cities as Lafayette and Lake Charles, which became metropolitan areas with economic influence extending for a radius of fifty miles or more, in the post-World War II period, were small towns at the turn of the century. In 1900, Lafayette had a population of just over 3,000 while Lake Charles had expanded to nearly 7,000. Donald J. Millet, "Town Development in Southwest Louisiana, 1865-1900," *Louisiana History*, 13 (Spring 1972): 165; U. S. Bureau of the Census, *Twelfth Census of the United States: 1900; Population*, Vol. I, Pt. I (Washington, D.C., 1904), 454.

[33]Baudier, *The Catholic Church*, 537-551; Diocese of Lafayette, *Initial Report of the Lafayette Diocesan Schools, 1943-1944* (Lafayette, La., 1944), 8; Diocese of Lafayette, *Annual School Report, 1947-48* (Lafayette, La., 1948), 5.

[34]North Louisiana's attendance rate was higher than that of South Louisiana (42 per cent to 28 per cent). Louisiana Department of Education, *Biennial Report of the State Superintendent of Public Education, 1902-03* (Baton Rouge, La., 1904), 55-57, 66.

[35]Robertson, *Public Education*, 183.

[36]Ibid.; Smith and Hitt, *The People of Louisiana*, 88-89; Robertson, *Public Education*, 116-117.

[37]*1930 Census*, 980-984; Smith and Hitt, *The People of Louisiana*, 88-89.

[38]Smith and Hitt, *The People of Louisiana*, 102-107.

[39]James H. Dormon points out that the low educational aspirations of Cajuns would persist as a cultural characteristic until changed economic conditions required better educational attainment, at the same time that small-scale agriculture became an increasingly difficult way

to make a living. Dormon, *The People Called Cajuns*, 74-76; Walter H. Primeaux, Jr., "The Small Louisiana Farmer, A Vanishing Breed," *Louisiana Studies*, 8 (1969): 186, 189-193.

[40]John C. Murphy, "An Analysis of Attitudes of American Catholics Toward the Immigrant and the Negro, 1825-1925" (Ph.D. dissertation, The Catholic University of America, 1940), 137; Randall M. Miller, *Catholics in the Old South: Some Speculations on Catholic Identities* (Notre Dame, Ind., 1981), 3-4, 13, 37; Diocese of Lafayette, *Course of Studies for the Elementary Grades of the Parochial Schools of the Diocese of Lafayette* (Lafayette, La., 1920), contained at Archives, Diocese of Lafayette; *New Catholic Encyclopedia*, 5 (????): 145; Larson, *When Parochial Schools Close*, 184.

[41]Edwin L. Stephens, "The Story of Acadian Education in Louisiana," *Louisiana Historical Quarterly*, 18 (April, 1935): 398-399, 404.

[42]T.H. Harris Papers, 3:3s.

[43]Baudier, *The Catholic Church*, 524, 537. A barrier to recruiting a native clergy was the absence of preparatory seminaries within the state. Establishment of such a seminary in the See city of the Diocese of Lafayette in 1947 resulted, by the 1960s, in a new generation of priests from the Southwestern Louisiana area. Diocese of Lafayette, *Annual School Report, 1947-1948* (Lafayette, La, 1948), 6.

Chapter VII

[1]Louisiana historian, Joe Gray Taylor, commented that many of the non-denominational private schools "could almost be termed Protestant parochial schools, because they were taught by Protestant clergymen to supplement their meager incomes." Joe Gray Taylor, *Louisiana: A Bicentennial History* (New York, 1976), 81-82; Roger A. Fischer, *The Segregation Struggle in Louisiana, 1862-77* (Urbana, Ill., 1974), 90.

[2]Taylor, *Louisiana*, 81; J. Carlyle Sitterson, *Sugar Country: The Cane Sugar Industry in the South, 1753-1950* (Lexington, 1953), 84-86; In referring to Bourbon neglect of education, William Ivy Hair has suggested "that there was probably some truth to the charge, made by Populist reformers in the 1890s, that the Bourbon Democracy deliberately sabotaged Louisiana's school system; and sabotaged it not so much for the sake of economy, but in order to hold public intelligence down to the lowest common denominator and so keep rural people of both races docile." William Ivy Hair, *Bourbonism and Agrarian Protest: Louisiana Politics, 1877-1900* (Baton Rouge, La., 1969), 124.

[3]Fischer, *The Segregation Struggle*, 90-99.

[4]Presently, New Orleans is about fifty-five per cent black. Fred B. Kniffen and Sam Bowers Hilliard, *Louisiana: Its Land and People*, revised edition (Baton Rouge, La., 1988), 193; U. S. Bureau of the Census, *Historical Statistics of the United States, Colonial Times to 1970* (Washington, D.C., 1975), Part I, 28; U. S. Bureau of the Census, *Compendium of the Eleventh Census: 1890; Population* (Washington, D.C., 1892), Part I, 489-490.

[5]Fischer, *The Segregation Struggle*, 115-116; Roger Baudier, *The Catholic Church in Louisiana* (New Orleans, 1939), 461, 501, 507-508.

[6]Louisiana Department of Education, *Annual Report of the State Superintendent of Public Education, 1874* (Baton Rouge, La., 1875), xv, xix-xx; Fischer, *The Segregation Struggle*, 131.

[7]Fischer, *The Segregation Struggle*, 16-18.

[8]Louisiana Department of Education, *Annual Report, 1874*, xxi; The Orleans Parish School Board reported in 1893: "It is a matter of great pride to our Board that the Public schools of New Orleans have arrived at a degree of intrinsic excellence and general popularity never before attained, and they compare most favorably with any system of schools to be found elsewhere." Quoted in: Louisiana State Board of Education, *Official Proceedings, 1869-*

1909, State Board minutes of May 24, 1893, Louisiana State University Library; Taylor, *Louisiana*, 120, 134; C. Vann Woodward, *Origins of the New South, 1877-1913* (Baton Rouge, La., 1951), 61-63, 66.

[9]Louisiana Department of Education, *Annual Report, 1874*, 80-81, 89, 96, 98-99, 129-133; Taylor, *Louisiana*, 120.

[10]T.H. Harris Papers, 3:3o, Southwestern Archives, University of Southwestern Louisiana; Fischer, *The Segregation Struggle*, 101-102; Roger Baudier, *One Hundred Years of the Upper Teche* (Arnaudville, La., 1953), 43-44; Hair, *Bourbonism*, 122-123; As late as 1898, when, now, parishes were constitutionally mandated to collect local taxes of at least one and one-quarter mill of property assessments for education, private schools still flourished in even non-Catholic areas of the state. For example, Jackson Parish, with no Catholics in its population, had thirty white private schools. Red River Parish, also with no Catholics, had fifteen white private schools. Union and Winn Parishes, with no Catholics, had forty-four and thirty white private schools, respectively. Louisiana Department of Education, *Biennial Report of the State Superintendent of Public Education, 1898-99* (Baton Rouge, La., 1900), 32-35.

[11]National Baptist Convention, *Annual*, 1899, 96; ibid., 1900, 181; ibid., 1901, 98, 165; Thomas Jesse Jones, *Negro Education: A Study of the Private and Higher Schools for Colored People in the United States*, Vol. One (Washington, D.C., 1917), 345, 374-375.

[12]Negro Methodists had eighteen academies in Alabama, Georgia, and the Carolinas. Ibid., 155-158; L.M. Hagood, *The Colored Man in the Methodist Episcopal Church* (Westport, Conn., 1970), 88, 142-147, 299, 306. In 1890, three Negro denominations (African Methodist Episcopal, African Methodist Episcopal Zion, and Colored Methodist Episcopal), plus the predominantly black Methodist Episcopal Church (northern Methodists), represented thirty per cent of Louisiana's black religious communicants, as compared to sixty-four per cent for Negro Baptists. By 1936, Negro Methodists declined to fifteen per cent of the black religious, compared to sixty-six per cent for Negro Baptists. In 1936, over forty per cent of all members of the Negro Methodist denominations, nationally, resided in Alabama, Georgia, and the Carolinas. U. S. Bureau of the Census, *Report on Statistics of Churches in the United States at the Eleventh Census: 1890* (Washington, D.C., 1894); hereafter cited as *Religious Census*, 1890; U. S. Bureau of the Census, *Religious Bodies: 1936; Denominations A to J: Statistics, History, Doctrine, Organization, and Work* (Washington, D.C., 1941), II, Part I, 1179, 1183, 1190, 1213; U. S. Bureau of the Census, *Religious Bodies: 1936; Summary and Detailed Tables* (Washington, D.C., 1941), Vol. I; hereafter cited as *Religious Census*, 1936.

[13]Jones, *Negro Education*, Vol. one, 138; ibid., Vol. two, 313; *Religious Census*, 1936.

[14]*Religious Census*, 1890; *Religious Census*, 1936. Jones, *Negro Education*, Vol. one, 345; Sue L. Eakin, "The Black Struggle for Education in Louisiana, 1877-1930s" (Ph.D. dissertation, University of Southwestern Louisiana, 1980), 192.

[15]Jones, *Negro Education*, Vol. two, 304-305; *Religious Census*, 1890; *Religious Census*, 1936.

[16]Richard Ognibene, "Catholic and Protestant Education in the Late Nineteenth Century," *Religious Education*, 77 (Jan./Feb., 1982): 14-16; There were twenty-six Episcopalian schools in the North and Northeast, in 1930. Of nineteen Episcopalian schools outside of the North and Northeast in 1930, three were in the West, eight in Maryland and Virginia, three in the District of Columbia, two in Tennessee, and one each in Georgia, North Carolina, and Texas. Porter Sargent, *A Handbook of Private Schools for American Boys and Girls: An Annual Survey*, 14th ed. (Boston, 1930), 791, 805-806, 823.

[17]*Religious Census*, 1890; *Religious Census*, 1936. Beginning with a high school in Metairie in 1947, the Episcopal Church has since sponsored several more denominational schools in both North and South Louisiana. Rebecca A. Shepherd, ed., *Peterson's Annual Guide to Independent Secondary Schools* (Princeton, N.J., 1982), 119, 297; Episcopal School of Acadiana, "School Profile," (informational sheets on mission of the school, in personal possession of author); John T. Russell maintains that the Episcopal school movement, resulting in the establishment of schools across the country, was a reaction to the Supreme Court decision of 1947, in *McCollum v Illinois*, which banned prayer in public schools–and not a

reaction to the Brown decision of 1954. John T. Russell, "The Parish School Movement: An Appraisal," in Kendig Brubaker Cully, ed., *The Episcopal Church and Education* (New York, 1966), 73-86.

[18]*Religious Census*, 1890; *Religious Census*, 1936; Synod of Louisiana of the Presbyterian Church in the United States, *Presbyterian Activities in Louisiana: A Synopsis for Use as a Study Book by Auxiliaries, Sunday Schools, Young People's Societies, and Others* (New Orleans, 1927), 14-17; *Records* of First Presbyterian Church, Lafayette, Louisiana, August 1875-May 1975, Southwestern Archives, University of Southwestern Louisiana (hereafter cited as Presbyterian *Records*), April 25, 1920, April 13, 1924.

[19]Synod of Louisiana, *Presbyterian Activities*, 49-50; The Presbyterian Church in Lafayette collected contributions of $4,738.50 in 1924. All but $430 of this went to paying the salary of the pastor and expenses on the church building. $42.50 went to conducting the Sunday School, which had an enrollment of 87. During the Depression, contributions were lower, but topped $6400 in 1946. A new church was built in 1947 and contributions rose to $24,735 in 1954, $64,667 in 1958, and ever higher after that time. Presbyterian *Records*; William B. Kennedy, "New Orthodoxy Goes to Sunday School: The Christian Faith and Life Curriculum," *Journal of Presbyterian History*, 58 (1980): 326-328, 365-367.

[20]Paul W. Koper, "The United Presbyterian Church and Christian Education—An Historical Overview," *Journal of Presbyterian History*, 59 (Fall 1981): 304.

[21]Taylor, *Louisiana*, 82; William A. Poe, "Religion and Education in North Louisiana, 1800-1865," in B. H. Gilley, ed., *North Louisiana; Essays on the Region and Its History, Vol. One: To 1865* (Ruston, La., 1984), 121.

[22]Poe, "Religion and Education in North Louisiana," 128; Hagood, *The Colored Man in the Methodist Church*, 306.

[23]Taylor, *Louisiana*, 82; *Baptist Message*, October 25, 1962, 14; *Annual* of the Louisiana Conference of the Methodist Episcopal Church, South (hereafter cited as MECS, *Annual*), 1930, 43.

[24]Sue L. Eakin, *Avoyelles Parish . . . Crossroads of Louisiana Where All Cultures Meet* (Baton Rouge, La., 1981), 87; Centenary's importance was in its mission to train more and better ministers, as well as to conduct a new correspondence course to improve the training of Sunday School teachers. MECS, *Annual*, 1919, 23.

[25]MECS, *Annual*, 1919, 22-23; ibid., 1928, 77; Sunday School enrollments climbed from about 33,000 in 1920 to over 42,000 in 1927. Only slight decline in enrollments were experienced during the early years of the Depression, as enrollment hit its low of 37,000 in 1937, climbing thereafter to an all-time high of over 45,000 in 1940. By 1955, enrollment had increased to over 73,000, a figure representing nearly seventy per cent of the entire church membership in the state. Ibid., 1920, 44; ibid., 1927, 71; ibid., 1937, 92-93; ibid., 1940, 20-21; ibid., 1955, 105.

[26]Ibid., 1938, 57; ibid., 1939, 67.

[27]Ibid., 1926, 51; *Time*, April 16, 1945, quoted in Porter Sargent, *The Continuing Battle for the Control of the Mind of Youth* (Boston, 1945), 95; Centenary enjoyed some good fortune that Louisiana College did not. Having been selected by the U. S. Army as a site for training schools for aviators and nurses during World War II, Centenary enjoyed the benefits of government military spending. In addition, the college's endowment fund was tripled in 1951 by a two million dollar bequest, left in the will of William Arch Haynes of Shreveport. Haynes had earlier donated over $105,000, in 1942, for the purchase of Dodd College, a Baptist women's junior college in Shreveport, which became the Haynes Campus of Centenary College in 1944. MECS, *Annual*, 1943, 35; ibid., 1944, 36; ibid., 1951, 58. Louisiana College, having to struggle to raise endowment funds to meet the standards of the Southern Association, could not qualify academically for membership. In 1953, the Southern Association required that at least twenty-five per cent of college faculties hold a Ph.D. Ibid., 1953, 73; Greene, *House Upon a Rock*, 267.

[28]One reason for the small growth of the Jewish population was the Civil War, which split the Jewish population. Those Jews in New Orleans in 1890 were apparently the ones who chose to cast their fortunes with the Confederacy in 1861, such as Judah P. Benjamin, Attorney-General, Secretary of War, and Secretary of State of the Confederate government during the war. Leo Shpall, *The Jews in Louisiana* (New Orleans, 1936), 9-12, 17; *Religious Census*, 1890; *Religious Census*, 1936.

[29]Shpall, *The Jews in Louisiana*, 13, 43-44; Beverly S. Williams, "Anti-Semitism and Shreveport, Louisiana: The Situation in the 1920s," *Louisiana History*, 21 (1980): 389-392; Elliott Ashkenazi, *The Business of Jews in Louisiana, 1840-1875* (Tuscaloosa, Ala., 1988), 1-4, 77.

[30]Shpall, *The Jews in Louisiana*, 13, 24, 27-28, 43-44. Isaac Delgado, the philanthropist who endowed the Delgado Trade School in New Orleans in 1912, is presented as Jewish in Shpall's book. The Delgado Trade School became very influential as a model for other such schools, which came into vogue in the wake of the Smith-Hughes Act of 1917. Although possibly of Jewish descent, Delgado was also of Spanish-Portuguese descent, and was a member, in New Orleans, of the Episcopal Church. Glenn R. Conrad, ed., *A Dictionary of Louisiana Biography*, 2 vols. (New Orleans, La., 1988), I:230-231.

[31]*Dictionary of Louisiana Biography*, II:600; Robert Nielson, Headmaster at the Episcopal School of Acadiana (an academically rigorous college-prep school) wrote in 1987 that he has "always considered Newman to be the finest high school in Louisiana, public or private." However, the preceding was written in a context of introducing a new faculty member from the Newman School, who claimed that the Episcopal School was better academically, because of the more rounded nature of the curriculum at a religious school, which can attempt to impart moral values. Episcopal School of Acadiana (Informational sheets on the school in personal possession of author).

[32]Interestingly, an Alexandria lawyer, H.H. White, defended the state's interest in the free textbook case. White was prominent in the Southern Methodist Church, becoming involved with the unification of several Southern Methodist denominations in 1939. White was also a long-time president of the Louisiana State Board of Education. Beverly S. Williams, "Anti-Semitism and Shreveport, Louisiana: The Situation in the 1920s," *Louisiana History*, 21 (1980): 392-394; *Herold v. Parish Board of School Directors* 136 La. 1034, 68 So. 116 (1913); *Bossier Parish School Board, et. al., Caddo Parish School Board, et. al. v. Louisiana State Board of Education, et. al.* 123 So. 665 (1929); *Cochran v. Louisiana State Board of Education* 281 U. S. 370 (1930).

[33]*Religious Census*, 1890.

[34]Walter Brownlow Posey, *Religious Strife on the Southern Frontier* (Baton Rouge, La., 1965), 33-34.

[35]Rodney Cline, *Education in Louisiana–History and Development* (Baton Rouge, La., 1974), 29; Minns Sledge Robertson, *Public Education in Louisiana After 1898* (Baton Rouge, La., 1952), 3-4; For a breakdown, in 1901, of parishes collecting special school taxes, and the amounts, see minutes of State Board of Education meeting of April 29, 1902, in Louisiana State Board of Education, *Official Proceedings, 1869-1909*, Louisiana State University Library.

[36]Ibid., 3-4, 188; Woodward, *Origins*, 321, 326-328, 340, 342.

[37]Dewey W. Grantham explained that Southern progressives faced the challenge of reconciling urban, industrial progress with Southern tradition. They were "in no sense involved in the promotion of fundamental social change. Nor were they, as a rule, democrats with an implicit faith in the masses or a concrete program for assisting the poor and disadvantaged. . . ." As representatives of "the emerging professional and bourgeois elements of the South's social structure, . . ." they ". . . accepted or accommodated themselves to a system whose major institutions were dominated by powerful economic and political interests." Dewey W. Grantham, *Southern Progressivism: The Reconciliation of Progress and Tradition* (Knoxville, Tenn., 1983), 417-418, 422.

[38]In support of J. Morgan Kousser, in *The Shaping of Southern Politics: Suffrage Restriction and the Establishment of the One-Party South, 1880-1910* (New Haven, 1974), Matthew J. Schott pointed out that in Louisiana, as in the rest of the South, electoral reform and progressivism were tied in with each other. Use of the Australian (secret) ballot was an effective disfranchiser of both whites and blacks in such states as Louisiana, with large rural and uneducated populations, unable to use secret ballots that required English literacy. Both Kousser and Schott submit that Louisiana's elites instituted the secret ballot with full knowledge of the high rates of illiteracy in the state, and that the success of the Australian ballot, as a tool for disfranchisement of the rural people, provided motivation to prolong illiteracy in the non black-belt, rural parishes. Progressive educational reform after 1898, tended to benefit mostly the urban population, as well as the white population of the black-belt parishes. As Schott aptly wrote, progressivism in Louisiana ". . .was motivated and influenced by upper-class, elite reformers with undemocratic attitudes and goals: That is to say, by progressives against democracy." Matthew J. Schott, "Progressives Against Democracy: Electoral Reform in Louisiana, 1894-1921," *Louisiana History*, 20 (1979): 249-251.

Chapter VIII

[1]Mencken became famous for his bashing of Southern society and culture as a widely read journalist of the 1920s and 30s. For a more recent and more scholarly example of criticism of the impact of religion on Southern society see Ernest Kurtz, "The Tragedy of Southern Religion," *Georgia Historical Quarterly*, 66 (1982): 217-247.

[2]Wilbur J. Cash, *The Mind of the South* (New York, 1941).

[3]Kenneth K. Bailey, *Southern White Protestantism in the Twentieth Century* (Gloucester, Mass., 1968). Samuel S. Hill, Jr., *Religion and the Solid South* (Nashville, Tenn., 1972).

[4]A recent example of a book that does examine the cultural impact of religion on society, though it is not concerned with religious education, is Ted Ownby, *Subduing Satan: Religion, Recreation, and Manhood in the Rural South, 1865-1920* (Chapel Hill, N. C., 1990).

[5]William Ivy Hair, *Bourbonism and Agrarian Protest: Louisiana Politics, 1877-1900* (Baton Rouge, La., 1969), 124; V.O. Key, Jr., *Southern Politics in State and Nation* (Knoxville, Tenn., 1984), 160-161.

[6]Archbishop Francis Janssens criticized public schools in rather strong terms in a pastoral letter of 1896: "Secular teaching, which trains the mind and leaves the heart and the soul untouched by the saving teachings of Christian faith, is not only insufficient, but often proves dangerous to our eternal interests." "Pastoral Letter of the Most Rev. Archbishop of New Orleans" (New Orleans, 1896), 6.

[7]Key, *Southern Politics*, 159-160, 180-182. Harnett Kane assessed the political problem of Louisiana's voters in a succinct manner: "On one hand, they could count the progress that had been achieved; but they could mark off, also, the losses that had gone with the period [1928-1940]: the fitting of the lives of two million men, women, and children into the pattern of totalitarianism, the extension of personal power during the life of the dictator, the continuation of group control and the same pattern after his death; and the inevitable abuses of power in both periods." Harnett T. Kane, *Louisiana Hayride: The American Rehearsal for Dictatorship, 1928-1940* (New York, 1941).

[8]George D. Kelsey, *Social Ethics Among Southern Baptists, 1917-1969* (Metuchen, N.J., 1972), 17-18.

[9]"Chapel Cars of the Catholic Church Extension Society; Journeys of St. Paul, 1916-18," Baudier Papers, AANO.

[10]It is interesting to note that in Long's first gubernatorial campaign, the 1924 election won by Henry L. Fuqua, the voting was split along religious lines. Of three candidates in the race, two were Protestant (Long and Fuqua), and one was Catholic (Hewitt Bouanchaud).

Because the anti-Catholic Ku Klux Klan was an issue in this race, South Louisiana's Catholic areas voted en masse for Bouanchaud, who had almost no support in Protestant areas. Yet, four years later, Huey Long became able to find support in all rural areas of the state, North and South. Perry H. Howard, ***Political Tendencies in Louisiana***, revised edition (Baton Rouge, La., 1971), 228, 230.

[11]Joe L. Green, "The Educational Significance of Huey P. Long," *Louisiana Studies*, 13 (1974): 275.

[12]T. Harry Williams, *Huey Long* (New York, 1981), 693.

[13]Williams, *Huey Long*, 521-523; Glen Jeansonne, "Challenge to the New Deal: Huey P. Long and the Redistribution of National Wealth," *Louisiana History*, 21 (1980): 338; Allan P. Sindler, *Huey Long's Louisiana: State Politics, 1920-1952* (Baltimore, 1956), 104, 108, 122, 179, 193.

[14]Williams, *Huey Long*, 308-310, 720, 738; Sindler, *Huey Long's Louisiana*, 58-59. The 1879 Louisiana Constitution provided for educational funds from proceeds on a poll tax, but contained no provision for enforcing collection of the tax. The same Constitution declared elsewhere that "No qualification of any kind of suffrage or office shall be made by law." However, in 1892, the Louisiana State Board of Education began urging parish school boards to insist on collection of the poll taxes, authorizing these local boards to bring suit against the tax collector, if he failed to comply. Whereas $29,767 was collected in poll taxes in 1880, $109,411 was collected in 1895. Louisiana State Board of Education, *Official Proceedings, 1869-1925*, minutes of August 19, 1892, February 10, 1897. It is interesting to speculate that the State Board of Education's sudden insistence on poll tax collection in 1892 came in response to the challenge of populism in the white, rural parishes of North Louisiana. Since the state governor was a member of the State Board of Education, it would not have been difficult to use the Board as a vehicle for the attainment of larger political goals.

[15]Lawrence Goodwyn, *The Populist Moment: A Short History of the Agrarian Revolt in America* (Oxford and New York, 1978), vii-xxiv.

[16]Edwin Scott Gaustad, *Historical Atlas of Religion in America* (New York, 1976). A demographic map of religion in the United States, within a flap on the back cover of Gaustad's atlas shows that, in 1970, every parish in the state, except East Baton Rouge, was solidly either majority Baptist or majority Catholic.

[17]The proliferation of sects, dissatisfied with changes within the major denominations, is a national phenomenon of the post-World War II period. Robert Wuthnow, "Religious Movements and Counter-Movements in North America," in James A. Beckford, ed., *New Religious Movements and Rapid Social Change* (London, 1986), 1-3.

[18]Ibid.

[19]Charles Y. Glock, "The Role of Deprivation in the Origin and Evolution of Religious Groups," in Robert Lee and Martin E. Marty, eds., *Religion and Social Conflict* (New York, 1964), 24-28, 30-31, 35.

[20]Letter from Paul D. Williams, Secretary, Committee on South, National Catholic Social Action Congress to Gerald P. O'Hara, Bishop of Savannah-Atlanta, May 3, 1939. Catholic Committee of the South, *Records, 1939-1956*, contained at Amistad Research Center, Tulane University, New Orleans, Louisiana.

Bibliography

I. Primary Sources

A. Archival Materials

American Missionary Association. Archives. Amistad Research Center. Tilton Hall, Tulane University. New Orleans, Louisiana.

American Missionary Association. Archive, Addendum. Records, 1887-1977. Tilton Hall, Tulane University. New Orleans, Louisiana.

Baudier, Roger. Papers. Archives of the Archdiocese of New Orleans. New Orleans, Louisiana.

Catholic Committee of the South. Records, 1939-1956. Amistad Research Center. Tilton Hall, Tulane University. New Orleans, Louisiana.

Harris, Thomas H. Papers. Southwestern Archives and Manuscripts Collection. University of Southwestern Louisiana. Lafayette, Louisiana.

Jeanmard, Jules B. Bishop of Lafayette. Correspondence, 1919-1927. The Roman Catholic Diocese of Lafayette. Archives. Lafayette, Louisiana.

Lawrence, Una Roberts. Resource Files. Series of the Home Mission Board Records, American Baptist Home Missionary Society. Southern Baptist Historical Library and Archives. Nashville, Tennessee.

Louisiana Baptist Convention. Archives and Mae Lee Memorial Library. Louisiana Baptist Building. Alexandria, Louisiana.

Newbrough, J.W. Biographical Data, Articles, Correspondence, 1932-1936. Southern Baptist Historical Library and Archives. Nashville, Tennessee.

Southern Baptist Convention. Historical Commission Archives. Southern Baptist Historical Library and Archives. Nashville, Tennessee.

B. Government Documents

Louisiana Department of Education. *Annual Report of the State*

Superintendent of Public Education, 1874. New Orleans: The *Republican* Office, 1875.

Louisiana. *Revised Statutes*, 1915. Vol. I, Section 2528.

Louisiana State Board of Education. *Official Proceedings, 1869-1925*. Microfilm 1173. Louisiana State University Archives. Baton Rouge, Louisiana.

United States Bureau of the Census. *Census of Population: 1960*, Vol. I: *Characteristics of the Population*, Part 20: *Louisiana*. Washington, D.C.: Government Printing Office, 1963.

United States Bureau of Education. *Biennial Survey of Education, 1922-24*. Washington, D.C.: Government Printing Office, 1927.

C. Religious Records

Annual. National Baptist Educational Convention, 1892. Southern Baptist Historical Library and Archives. Nashville, Tennessee.

Annuals. Acadia Baptist Association, 1919-1940. Southern Baptist Historical Library and Archives. Nashville, Tennessee.

Benedictine Monks of Solesmes. *Papal Teachings: Education*. New York: St. Paul Editions, 1960.

Ellis, John Tracy. *Documents of American Catholic History*, second edition. Milwaukee: The Bruce Publishing Co., 1962.

Gillard, John T. *The Catholic Church and the American Negro*. Baltimore: St. Joseph's Society Press, 1929.

Guilday, Peter, ed. *National Pastorals of the American Hierarchy, 1792-1919*. Washington, D.C.: National Catholic Welfare Council, 1923.

Huber, Raphael M., ed. *Our Bishops Speak: National Pastorals and Annual Statements of the Hierarchy of the United States, 1919-1951*. Milwaukee: The Bruce Publishing Co., 1952.

Journals. American National Baptist Convention, 1889-1891. Southern Baptist Historical Library and Archives. Nashville, Tennessee.

Louisiana Baptist Convention. *Acadia Baptist Academy: A Denominational Asset; Some Facts You Would Like to Know About Your School.* Alexandria, La.: Standard Printing, 1929.

McCants, Sister Dorothea Olga, editor and translator. *They Came to Louisiana: Letters of a Catholic Mission, 1854-1882.* Baton Rouge: Louisiana State University Press, 1970.

McCluskey, Neil G. *Catholic Education in America: A Documentary History.* New York: Teacher's College, Columbia University, 1964.

Pope Pius XI. *Christian Education of Youth.* New York: The America Press, 1936.

Records. First Presbyterian Church of Lafayette, Louisiana. August 1875-May 1975. Southwestern Archives and Manuscripts Collection. University of Southwestern Louisiana. Lafayette, Louisiana.

Synod of Louisiana of the Presbyterian Church in the United States. *Presbyterian Activities in Louisiana: A Synopsis for Use as a Study Book by Auxiliaries, Sunday Schools, Young People's Societies, and Others.* New Orleans: Louisiana Synod's Board of Education, 1927.

D. Books

Baudier, Roger. *The Catholic Church in Louisiana.* New Orleans: Archdiocese of New Orleans, 1939.

Crowley, Jeremiah J. *The Parochial School: A Curse to the Church, A Menace to the Nation; An Expose of the Parochial School—An Appalling Account of Priestly Graft, Sacrilege and Immorality—The Loss of Thirty Million Catholics in the United States, Etc.* Chicago: published by the author, 1904.

Davis, Edwin Adams. *Plantation Life in the Florida Parishes of Louisiana, 1836-1846: As Reflected in the Diary of Bennet H. Barrow.* New York: Columbia University Press, 1943.

Dennett, Daniel. *Louisiana As It Is: Its Topography and Material Resources . . . and People of the State.* New Orleans: Eureka Press, 1876.

Dillard, James Edgar. *We Southern Baptists, 1937-38.* Nashville: Executive Committee, Southern Baptist Convention, 1938.

Durham, John Pinckney and Ramond, John S., compilers. *Baptist Builders in Louisiana.* Shreveport: Art Craft Press, 1934.

General Education Board. *An Account of Its Activities, 1902-1914.* New York: General Education Board, 1915.

Gerow, Richard Oliver, Bishop of Natchez, compiler. *Catholicity in Mississippi.* Natchez: Hope Haven Press, 1939.

Hagood, L. M. *The Colored Man in the Methodist Episcopal Church.* 1890; reprint edition, Westport, Conn.: Negro Universities Press, 1970

Hicks, William. *History of Louisiana Negro Baptists: 1804-1914.* Nashville: National Baptist Publishing Board, 1914.

Louisiana Work Projects Administration. *Louisiana: A Guide to the State; Compiled by Workers of the Writers' Program of the Work Projects Administration in the State of Louisiana.* New York: Hastings House Publishers, 1941.

Pitkin, R. S. *Public School Support in the United States during Periods of Economic Depression.* New York: Stephen Daye Press, 1933.

Rousseve, Charles Barthelemy. *The Negro in Louisiana: Aspects of His History and His Literature.* New Orleans: Xavier University Press, 1937.

Shpall, Leo. *The Jews in Louisiana.* New Orleans: Steeg Printing and Publishing, 1936.

Woodson, Carter Godwin. *The Mis-Education of the Negro.* Washington, D.C.: The Associated Publishers, Inc., 1938.

E. Articles

Braden, John. "Introduction," in *The Colored Man in the Methodist Episcopal Church*. pp. 1-18. Authored by L. M. Hagood. 1890; reprint edition, Westport, Conn.: Negro Universities Press, 1970.

Dunbar-Nelson, Alice. "People of Color in Louisiana," part one, *Journal of Negro History*, Vol. one, No. 4 (1916): 361-76. Part two, *Journal of Negro History*, Vol. two, No. 1 (1917): 51-78.

Embree, Edwin R. "Every Tenth Pupil," *Survey Graphic* 23 (1934): 538-41.

Stephens, Edwin L. "The Story of Acadian Education in Louisiana," *Louisiana Historical Quarterly* 18 (1935): 397-406.

II. Secondary Sources

A. Books

Albanese, Catherine L. *Corresponding Motion: Transcendental Religion and the New America*. Philadelphia: Temple University Press, 1977.

Arceneaux, George. *Youth in Acadie: Reflections on Acadian Life and Culture in Southwest Louisiana*. Baton Rouge: Claitor's Publishing Division, 1974.

Ashkenazi, Elliott. *The Business of Jews in Louisiana, 1840-1875*. Tuscaloosa: University of Alabama Press, 1988.

Baer, Hans A. *The Black Spiritual Movement: A Religious Response to Racism*. Knoxville: University of Tennessee Press, 1984.

Bailey, Hugh C. *Liberalism in the New South: Southern Social Reformers and the Progressive Movement*. Coral Gables, Fla.: University of Miami Press, 1969.

Bailey, Kenneth K. *Southern White Protestantism in the Twentieth Century*. 1964; reprint ed., Gloucester, Mass.: Peter Smith, 1968.

Bailyn, Bernard and Fleming, Donald, eds. *Perspectives in American History*, vol. 6. Cambridge, Mass.: Harvard University Press, 1972.

Baker, Robert A. *The Southern Baptist Convention and Its People, 1607-1972*. Nashville: Broadman Press, 1974.

Baker, Tod A., Steed, Robert P., and Moreland, Laurence W., eds. *Religion and Politics in the South: Mass and Elite Perspectives*. New York: Frederick A. Praeger, 1983.

Banton, Michael P., ed. *Anthropological Approaches to the Study of Religion*. London: Tavistock Publications, 1966.

Banton, Michael. *Racial and Ethnic Competition*. Cambridge: Cambridge University Press, 1983.

Barth, Fredrik, ed. *Ethnic Groups and Boundaries: The Social Organization of Culture Difference*. Boston: Little, Brown and Co., 1969.

Baudier, Roger. *One Hundred Years of the Upper Teche*. Arnaudville, La.: St. Francis Regis Church, 1952.

Baudier, Roger and Everett, Millard F. *Knights of Columbus in Louisiana, 1902-1962*. New Orleans: A. F. Laborde and Sons, 1965.

Benoist, Jean-Marie. *The Structural Revolution*. New York: St. Martin's Press, 1975.

Berger, Peter L. *A Rumor of Angels: Modern Society and the Rediscovery of the Supernatural*. Garden City, N. Y.: Doubleday and Co., 1970.

Billington, Ray Allen. *The Protestant Crusade, 1800-1860: A Study of the Origins of American Nativism*. 1938; reprint edition, Chicago: Quadrangle Books, 1964.

Bohannon, Paul and Plog, Fred, eds. *Beyond the Frontier: Social Process and Cultural Change*. Garden City, N. Y.: The Natural History Press, 1967.

Bond, Horace Mann. *Negro Education in Alabama: A Study in Cotton and Steel*. 1939; reprint edition, New York: Octagon Books, 1969.

Bowers, C. A. *The Progressive Educator and the Depression: The Radical Years*. New York: Random House, 1969.

Brigham, Judith. *A Historical Study of the Educational Agencies of the Southern Baptist Convention, 1845-1945*. 1951; reprint edition, New York: Arno Press, 1972.

Brown, Arlo A. *A History of Religious Education in Recent Times*. New York: Abingdon-Colesbury Press, 1923.

Brown, Samuel W. *The Secularization of American Education*. New York: Teacher's College, Columbia University, 1912.

Brownell, Blaine A. *The Urban South in the Twentieth Century*. St. Charles, Mo.: Forum Press, 1974.

Brubacher, John Seiler. *A History of the Problems of Education*, second edition. New York: McGraw-Hill, 1966.

Bucke, Emory Stevens, ed. *The History of American Methodism*, 3 volumes. New York and Nashville: Abingdon Press, 1964.

Buetow, Harold A. *Of Singular Benefit: The Story of Catholic Education in the United States*. New York: Macmillan, 1970.

Bullock, Henry Allen. *A History of Negro Education in the South; From 1619 to the Present*. Cambridge, Mass.: Harvard University Press, 1967.

Butler, J. Donald. *Religious Education: The Foundations and Practice of Nurture*. New York: Harper and Row, 1962.

Clayton, Bruce. *The Savage Ideal: Intolerance and Intellectual Leadership in the South, 1890-1914*. Baltimore: Johns Hopkins University Press, 1972.

Cline, Rodney. *Builders of Louisiana Education: Sketches of Some of the Persons Who Have Made Significant Contributions to Education in Louisiana*. Baton Rouge: College of Education, Louisiana State University, 1963.

Cobb, James C. and Namorato, Michael, V., eds. *The New Deal and the South*. Jackson: University Press of Mississippi, 1984.

Confrey, Burton. *Secularism in American Education: Its History.* Washington, D.C.: The Catholic University of America Press, 1931.

Conrad, Glenn R., ed. *The Cajuns: Essays on Their History and Culture.* Lafayette, La.: Center for Louisiana Studies, University of Southwestern Louisiana, 1978.

Conrad, Glenn R., gen. ed. *Readings in Louisiana History.* New Orleans: Louisiana Historical Association, 1978.

Cremin, Lawrence A. *Traditions of American Education.* New York: Basic Books, 1977.

Cubberley, Ellwood P. *Public Education in the United States.* New York: Houghton Mifflin Co., 1934.

Cully, Kendig Brubaker, ed. *The Episcopal Church and Education.* New York: Morehouse-Barlow, 1966.

Dabney, Charles William. *Universal Education in the South.* Two volumes. 1936; reprint edition, New York: Arno Press, 1969.

Despres, Leo A., ed. *Ethnicity and Resource Competition in Plural Societies.* The Hague and Paris: Mouton Publishers, 1975.

Dolan, Jay P., ed. *The American Catholic Parish: A History from 1850 to the Present.* New York: Paulist Press, 1987.

Dollard, John. *Caste and Class in a Southern Town,* Third Edition. 1937; reprint edition, Garden City, N.Y.: Doubleday and Co., 1957.

Dormon, James H. *The People Called Cajuns: An Introduction to an Ethnohistory.* Lafayette, La.: Center for Louisiana Studies, University of Southwestern Louisiana, 1983.

Eakin, Sue L. *Avoyelles Parish . . . Crossroads of Louisiana Where All Cultures Meet.* Baton Rouge: Moran Publishing, 1981.

Egerton, John. *The Americanization of Dixie: The Southernization of America.* New York: Harper's Magazine Press, 1974.

Eighmy, John Lee. *Churches in Cultural Captivity: A History of the*

Social Attitudes of Southern Baptists. Knoxville: University of Tennessee Press, 1972.

Ellis, John Tracey. *American Catholicism.* Chicago: University of Chicago Press, 1956.

Faust, Drew Gilpin. *A Sacred Circle: The Dilemma of the Intellectual in the Old South, 1840-1860.* Baltimore: Johns Hopkins University Press, 1977.

Feinberg, Walter. *Reason and Rhetoric: The Intellectual Foundations of 20th Century Liberal Educational Policy.* New York: John Wiley and Sons, 1975.

Fischer, Roger A. *The Segregation Struggle in Louisiana, 1862-77.* Urbana: University of Illinois Press, 1974.

Fite, Gilbert C. *Cotton Fields No More: Southern Agriculture, 1865-1980.* Lexington: University of Kentucky Press, 1984.

Fraser, Walter L., Jr., et. al., eds. *The Web of Southern Social Relations: Women, Family, and Education.* Athens: University of Georgia Press, 1985.

Galbraith, John Kenneth. *The Affluent Society.* Boston: Houghton Mifflin, 1958.

Gatewood, Willard B., compiler. *Controversy in the Twenties: Fundamentalism, Modernism, and Evolution.* Nashville: Vanderbilt University Press, 1969.

Gaustad, Edwin Scott. *Historical Atlas of Religion in America.* New York: Harper and Row, 1976.

Gilley, B. H., ed. *North Louisiana: Essays on the Region and Its History,* volume one: *To 1865.* Ruston, La.: McGinty Trust Fund Publications, 1984.

Goldfield, David R. *Cotton Fields and Skyscrapers: Southern City and Region, 1607-1980.* Baton Rouge: Louisiana State University Press, 1982.

Goodenow, Ronald K. and White, Arthur O., eds. *Education and the Rise of the New South.* Boston: G. K. Hall, 1981.

Goodwyn, Lawrence. *The Populist Moment: A Short History of the Agrarian Revolt in America.* Oxford and New York: Oxford University Press, 1978.

Grantham, Dewey W. *Southern Progressivism: The Reconciliation of Progress and Tradition.* Knoxville: University of Tennessee Press, 1983.

Greene, Glen Lee. *House Upon a Rock: About Southern Baptists in Louisiana.* Alexandria, La.: Executive Board of the Louisiana Baptist Convention, 1973.

Hair, William Ivy. *Bourbonism and Agrarian Protest: Louisiana Politics, 1877-1900.* Baton Rouge: Louisiana State University Press, 1969.

Hallowell, Christopher. *People of the Bayou: Cajun Life in Lost America.* New York: E. P. Dutton, 1979.

Harlan, Louis R. *Separate and Unequal: Public School Campaigns and Racism in the Southern Seaboard States, 1901-1915.* Chapel Hill: University of North Carolina Press, 1958.

Harrell, David Edwin, Jr. *White Sects and Black Men in the Recent South.* Nashville: Vanderbilt University Press, 1971.

Harrell, David Edwin, Jr., ed. *Varieties of Southern Evangelicalism.* Macon: Mercer University Press, 1981.

Higham, John. *Strangers in the Land: Patterns of American Nativism, 1860-1925.* New Brunswick, N.J.: Rutgers University Press, 1955.

Hill, Samuel S., Jr., ed. *Religion in the Southern States: A Historical Study.* Macon: Mercer University Press, 1983.

Hill, Samuel S., Jr. *Religion and the Solid South.* Nashville: Abingdon Press, 1972.

Hiller, Harry H. *Canadian Society: A Macro Analysis.* Scarborough, Ontario: Prentice-Hall Canada, Inc., 1986.

Hofstadter, Richard. *Anti-Intellectuallism in American Life*. New York: Alfred A. Knopf, 1963.

Hopkins, Charles H. *The Rise of the Social Gospel in American Protestantism, 1865-1915*. 1940; reprint edition, New Haven: Yale University Press, 1967.

Howard, Perry H. *Political Tendencies in Louisiana*. Revised Edition. Baton Rouge: Louisiana State University Press, 1971.

Johnson, Alvin and Yost, Frank. *Separation of Church and State in the United States*. Minneapolis: University of Minnesota Press, 1948.

Johnson, Charles D. *Higher Education of Southern Baptists: An Institutional History, 1826-1954*. Waco: Baylor University Press, 1955.

Johnson, Harry M., ed. *Religious Change and Continuity*. San Francisco: Jossey-Bass Publishers, 1979.

Kane, Harnett T. *The Bayous of Louisiana*. New York: William Morrow and Co., 1944.

Katz, Michael B. *The Irony of Early School Reform: Educational Innovation in Mid-Nineteenth Century Massachusetts*. Cambridge, Mass.: Harvard University Press, 1968.

Kelsey, George D. *Social Ethics Among Southern Baptists, 1917-1969*. Metuchen, N. J.: The Scarecrow Press, 1972.

Key, V. O., Jr. *Southern Politics in State and Nation*. 1949; reprint edition, Knoxville: University of Tennessee Press, 1984.

Kniffen, Fred B. and Hilliard, Sam Bowers. *Louisiana: Its Land and People*, revised edition. Baton Rouge: Louisiana State University Press, 1988.

Kousser, J. Morgan. *The Shaping of Southern Politics: Suffrage Restriction and the Establishment of the One-Party South, 1880-1910*. New Haven: Yale University Press, 1974.

Krug, Edward A. *The Shaping of the American High School*, vol. 2: *1920-1941*. Madison: University of Wisconsin Press, 1972.

Labbé, Dolores Egger. *Jim Crow Comes to Church: The Establishment of Segregated Catholic Parishes in South Louisiana*. 1971; reprint edition, New York: Arno Press, 1978.

Larson, Martin A. *When Parochial Schools Close: A Study in Educational Financing*. Washington and New York: Robert B. Luce, Inc., 1972.

Lazerson, Marvin and Grubb, W. Norton, eds. *American Education and Vocationalism: A Documentary History, 1870-1970*. New York: Teachers College Press, Columbia University, 1974.

Lee, Robert and Marty, Martin E., eds. *Religion and Social Conflict*. New York: Oxford University Press, 1964.

Lincoln, C. Eric. *Race, Religion, and the Continuing American Dilemma*. New York: Hill and Wang, 1984.

Liston, R. T. L., ed. *The Neglected Educational Heritage of Southern Presbyterians*. Bristol, Tenn.: n. p., 1956.

Macksey, Richard and Donato, Eugenio, eds. *The Structuralist Controversy: The Languages of Criticism and the Sciences of Man*. Baltimore: The Johns Hopkins University Press, 1972.

Magruder, Edith C. *A Historical Study of the Educational Agencies of the Southern Baptist Convention, 1845-1945*. New York: Teachers College Press, Columbia University, 1951.

Mandle, Jay R. *The Roots of Black Poverty: The Southern Planatation Economy After the Civil War*. Durham, N.C.: Duke University Press, 1978.

McLaughlin, Sister Raymond. *A History of State Legislation Affecting Private Elementary and Secondary Schools in the United States, 1870-1945*. Washington, D.C.: The Catholic University of America Press, 1946.

McLoughlin, William G. *Revivals, Awakenings, and Reform: An Essay on Religion and Social Change in America, 1607-1977*. Chicago:

University of Chicago Press, 1978.

Michaelson, Robert. *Piety in the Public School: Trends and Issues in the Relationship Between Religion and the Public School in the United States.* New York: Macmillan, 1970.

Miller, Alexander F. and Hill, Mozell. *Safety, Security and the South.* Atlanta: Southern Regional Council, 1951.

Miller, Randall M. *Catholics in the Old South: Some Speculations on Catholic Identities.* Notre Dame, Ind.: Charles and Margaret Hall Cushwa Center for the Study of American Catholicism, University of Notre Dame, 1981.

Miller, Robert Moats. *American Protestantism and Social Issues.* Chapel Hill: University of North Carolina Press, 1958.

Mills, Gary B. *The Forgotten People: Cane River's Creoles of Color.* Baton Rouge: Louisiana State University Press, 1977.

Nash, Paul, ed. *History and Education: The Educational Uses of the Past.* New York: Random House, 1970.

Newton, Lewis William. *The Americanization of French Louisiana: A Study of the Process of Adjustment Between the French and the Anglo-American Populations of Louisiana, 1803-1860.* New York: Arno Press, 1980.

Nolan, Charles E. *Mother Clare Coady: Her Life, Her Times and Her Sisters.* New Orleans: Academy Enterprises of New Orleans, Inc., 1983.

Ownby, Ted. *Subduing Satan: Religion, Recreation, and Manhood in the Rural South, 1865-1920.* Chapel Hill: University of North Carolina Press, 1990.

Parker, Inez Moore. *The Rise and Decline of the Program of Education for Black Presbyterians of the United Presbyterian Church, U. S. A., 1865-1970.* San Antonio: Trinity University Press, 1977.

Patterson, Orlando. *Slavery and Social Death: A Comparative Study.* Cambridge, Mass.: Harvard University Press, 1982.

Pickering, W. S. F. *Durkheim's Sociology of Religion: Themes and Theories*. London: Routledge and Kegan Paul, 1984.

Posey, Walter Brownlow. *The Baptist Church in the Lower Mississippi Valley, 1776-1845*. Lexington: University of Kentucky Press, 1957.

Prather, H. Leon, Jr. *Resurgent Politics and Educational Progressivism in the New South: North Carolina, 1890-1913*. Rutherford, N. J.: Fairleigh Dickinson University Press, 1979.

Raboteau, Albert J. *Slave Religion: The "Invisible Institution" in the Antebellum South*. Oxford and New York: Oxford University Press, 1978.

Reed, John Shelton. *The Enduring South: Sub-Cultural Persistence in a Mass Society*. Chapel Hill: University of North Carolina Press, 1972.

Reilly, Daniel F. *The School Controversy, 1891-1893*. Washington, D. C.: Catholic University of America Press, 1943.

Rice, Madeleine H. *American Catholic Opinion in the Slavery Controversy*. New York: Columbia University Press, 1944.

Richey, Russell E. and Jones, Donald G., eds. *American Civil Religion*. New York: Harper and Row, 1974.

Robertson, Minns Sledge. *Public Education in Louisiana After 1898*. Baton Rouge: College of Education, Louisiana State University, 1952.

Roland, Charles P. *The Improbable Era: The South Since World War II*. Lexington: University of Kentucky Press, 1975.

Rushton, William Faulkner. *The Cajuns: From Acadia to Louisiana*. New York: Farrar, Straus, Giroux, 1979.

Sargent, Porter. *The Continuing Battle for the Control of the Mind of Youth*. Boston: Porter Sargent, 1945.

Shugg, Roger W. *Origins of Class Struggle in Louisiana: A Social History of White Farmers and Laborers during Slavery and After, 1840-1875*. Baton Rouge: Louisiana State University Press, 1939.

Simmons, Loyed R. *Southern Baptists and Federal Aid.* Washington, D. C.: Americans United for Separation of Church and State, 1968.

Simpson, George Eaton. *Black Religions in the New World.* New York: Columbia University Press, 1978.

Sindler, Allan P. *Huey Long's Louisiana: State Politics, 1920-1952.* Baltimore: The Johns Hopkins University Press, 1956.

Sitterson, J. Carlyle. *Sugar Country: The Cane Sugar Industry in the South, 1753-1950.* Lexington: University of Kentucky Press, 1953.

Slaght, Laurence T. *Multiplying the Witness: 150 Years of American Baptist Educational Ministries.* Valley Forge, Pa.: Judson Press, 1974.

Smith, H. Shelton. *In His Image, But . . .: Racism in Southern Religion, 1780-1910.* Durham. N. C.: Duke University Press, 1972.

Smith, T. Lynn and Hitt, Homer L. *The People of Louisiana.* Baton Rouge: Louisiana State University Press, 1952.

Spitzer, Nicholas R., ed. *Louisiana Folklife: A Guide to the State.* Baton Rouge: Louisiana Folklife Program, Office of Cultural Development, Department of Culture, Recreation, and Tourism, 1985.

Spring, Joel. *The American School, 1642-1985: Varieties of Historical Interpretation of the Foundations and Development of American Education.* New York: Longman, 1986.

St. Amant, C. Penrose. *A Short History of Louisiana Baptists.* Nashville: Broadman Press, 1948.

Sugg, Redding S. and Jones, George Hilton. *The Southern Regional Education Board: Ten Years of Regional Cooperation in Higher Education.* Baton Rouge: Louisiana State University Press, 1960.

Taylor, Joe Gray. *Louisiana: A Bicentennial History.* New York: W.W. Norton, 1977.

Thompson, James M., Jr. *Tried as by Fire: Southern Baptists and the*

Religious Controversies of the 1920s. Macon, Ga.: Mercer University Press, 1982.

Tindall, George Brown. *The Emergence of the New South, 1913-1945.* Baton Rouge: Louisiana State University Press, 1967.

Tyack, David and Hansot, Elisabeth. *Managers of Virtue: Public School Leadership in America, 1820-1980.* New York: Basic Books, 1982.

Violas, Paul C. *The Training of the Urban Working Class: A History of Twentieth-Century American Education.* Chicago: Rand McNalley College Publishing Co., 1978.

Wheat, Leonard F. *Urban Growth in the Nonmetropolitan South.* Lexington, Mass.: D. C. Heath and Co., 1976.

Williams, T. Harry. *Huey Long.* 1969; reprint edition, New York: Vintage Books, 1981.

Wilson, Charles Reagan. *Baptized in Blood: The Religion of the Lost Cause, 1865-1920.* Athens: University of Georgia Press, 1980.

Wilson, John F. *Public Religion in American Culture.* Philadelphia: Temple University Press, 1979.

Wilson, John F. and Drakeman, Donald L., eds. *Church and State in American History: The Burden of Religious Pluralism*, second edition. Boston: Beacon Press, 1987.

Wilson, William Julius. *The Declining Significance of Race: Blacks and Changing American Institutions.* Chicago: University of Chicago Press, 1978.

Wise, Ivan M. *Footsteps of the Flock, or, Origins of Louisiana Baptists.* Vol. II: *South Louisiana Baptists.* N.p., n.d. Contained at Mae Lee Memorial Library, Louisiana Baptist Building. Alexandria, Louisiana.

Woodward, C. Vann. *Origins of the New South: 1877 to 1913.* Baton Rouge: Louisiana State University Press, 1951.

Wyatt-Brown, Bertram. *Yankee Saints and Southern Sinners.* Baton Rouge: Louisiana State University Press, 1985.

Yance, Norman A. *Religion Southern Style: Southern Baptists and Society in Historical Perspective.* Macon, Ga.: Mercer University Press, 1978.

B. Articles

Abernathy, Mollie C. "Southern Women, Social Reconstruction, and the Church in the 1920s," *Louisiana Studies,* 13 (1974): 289-312.

Adams, William H. "The Louisiana Whigs," *Louisiana History,* 15 (1974): 213-28.

Anderson, James. "Northern Foundations and the Shaping of Southern Black Rural Education, 1902-1935," *History of Education Quarterly,* 18 (1978): 371-96.

Barth, Fredrik. "Introduction," in *Ethnic Groups and Boundaries: The Social Organization of Culture Difference.* pp. 1-36. Edited by Fredrik Barth. Boston: Little, Brown and Co., 1969.

Beales, A. C. F. "Church and State in Education: Public Support for Confessional Schools in Some English-Speaking Countries," in *History and Education: The Educational Uses of the Past.* pp. 257-82. Edited by Paul Nash. New York: Random House, 1970.

Bellah, Robert N. "Civil Religion," *Daedalus,* 96 (1967): 1-26.

Betts, John Rickards. "Darwinism, Evolution, and American Catholic Thought, 1860-1900," *Catholic Historical Review,* 45 (1959): 161-85.

Brasseaux, Carl A. "Acadian Education: From Cultural Isolation to Mainstream America," in *The Cajuns: Essays on Their History and Culture*, 212-24. Edited by Glenn R. Conrad. Lafayette, La.: Center for Louisiana Studies, University of Southwestern Louisiana, 1978.

Brickman, William W. "Public and Private Education as Co-Partners in the Formation of American Society, 1875-1964," *Religious Education,* 49 (1964): 294-304.

Broom, Leonard, Siegel, Bernard J., Vogt, Evon Z., and Watson, James B. "Acculturation: An Exploratory Formulation," in *Beyond the Frontier:*

Social Process and Cultural Change, 255-86. Edited by Paul Bohannon and Fred Plog. Garden City, N. Y.: The Natural History Press, 1967.

Carrigan, Jo Ann. "Mass Communication and Public Health: The 1905 Campaign Against Yellow Fever in New Orleans," *Louisiana History*, 29 (1988): 5-20.

Carter, Doris Dorcas. "Charles P. Adams and Grambling State University: The Formative Years (1901-1928)," *Louisiana History*, 17 (1976): 401-412.

Cassidy, Francis P. "Catholic Education in the Third Plenary Council of Baltimore," *Catholic Historical Review*, 34 (1948-1949): 257-305, 414-436.

Conrad, Carl E. "Lucien C. Smith," unpublished, undated biographical sketch in possession of author. Contained at Mae Lee Memorial Library, Louisiana Baptist convention Archives, Alexandria, Louisiana. 4 pp.

Conrad, Glenn R. "The Acadians: Myths and Realities," in *The Cajuns: Essays on Their History and Culture*. pp. 1-18. Edited by Glenn R. Conrad. Lafayette, La.: Center for Louisiana Studies, University of Southwestern Louisiana, 1978.

Davis, O. L. "A History of the Religious Education Association," *Religious Education*, 44 (1949): 41-54.

Dennis, Rutledge M. "Dubois and the Role of the Educated Elite," *Journal of Negro Education*, 46 (1977): 388-402.

Despres, Leo A. "Introduction," in *Ethnicity and Resource Competition in Plural Societies*. pp. 1-8. Edited by Leo A. Despres. The Hague and Paris: Mouton Publishers, 1975.

Dormon, James H. "The Cajuns: Ethnogenesis and the Shaping of Group Consciousness," in *The Cajuns: Essays on Their History and Culture*. pp. 233-51. Edited by Glenn R. Conrad. Lafayette, La.: Center for Louisiana Studies, University of Southwestern Louisiana, 1978.

Dyson-Hudson, Neville. "Structure and Infrastructure in Primitive Society: Levi-Strauss and Radcliffe-Brown," in *The Structuralist Controversy:*

The Languages of Criticism and the Sciences of Man. pp. 218-241. Edited by Richard Macksey and Eugenio Donato. Baltimore: The Johns Hopkins University Press, 1972.

Eighmy, John Lee. "Religious Liberalism in the South During the Progressive Era," *Church History,* 38 (1969): 359-372.

Ellis, John Tracy. "Church and State in the United States: A Critical Appraisal," *Catholic Historical Review,* 38 (1952): 285-316.

Estaville, Lawrence E., Jr. "Changeless Cajuns: Nineteenth-Century Reality or Myth?" *Louisiana History,* 28 (1987): 117-140.

Evans, John Whitney. "Catholics and the Blair Education Bill," *Catholic Historical Review,* 46 (1960): 273-298.

Flynt, J. Wayne. "Dissent in Zion: Alabama Baptists and Social Issues, 1900-1914," *Journal of Southern History,* 35 (1969): 523-542.

Gerard, Ginny. "A History of the Protestant Episcopal Church in Shreveport, Louisiana, 1839-1916," *North Louisiana Historical Association Journal,* Vol. 9, No. 2 (1978): 193-203.

Gershenberg, Irving. "Southern Values and Public Education: A Revision," *History of Education Quarterly,* 10 (1970): 413-422.

Glenn, Norval D. and Hyland, Ruth. "Religious Preference and Worldly Success: Some Evidence from National Surveys," *American Sociological Review,* 32 (1967): 73-85.

Glock, Charles Y. "The Role of Deprivation in the Origin and Evolution of Religious Groups," in *Religion and Social Conflict.* pp. 24-36. Edited by Robert Lee and Martin E. Marty. New York: Oxford University Press, 1964.

Going, Allen J. "The South and the Blair Education Bill," *Mississippi Valley Historical Review,* 44 (1958): 267-290.

Goodenow, Ronald K. "The Progressive Educator, Race and Ethnicity in the Depression Years: An Overview," *History of Education Quarterly,* 15 (1975): 365-394.

Green, Joe L. "The Educational Significance of Huey P. Long," *Louisiana Studies*, 13 (1974): 263-277.

Harlan, Louis R. "Desegregation in New Orleans Schools During Reconstruction," *American Historical Review*, LXVII (1962): 663-675.

Harrell, David E., Jr. "The South: Seedbed of Sectarianism," in *Varieties of Southern Evangelicalism*. pp. 45-57. Edited by David E. Harrell, Jr. Macon, Ga.: Mercer University Press, 1981.

Hebert, Wallace. "Louisiana Baptists and the Scopes Trial," *Louisiana Studies*, 7 (1968): 329-346.

Herberg, Will. "America's Civil Religion: What It is and Whence It Comes," in *American Civil Religion*, pp. 76-88. Edited by Russell E. Richey and Donald G. Jones. New York: Harper and Row, 1974.

Hill, Samuel S., Jr. "Epilogue," in *Churches in Cultural Captivity: A History of the Social Attitudes of Southern Baptists*. pp. 202-209. Authored by John Lee Eighmy. Knoxville: University of Tennessee Press, 1972.

Hoetink, Harmannus. "Resource Competition, Monopoly, and Socioracial Diversity," in *Ethnicity and Resource Competition in Plural Societies*. pp. 9-26. Edited by Leo A. Despres. The Hague and Paris: Mouton Publishers, 1975.

Holloman, Regina E. "Ethnic Boundary Maintenance, Readaptation and Societal Evolution," in *Ethnicity and Resource Competition in Plural Societies*. pp. 27-40. Edited by Leo A. Despres. The Hague and Paris: Mouton Publishers, 1975.

Jeansonne, Glen. "Challenge to the New Deal: Huey P. Long and the Redistribution of National Wealth," *Louisiana History*, 21 (1980): 331-339.

Johnson, Harry M. "Religion in Social Change and Social Evolution," in *Religious Change and Continuity*. pp. 313-339. Edited by Harry M. Johnson. San Francisco: Josey-Bass Publishers, 1979.

Jordan, Rosan A. "Folklore and Ethnicity: Some Theoretical Considerations," in *Louisiana Folklife: A Guide to the State*. pp. 49-

54. Edited by Nicholas R. Spitzer. Baton Rouge: Louisiana Folklife Program, Office of Cultural Development, Department of Culture, Recreation, and Tourism, 1985.

Judges, A. V. "The Meaning of Equality in Education," in *History and Education: The Educational Uses of the Past*. pp. 160-191. Edited by Paul Nash. New York: Random House, 1970.

Katz, Michael B. "Education and Social Development in the Nineteenth Century: New Directions for Enquiry," in *History and Education: The Educational Uses of the Past*. pp. 83-114. Edited by Paul Nash. New York: Random House, 1970.

Kennedy, William B. "New Orthodoxy Goes to Sunday School: The Christian Faith and Life Curriculum," *Journal of Presbyterian History*, 58 (1980): 326-370.

Keyes, Charles F. "Towards a New Formulation of the Concept of Ethnic Group," *Ethnicity*, 3 (1976): 202-213.

Klinkhamer, Sister Marie Carolyn. "The Blaine Amendment of 1975: Private Motives for Political Action," *Catholic Historical Review*, 42 (1956): 15-49.

Koper, Paul W. "The United Presbyterian Church and Christian Education—An Historical Overview," *Journal of Presbyterian History* 59 (1981): 288-308.

Kunkel, Paul A. "Modifications in Louisiana Negro Legal Status under Louisiana Constitutions, 1812-1957," *Journal of Negro History*, 44 (1959): 1-25.

Kurtz, Ernest. "The Tragedy of Southern Religion," *Georgia Historical Quarterly*, 66 (1982): 217-247.

Lawrence, William Francis. "European Immigration Trends of Northeast Louisiana, 1880-1900," *Louisiana History*, 26 (1985): 41-52.

Leonard, Henry B. "Ethnic Tensions, Episcopal Leadership, and the Emergence of the Twentieth-Century American Catholic Church: The Cleveland Experience," *Catholic Historical Review*, 71 (1985): 394-412.

Lidz, Victor M. "Secularization, Ethical Life, and Religion in Modern Societies," in *Religious Change and Continuity*. pp. 191-217. Edited by Harry M. Johnson. San Francisco: Jossey-Bass Publishers, 1979.

Loveland, Anne C. "The 'Southern Work' of the Reverend Joseph C. Hartzell, Pastor of Ames Church in New Orleans, 1870-1873," *Louisiana History*, 16 (1975): 391-407.

Martin, Robert F. "Critique of Southern Society and Vision of a New Order: The Fellowship of Southern Churchmen, 1934-1957," *Church History*, 52 (1983): 66-80.

Marty, Martin E. "Two Kinds of Two Kinds of Civil Religion," in *American Civil Religion*. pp. 139-57. Edited by Russell E. Richey and Donald G. Jones. New York: Harper and Row, 1974.

Marx, Gary T. "Religion: Opiate or Inspiration of Civil Rights Militancy Among Negroes?" *American Sociological Review*, 32 (1967): 64-72.

Meng, John J. "Cahenslyism: The Second Chapter, 1891-1910," *Catholic Historical Review*, 32 (1946): 302-340.

Millet, Donald J. "Town Development in Southwest Louisiana, 1865-1900," *Louisiana History*, 13 (1972): 139-168.

Moore, Raymond S. "Protestant Full-Time Weekday Schools," in *Religious Education: A Comprehensive Survey*. pp. 236-246. Edited by Marvin J. Taylor. New York and Nashville: Abingdon Press, 1960.

Moreau, John Adam. "Huey Long and His Chroniclers," *Louisiana History*, 6 (1965): 121-140.

Murvar, Vatro. "Integrative and Revolutionary Capabilities of Religion," in *Religious Change and Continuity*. pp. 74-86. Edited by Harry M. Johnson. San Francisco: Jossey-Bass Publishers, 1979.

Newton, Lewis W. "Creoles and Anglo-Americans in Old Louisiana—A Study in Culture Conflicts," *Southwestern Social Science Quarterly*, 14 (1933): 31-48.

Ognibene, Richard. "Catholic and Protestant Education in the Late Nineteenth Century," *Religious Education,* 77 (1982): 5-20.

Oneal, Marion Sherrard. "A School Ma'am in Louisiana's Piney Woods, 1902-1903," *Louisiana History,* 5 (1964): 135-142.

Otite, Onigu. "Resource Competition and Inter-Ethnic Relations in Nigeria," in *Ethnicity and Resource Competition in Plural Societies.* pp. 119-130. Edited by Leo A. Despres. The Hague and Paris: Mouton Publishers, 1975.

Painter, Nell Irvin. "'Social Equality,' Miscegenation, Labor, and Power," in *The Evolution of Southern Culture.* pp. 47-67. Edited by Numan V. Bartley. Athens, Ga.: University of Georgia Press, 1988.

Peoples, Morgan D. "'Kansas Fever' in North Louisiana," *Louisiana History,* 11 (1970): 121-136.

Pies, Timothy Mark. "The Parochial School Campaigns in Michigan, 1920-1924: The Lutheran and Catholic Involvement," *Catholic Historical Review,* 72 (1986): 222-238.

Poe, William A. "Religion and Education in North Louisiana, 1800-1865," in *North Louisiana; Essays on the Region and Its History.* Volume one: *To 1865.* pp. 113-30. Edited by B. H. Gilley. Ruston, La.: McGinty Trust Fund Publications, 1984.

Primeaux, Walter J., Jr. "The Small Louisiana Farmer, A Vanishing Breed," *Louisiana Studies,* 8 (1969): 185-193.

Reilly, Timothy F. "Benjamin M. Palmer: Secessionist Becomes Nationalist," *Louisiana History,* 18 (1977): 287-301.

Richardson, Herbert. "Civil Religion in Theological Perspective," in *American Civil Religion.* pp. 161-84. Edited by Russell E. Richey and Donald G. Jones. New York: Harper and Row, 1974.

Russell, John T. "The Parish School Movement: An Appraisal," in *The Episcopal Church and Education.* pp. 73-86. Edited by Kendig Brubaker Cully. New York: Morehouse-Barlow, 1966.

Schott, Mathew J. "Class Conflict in Louisiana Voting Since 1877: Some

New Perspectives," in *Readings in Louisiana History*. Edited by Glenn R. Conrad. pp. 269-273. New Orleans: Louisiana Historical Association, 1978.

Shanabruch, Charles. "The Louisiana Immigration Movement, 1891-1907: An Analysis of Efforts, Attitudes, and Opportunities," *Louisiana History*, 18 (1977): 203-226.

Smith, Elwyn A. "The Fundamental Church-State Tradition of the Catholic Church in the United States," *Church History*, 38 (1969): 486-505.

Smith, Timothy L. "Parochial Education and American Culture," in *History and Education; The Educational Uses of the Past*. pp. 192-211. Edited by Paul Nash. New York: Random House, 1970.

Trout, Robert O. "Rural-Urban Dependency Ratios in Louisiana," *Louisiana Studies*, 5 (1966): 269-277.

Tyack, David B. "Onward Christian Soldiers: Religion in the American Common School," pp. 212-55 in *History and Education: The Educational Uses of the Past*. Edited by Paul Nash. New York: Random House, 1970.

Valentine, Jerry W. "The WPA and Louisiana Education," *Louisiana History*, 13 (1972): 391-395.

Washington, Joseph R., Jr. "The Peculiar Peril and Promise of Black Folk Religion," in *Varieties of Southern Evangelicalism*. pp. 59-69. Edited by David E. Harrell, Jr. Macon, Ga.: Mercer University Press, 1981.

Williams, Beverly S. "Anti-Semitism and Shreveport, Louisiana: The Situation in the 1920s," *Louisiana History*, 21 (1980): 387-98.

Wilson, Charles Reagan. "The Religion of the Lost Cause: Ritual and Organization of the Southern Civil Religion, 1865-1920," *Journal of Southern History*, 46 (1980): 219-238.

Wilson, John F. "A Historian's Approach to Civil Religion," in *American Civil Religion*. pp. 115-138. Edited by Russell E. Richey and Donald G. Jones. New York: Harper and Row, 1974.

Wingo, Barbara C. "The 1928 Presidential Election in Louisiana,"

Louisiana History 18 (1977): 405-435.

C. Theses and Dissertations

Butler, Loretta M. "A History of Catholic Elementary Education for Negroes in the Diocese of Lafayette, Louisiana." Ph.D. dissertation. The Catholic University of America, 1963.

Cline, Rodney. "The Life and Work of Seaman A. Knapp." M.A. thesis. Louisiana State University, 1936.

Condon, Sister M. Andrée. "The Development of the Financial Procedures for the Establishment and Maintenance of Catholic Schools in the Archdiocese of New Orleans, 1727-1958." Ph.D. dissertation. Louisiana State University, 1959.

Eakin, Sue L. "The Black Struggle for Education in Louisiana, 1877-1930s." Ph.D. dissertation. University of Southwestern Louisiana, 1980.

Fish, John Olen. "Southern Methodism in the Progressive Era: A Social History." Ph.D. dissertation. University of Georgia, 1969.

Kenney, Sister Mary Josephine. "Contributions of the Sisters of the Blessed Sacrament for Indians and Colored People to Catholic Negro Education in the State of Louisiana." M.A. thesis. The Catholic University of America, 1942.

Murphy, John C. "An Analysis of Attitudes of American Catholics Toward the Immigrant and the Negro, 1825-1925." Ph.D. dissertation. The Catholic University of America, 1940.

Nolan, Charles E. "Carmelite Dreams, Creole Perspectives: The Sisters of Mount Carmel of Louisiana (1833-1903)." Ph.D. dissertation. The Pontifical Gregorian University, Rome, Italy, 1970.

Storey, John W. "The Negro in Southern Baptist Thought, 1865-1900." Ph.D. dissertation. University of Kentucky, 1968.

Young, Sister Mary David. "A History of the Development of Catholic Education for the Negro in Louisiana." M.A. thesis. Louisiana State University, 1944.

D. Magazines

Baptist Chronicle. January 9, 1896. January 23, 1896.

Baptist Message. December 19, 1957. October 18, 1962. October 25, 1962. November 1, 1962. November 8, 1962.

Catholic Action of the South (Diocese of Alexandria). May, 1953.

Catholic Action of the South (Diocese of Lafayette). July, December, 1943. April, 1953.

Index